Introduction

From its beginning in December 1972, **Doll Reader** has prided itself on the variety and quality of articles on doll making and dressing as well as collecting. In 1983, due to many requests, we published *Doll Reader Make and Dress, Volume I*, which was a compilation of a number of outstanding making and dressing articles which had appeared in previous issues of the magazine. Because of the success of this publication, **Doll Reader** is pleased to present *Doll Reader Make and Dress, Volume II*, which we feel will prove to be an invaluable resource to the doll maker and costumer.

This volume is separated into three main chapters. The first chapter, Doll Dressing, is divided into five sections and here you will find 31 articles which include more than 23 patterns for costuming your antique dolls as well as your modern and collectible ones. There are patterns to fit your French fashion dolls, boys, girls, children, babies, chinas and others, as well as the more recent popular dolls such as *Ginny, Jill* and *Betsy McCall*. Bonnet and hat patterns are given as are instructions for a crocheted gown for a baby doll. To assist the seamstress in costuming and accessorizing her dolls, there are articles on everything from babies' wear to that of brides containing much helpful information, ideas and illustrations.

The second chapter, Doll Making, is divided into four sections. There are eight articles on porcelain doll making, six on cloth doll making and two showing you how to make dolls of other media. Also included are two articles on making doll bodies.

The third chapter on Doll Repair/Restoration provides helpful information on how to string a doll and do other minor repairs and includes an in-depth article on the hazards encountered by a doll doctor. Articles containing advice on caring for your doll collection and preventing damage to your dolls are also presented.

It is our hope that the doll costumer/doll maker will find this volume as enjoyable and helpful as Volume I. Articles on doll making and dressing continue to appear in the **Doll Reader** and if you do not already subscribe, we invite you to do so in order to further your enjoyment of making and dressing dolls.

Virginia Ann Heyerdahl
Editor - April 1988

Gary R. Ruddell
Publisher - April 1988

Doll Reader®
Make
and
Dress
Volume II

Edited by Virginia Ann Heyerdahl

Article Reprints 1980 - 1985

Published by Hobby House Press

Cumberland,
Maryland 21502

Additional copies of this book may be purchased at $12.95
from
HOBBY HOUSE PRESS, INC.
900 Frederick Street
Cumberland, Maryland 21502
or from your favorite bookstore or dealer.
Please add $2.25 per copy for postage.

Doll Reader® Make and Dress Volume II is a compendium of
articles which have been previously published in *Doll Reader* magazine. The research and publication of this book was not sponsored in
any way by the manufacturers of the dolls, doll costumes or accessories
mentioned in the articles.

TABLE OF CONTENTS

DOLL DRESSING:

SEWING FOR YOUR DOLLS:

Lisette Clanet — Normandy Bride of 1728
by Barbara Pickering 8

Polonaise and Petticoat, Circa 1775
by Kathleen Songal .15

A Traditional English Pedlar Doll To Make
by Barbara Pickering .17

Dressing an 11½in (29cm) China Head Doll
by Sandy Williams 25

Pattern from *Poupée Modèle*, August 1867
by Dorothy S. Coleman & Sandy Williams 28

Dress Pattern from *Poupée Modèle*, 15 June 1867
by Dorothy S. Coleman & Sandy Williams 32

Boy Doll's Suit Pattern from *La Poupée Modèle*, July 1881
by Dorothy S. Coleman & Sandy Williams 36

Dressing a Tiny Bisque Doll
by Sandy Williams 40

A Little German Schoolgirl, Part I
by Donna Miska 42

A Little German Schoolgirl, Part II
by Donna Miska 46

A Ball Gown of the 1890s
by Brenda Paske 51

Armand Marseille Baby Dressed in Early 1860s Style
by Barbara Pickering .55

Kate Greenaway Outfit
by Virginia Cross 63

Cinderella and Fairy Godmother Costumes for *Ginny* and *Jill*
by Lauren Welker 68

A Party Dress for Tiny 8in (20cm) *Betsy McCall*
by Lauren Welker 71

Crocheted Dress and Bonnet for a 12in (30cm) *Bye-Lo Baby*
by Pat Nelson 73

A Coat for a Dolls' House Man
by Jane Thompson 77

Pattern for Antique Doll Clothing for Dolls under 8in (20cm)
by Dorothy Noell De Campus [Kern] 78

COSTUMING AIDS:

The Fashionable Bride, 1330 to 1930
by Brenda Paske 82

Beautiful Brides, 1892 to 1908
by Lyn Alexander & Janice Miller 88

A Fashionable Wardrobe, 1836 to 1853
by Brenda Paske 91

Costume Guide for 1837 Day Dress
by Kathleen Songal 97

Fancy Needlework, 1900 to 1930
by Lyn Alexander 104

For New Arrivals From Storktown
by Lyn Alexander 110

On Dressing the Schoenhut Doll
by Ruth H. Zimmerman 113

Miniature Sewing Techniques
by Lauren Welker 116

BONNETS AND HAT:

Let's Make an 1898 Poke Bonnet
    by Dorothy Noell de Campus [Kern] 120
Doll Hat for a 12in (30cm) Head Size
    by Ruth Dougherty 125

ACCESSORIES:

The Subject of Sleeves and Collars
    by Albina Bailey 128
Miniature Ribbon Roses
    by Doris Rockwell Gottilly 133
Dolls' Shoes and Socks
    by Jeannie Sieg 137
Parasols For All
    by Barbara Guyette 144
Doll Stockings
    by Pat Nelson 147

DOLL MAKING:
PORCELAIN DOLLS:

Make Your Own Doll Collection: *Princess Elizabeth*
    by Artie Seeley 150
Make Your Own Doll Collection: *Shirley Temple* Doll
    by Artie Seeley 153
How to Model a Doll Head
    by Martha Armstrong-Hand 156
"La plus elegant jeune femme de France"
    by Joan Erdman 159
Royal Heir
    by Lauren Welker 162
How To Make An All-porcelain Doll
    by Marie L. Sitton 165
Cleaning Greenware
    by Marie L. Sitton 170
Make Your Own Doll Collection: *Bye-Lo*
    by Artie Seeley 172

CLOTH DOLLS:

***Queen Elizabeth I* — A Cloth Doll**
    by Bette Wells 176
***Christopher*, A Googlie-eyed Little Sailor Doll**
    by Doris Rockwell Gottilly 179
A Flapper of the Twenties
    by Bette Wells 183
Pincushion Dolls
    by Janet Carija Brandt 187
***Gabriella*, A Painted-face Cloth Doll**
    by Patricia Wilks 190

OTHER MEDIA:

Pincushion Needlework Companion Doll
    by Doris Rockwell Gottilly 197

DOLL BODIES:

German Kid Body
    by Elizabeth Andrews Fisher 202
Make Your Own Doll Collection: Costuming a Lady of the 1890s
    by Artie Seeley 205

DOLL REPAIR/RESTORATION:

Care of a Doll Collection
    by Robert & Karin MacDowell 212
Stringing Without Tears
    by G. P. Jones 215
Dolling Discoveries
    by Elizabeth Andrews Fisher 216
The Hazards of Being a Doll Doctor and Doll Maker — A Personal Account
    by Linda Greenfield 217
Notes on Preventing Avoidable Damage to Fine Antique Dolls
    by Robert & Karin MacDowell 222

DOLL DRESSING:

SEWING FOR YOUR DOLLS:

Lisette Clanet — Normandy Bride of 1728
  by Barbara Pickering

Polonaise and Petticoat, Circa 1775
  by Kathleen Songal

A Traditional English Pedlar Doll To Make
  by Barbara Pickering

Dressing an 11½in (29cm) China Head Doll
  by Sandy Williams

Pattern from *Poupée Modèle*, August 1867
  by Dorothy S. Coleman & Sandy Williams

Dress Pattern from *Poupée Modèle*, 15 June 1867
  by Dorothy S. Coleman & Sandy Williams

Boy Doll's Suit Pattern from *La Poupée Modèle*, July 1881
  by Dorothy S. Coleman & Sandy Williams

Dressing a Tiny Bisque Doll
  by Sandy Williams

A Little German Schoolgirl, Part I
  by Donna Miska

A Little German Schoolgirl, Part II
  by Donna Miska

A Ball Gown of the 1890s
  by Brenda Paske

Armand Marseille Baby Dressed in Early 1860s Style
  by Barbara Pickering

Kate Greenaway Outfit
  by Virginia Cross

Cinderella and Fairy Godmother Costumes for *Ginny* and *Jill*
  by Lauren Welker

A Party Dress for Tiny 8in (20cm) *Betsy McCall*®
  by Lauren Welker

Crocheted Dress and Bonnet for a 12in (30cm) *Bye-Lo Baby* head circumference 9in (23cm)
  by Pat Nelson

A Coat for a Dolls' House Man
  by Jane Thompson

Pattern for Antique Doll Clothing for Dolls under 8in (20cm)
  by Dorothy Noell De Campus [Kern]

Lisette Clanet — Normandy Bride of 1728

by **Barbara Pickering**

Photographs by **Lloyd Pickering**

Illustration 1. Front view of doll dressed as *Lisette Clanet.*

Illustration 2. Back view of doll dressed as *Lisette Clanet.*

Wedding Costume for a
19in (48cm) doll
Based on the costume doll created by
Elizabeth Haines

One of the most fascinating books on wedding customs and costumes must, undoubtedly, be *Early American Brides* by Frank and Elizabeth Haines, published by Hobby House Press, Inc., in 1982. The historical background given for each bride with its clear illustrations and drawings inspired me to copy Lisette Clanet, the Casket girl from Bayeaux (pages 112 to 119), as accurately as I possibly could. Alas, the doll itself is not as beautiful as the lovely model Frank Haines has created! He told me that after the death of his wife he gave all the brides made between them to the museum in Wilmington,

North Carolina, as a memorial to Elizabeth Haines. Perhaps some readers are able to study the brides in detail in the museum.

The doll I dressed is 19in (48cm) high. She has a porcelain face and a wired cloth body. Do remember: no two dolls are alike, so check your pattern pieces carefully and adjust them accordingly.

A seam allowance of 1/4in (.65cm) is included in each pattern piece. Iron all seams before putting the dress on the doll. As it is a costume doll, the clothes do not need to be made to take off.

MATERIALS:
18in (46cm) by 13in (33cm) lawn (chemise)
9in (23cm) by 1/8in (.31cm) white lace (edging of chemise neckline)
18in (46cm) by 1/4in (.65cm) white lace (edging of chemise hemline)
15in (38cm) by 8½in (22cm) light red woolen material (petticoat)
Red silk cord (for embroidering red petticoat)
17in (43cm) by 8¼in (21cm) white linen (petticoat)
17in (43cm) by 1½in (4cm) white lace (linen petticoat)
Approximately 1yd (.91m) narrow white tape (petticoats)
13in (33cm) by 9in (23cm) white cotton material (stockings)
Approximately 1yd (.91m) by 1/8in (.31cm) light blue velvet ribbon (garters)
14in (36cm) by 13in (33cm) red woolen material (bodice)
26in (66cm) by 9in (23cm) printed cotton (skirt)
26in (66cm) by 9in (23cm) peacock blue sateen (skirt lining)
10in (25cm) square paisley patterned woolen material (shawl)
28in (71cm) by 9in (23cm) black/violet silk material (apron)
10in (25cm) by 5in (13cm) white Vilene (foundation of headdress)
20½in (52cm) by 28in (71cm) white lace (headdress)
Approximately 21in (53cm) by 1/4in (.65cm) white lace (edging of headdress)
11in (28cm) by 1/8in (.31cm) black velvet ribbon (necklace)
Small gold cross
Two small gold-headed pins (apron)
6¾in (17cm) by 3¼in (3cm) black leather (shoes)
2¼in (6cm) by 1¼in (3cm) medium strong cardboard (shoe soles)
2in (5cm) by 1in (2cm) piece of 3/16in (.45cm) balsa wood (heels)
Black paint (heels)
Matching sewing cotton
Glue
CHEMISE: It is made of fine lawn, the top of which shows above the bodice. Stitch together shoulder and side seams (French seams) along broken lines. Fold sleeves in half and sew along broken lines. Gather top of sleeves to fit armholes and sew them into chemise. Hem edge of sleeves. Cut a bias strip of the same material approximately 1/2in (1.3cm) wide by neckline width. With

right sides together sew strip to neckline. Turn strip to wrong side of chemise, turn raw edges under and hem. Neaten both ends and sew up opening. Trim neckline with very narrow lace. Adjust length of chemise, turn under raw edges and hem neatly. Trim hemline with lace. Put chemise on the doll. Pull a gathering thread through neckline, pull tight and secure firmly. Do the same with the sleeves.

STOCKINGS: Wrap the material around the leg and tack together, stretching tightly as you go. Slip the material off the leg and sew along tacking line. Cut off any surplus material. Turn under raw edges at the top and hem. Stitch stockings (at the top) to both legs.

GARTERS: The stockings are supported by blue velvet garters which wind around the legs according to the sketch. Secure with a few invisible stitches.

RED AND WHITE PETTICOATS: It was customary to wear a light red wool petticoat with a lovely red silk cord embroidered band. The white linen petticoat is trimmed with a deep lace flounce. Both petticoats are made in the same way.

Fold the material in half and sew along broken lines (French seams). Hem the back opening with the narrowest hem that can be turned down. Neatly buttonhole stitch angle A (see diagram), then make a loop across the work over it closely in buttonhole stitch (see diagram). With right sides together sew waistbands to petticoats. Turn waistband to wrong side of petticoat, turn raw edges under and sew. Neaten both end openings. Adjust lengths of both petticoats, turn under raw edges and hem. Trim the white petticoat with lace. The red petticoat is, as mentioned above, embroidered with red silk cord. Either use an iron-on transfer pattern or design a lovely border yourself. Run a narrow tape through the waistbands, put the petticoats on the doll (red one first) and tie tapes at the back.

BODICE: Sew bodice front to the two back pieces at side and shoulder seams (French seams) along broken lines. Fold sleeves in half and sew along broken lines (French seams). Gather top of sleeves to fit armholes and sew sleeves into bodice. Adjust length of sleeves, turn under raw edges and hem. Cut a bias strip of the same material 1/2in (1.3cm) wide by neckline width and proceed as for chemise neckline.

Illustration 3. Doll dressed as *Lisette Clanet* showing construction of her clothes.

SKIRT: The skirt and the lining are cut out together and sewn as one piece. Proceed in exactly the same way as for the petticoats, but leave out the waistband. Gather of skirt to fit bodice. With right sides together sew skirt to bodice. Fit dress to doll, turn under back opening of bodice and stitch neatly to body. Adjust hemline, turn under raw edges and hem.

SHAWL: In wintertime light wool shawls were worn, in summertime printed cotton ones. I used a fine woolen material with a small paisley pattern as suggested in the book. Hem all four sides, fold into a triangle and place the shawl around the doll's shoulders. Tuck front ends into bodice and secure with a few stitches.

APRON: I was unable to find a piece of silk with the unusual color combination of black and violet as suggested in the book. I decided to buy a piece of white silk with a slightly raised flower pattern. I then dyed the material with black ink. Result: a beautiful dark gray with the flowers being slightly lighter.

Hem the two sides and bottom of apron. Gather top of apron as indicated on pattern (leave 4in [10cm] of material in the middle of the apron without gathers) to go approximately two-thirds around the waist. With right sides together sew waistband to apron top. Turn waistband to wrong side of apron, turn under raw edges and sew. Neaten and sew up both openings of ties.

Hem the two sides and top of the apron bib. Turn under raw edges of bottom and sew neatly to wrong side of apron, to the part without gathers. Tie apron around doll. The bib is held up by two gold-headed pins pinned to the bodice.

NECKLACE: Sew a little gold cross to a piece of narrow black velvet ribbon and place it round the doll's neck.

If you do not have a small gold cross, cut one out of thin balsa wood and paint or spray it gold.

HEADDRESS: Fold the foundation of the headdress in half and sew along broken lines. Stitch this piece to the doll's head. Next fold the main headdress in half and sew along center back seam. Hem all around dotted lines as indicated on the pattern and attach narrow lace to it. Fold the side "flaps" over so that point B meets A and hold together with a few stitches. Spray the "flaps" with starch. Pull headdress over foundation and secure with a few stitches. Now fold top of headdress in half and sew along broken lines. Pull a gathering thread along top and bottom

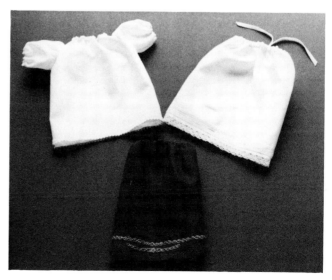

Illustration 4. Chemise and petticoats for doll dressed as *Lisette Clanet.*

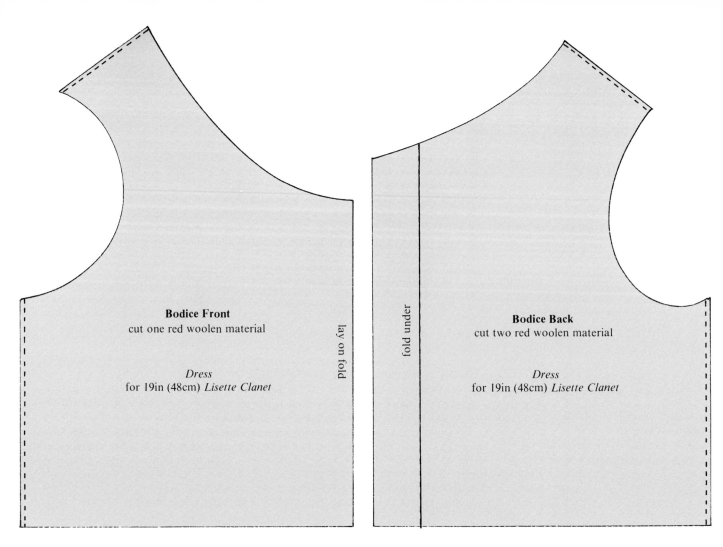

Bodice Front
cut one red woolen material

Dress
for 19in (48cm) *Lisette Clanet*

lay on fold

fold under

Bodice Back
cut two red woolen material

Dress
for 19in (48cm) *Lisette Clanet*

gather   do not gather   gather

cut one silk
actual measurements: 13in (33cm) by 7½in (19cm)

Apron
for 19in (48cm) *Lisette Clanet*

Bib
cut one silk
Actual measurements:
4in (10cm) by 3in (8cm)
Apron
for 19in (48cm)
Lisette Clanet

edges, place over headdress and pull gathering threads sufficiently tight. This gives you the top fullness. Secure threads firmly.

SHOES: Cut two soles in cardboard and two in leather. The cardboard ones should be slightly smaller. Pin soles temporarily to doll's feet. Place the top part of the shoe over her foot and fold the leather according to the diagram so that you obtain the square toe shape. Then glue the leather underneath the cardboard sole and glue the back together. Cover the cardboard sole with leather. Finally cut a pair of heels from a piece of 3/16in (.45cm) balsa wood to fit the shoes. Glue them underneath and paint black.

To complete the wedding costume Lisette should, by rights, have a small brass-studded chest containing "two bodices, two shirts, two petticoats, six headdresses, various other articles of clothing and some household linen." □

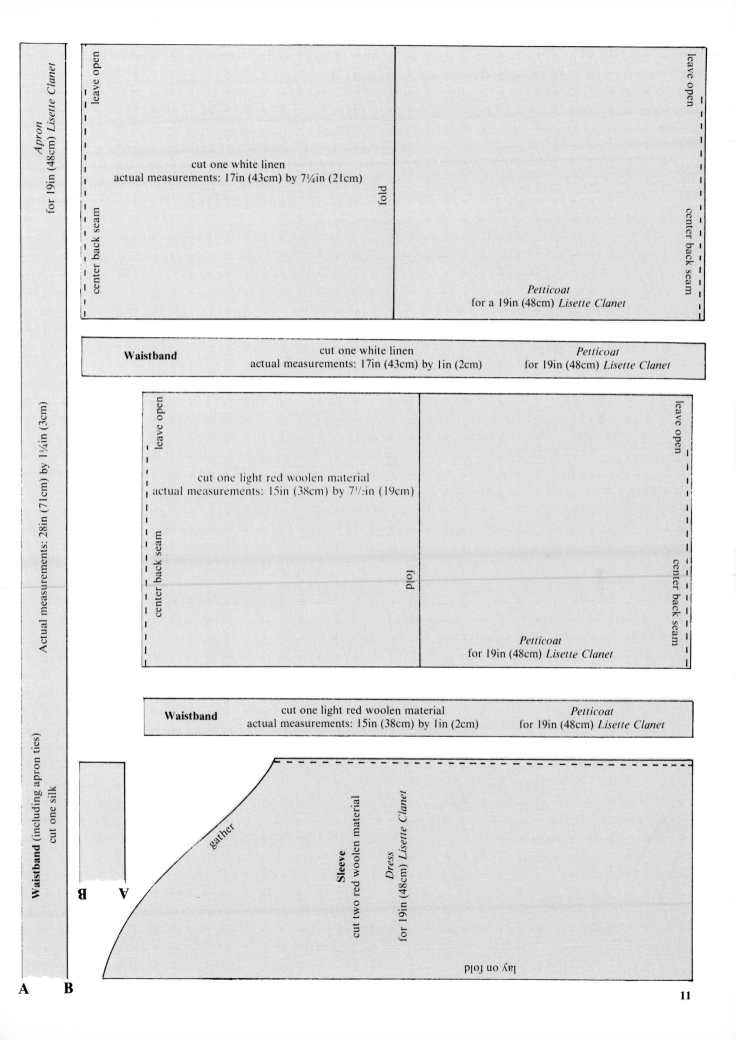

Apron
for 19in (48cm) *Lisette Clanet*

leave open

cut one white linen
actual measurements: 17in (43cm) by 7¼in (21cm)

fold

center back seam

leave open

center back seam

Petticoat
for a 19in (48cm) *Lisette Clanet*

Waistband   cut one white linen
actual measurements: 17in (43cm) by 1in (2cm)

Petticoat
for 19in (48cm) *Lisette Clanet*

leave open

cut one light red woolen material
actual measurements: 15in (38cm) by 7½in (19cm)

center back seam

fold

leave open

center back seam

Petticoat
for 19in (48cm) *Lisette Clanet*

Waistband   cut one light red woolen material
actual measurements: 15in (38cm) by 1in (2cm)

Petticoat
for 19in (48cm) *Lisette Clanet*

Actual measurements: 28in (71cm) by 1¼in (3cm)

Waistband (including apron ties)
cut one silk

gather

Sleeve
cut two red woolen material

Dress
for 19in (48cm) *Lisette Clanet*

lay on fold

B

A

A

B

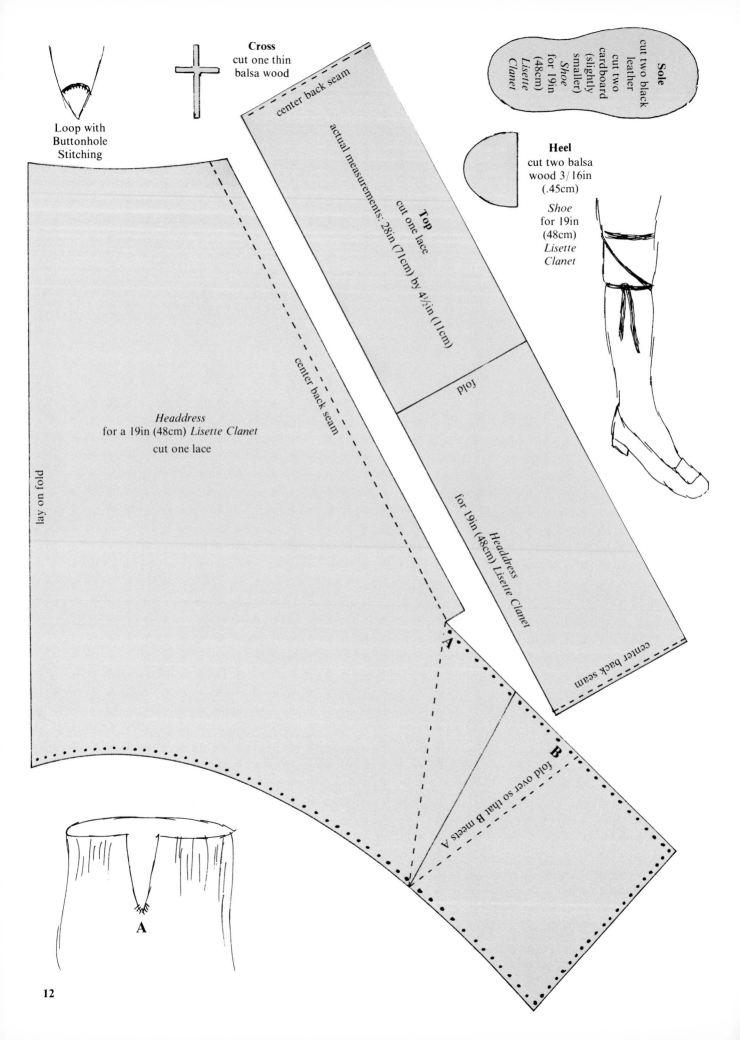

Loop with Buttonhole Stitching

Cross
cut one thin
balsa wood

Sole
cut two black
leather
cut two
cardboard
(slightly
smaller)
Shoe
for 19in
(48cm)
*Lisette
Clanet*

Heel
cut two balsa
wood 3/16in
(.45cm)

Shoe
for 19in
(48cm)
*Lisette
Clanet*

center back seam

Top
cut one lace

actual measurements: 28in (71cm) by 4½in (11cm)

fold

center back seam

Headdress
for a 19in (48cm) *Lisette Clanet*

cut one lace

lay on fold

Headdress
for 19in (48cm) *Lisette Clanet*

center back seam

A

B

fold over so that B meets A

A

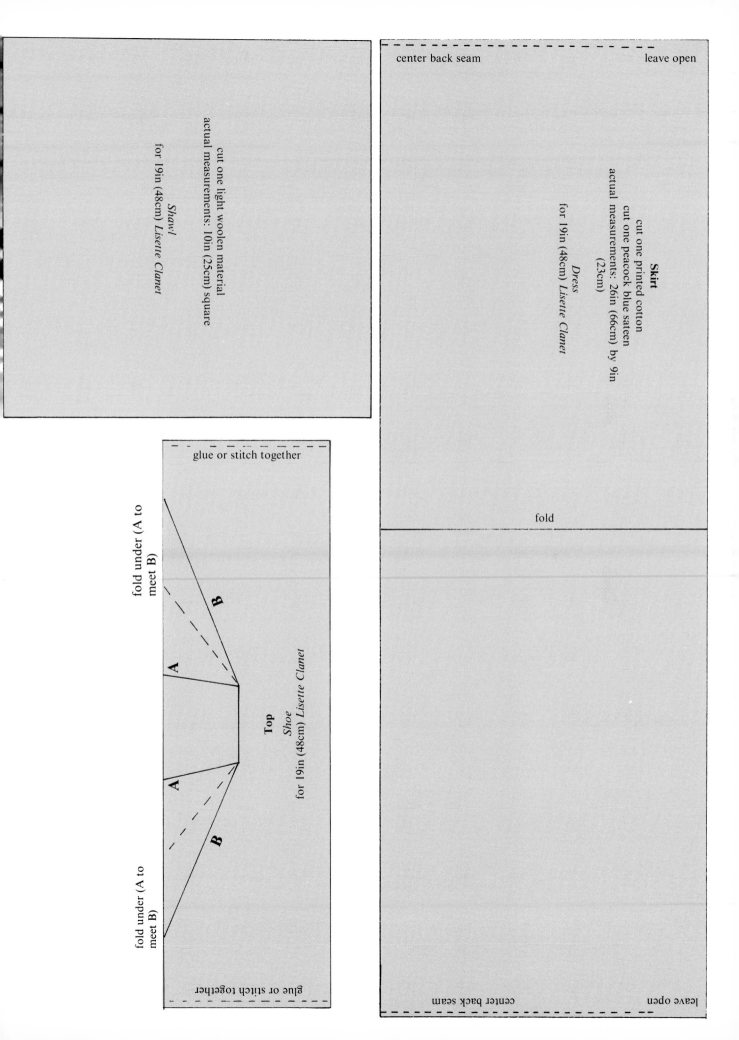

Shawl
for 19in (48cm) *Lisette Clanet*

actual measurements: 10in (25cm) square
cut one light woolen material

Skirt
actual measurements: 26in (66cm) by 9in (23cm)
cut one peacock blue sateen
cut one printed cotton
Dress
for 19in (48cm) *Lisette Clanet*

center back seam   leave open

fold

center back seam   leave open

---

glue or stitch together

fold under (A to meet **B**)

B

A

Top
Shoe
for 19in (48cm) *Lisette Clanet*

A

B

fold under (A to meet **B**)

glue or stitch together

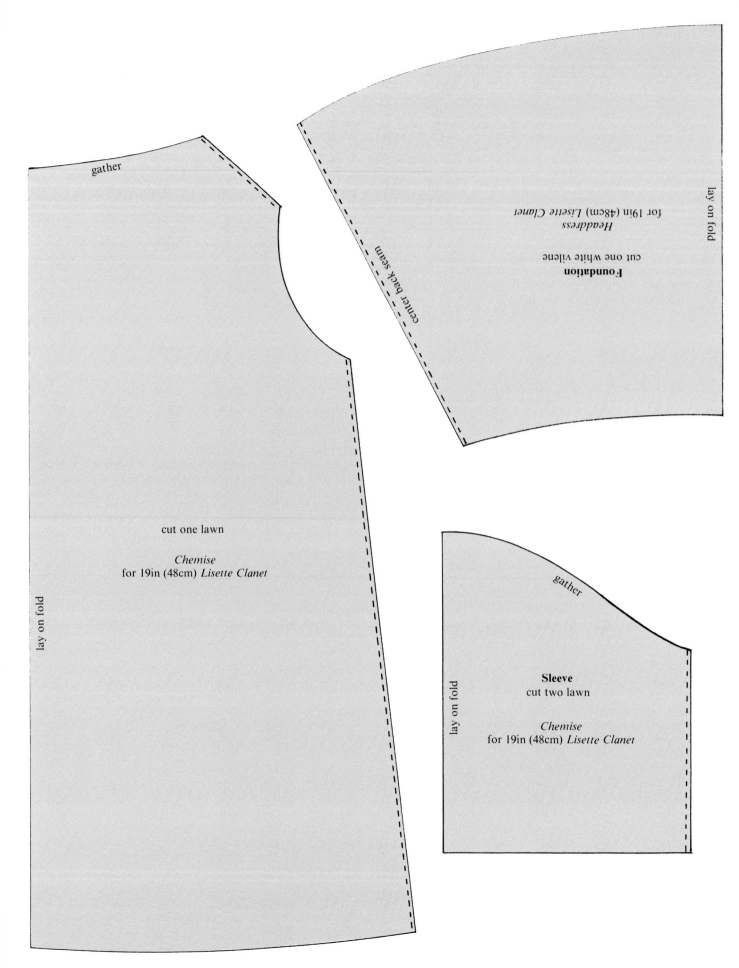

gather

lay on fold

cut one lawn

Chemise
for 19in (48cm) *Lisette Clanet*

center back seam

lay on fold

Foundation
cut one white vilene

Headdress
for 19in (48cm) *Lisette Clanet*

lay on fold

gather

lay on fold

Sleeve
cut two lawn

Chemise
for 19in (48cm) *Lisette Clanet*

14

Polonaise and Petticoat, Circa 1775
To fit a 12in (30cm) to 13in (33cm) lady doll.

by **Kathleen Songal**

The robe a la polonaise was a favorite daytime dress worn by fashionable ladies in France, England and the Americas in the 1770s. It was an informal walking dress characterized by being made shorter than its ankle-length petticoat with its overskirt caught up and draped in three puffs at the back. Marie Antoinette popularized this style playing milkmaid at the Petit Trianon and Marly and soon all fashionables adopted it. In keeping with its simple lines and its attempt to mimic dress of the common countrywoman, it was often made from calicoes, lovely printed and painted cotton fabrics.

DESCRIPTION OF CALICO POLONAISE WITH MATCHING PETTICOAT:

The polonaise bodice is cut tight fitted in both front and back with a very low front neckline. The bodice opens down the center front with an edge to edge opening, secured by either hooks and eyes or pins. It is deeply pointed in the front and back and exhibits a typical 1770 dress construction feature in having the bodice front and side piece cut in one resulting in no side seams, but rather, gored back seams. This cutting technique makes the bodice back waistline appear very slender. This illusion is further reinforced by the addition of trim outlining mock seams (indicated by dashed lines on the pattern) at center back and on either side of center back. Our bodice example is not boned but is interfaced to help retain its shape. Purists may wish to substitute small flat toothpicks sewn into a linen lining in order to obtain a boned bodice. The close-fitted sleeve extends just over the elbow in the back of the arm and curves in shorter in the front where the arm bends. The unlined overskirt is pleated to the bottom edge of the bodice leaving a gap in the center front that exposes the petticoat. The overskirt is then draped into three puffs at the back by arranging it into folds produced by drawing the fabric through narrow doubled bands attached under bows at the bodice back. The matching petticoat differs from authentic construction by opening in the center back rather than at the sides. A fine gauze neckerchief is tied at the bosom. In the 1770s self-fabric pleated and pinked ruffles and bands were the preferred trims for this style of dress. Likewise, this polonaise is outlined with a self-fabric ruffle along all outer edges of the overskirt. The ruffle is cut deeper at the skirt's bottom edges and narrows as it nears the front waistline. The bodice neckline edge and sleeve bottoms are finished off with self-material pleated bands.

HOW TO MAKE POLONAISE AND PETTICOAT:

BODICE:

Interface front and back bodice pieces.

Sew bodice fronts to bodice back at side and shoulder seams.

Narrowly hem neckline, front edge openings and bodice bottom.

Using three strands of embroidery thread outline with stem stitch mock seams (indicated by dashed lines on pattern) at the center back and at either side of center back.

For trim, closely pleat narrow band of self-material and sew to bodice neckline edge.

SLEEVES:

Sew sleeve together along arm seams.

Narrowly hem bottom sleeve edge.

Sew sleeve into armhole matching *a's.*

For trim, closely pleat narrow band of self-material and sew to lower edge of sleeve.

OVERSKIRT:

Narrowly hem bottom and center front edges of overskirt.

For trim, cut strip of self-material 3/4in (2cm) wide at center graduating to 1/2in (1.3cm) wide at ends. Gather strip into ruffle and sew to outer edges of overskirt.

Closely pleat top edge of overskirt. All pleats must face from center front toward center back. Add an additional row of staystitching 1/2in (1.3cm) below top row to hold pleats in place.

Pin overskirt UNDER bodice at the doll's natural waistline leaving a gap between *b's* in the center front.

Sew bottom edge of outside bodice to overskirt. This procedure will create an excess amount of pleated material at the inside waistline that can be eliminated by folding it down and clipping where necessary.

For loops, cut two lengths of narrow ribbon. Double the ribbon and sew one end inside the back bodice at the position marked X on the pattern and the other end of the doubled ribbon on the outside of the back bodice at the same position. These loops will hold the overskirt into three swags to create the polonaise.

Make three small bows out of ribbon. Place one bow at the center front of the bodice and another at either side of the back bodice over the ribbon loops at the position marked X on the pattern.

PETTICOAT:

Narrowly hem back opening and bottom edges of petticoat.

Closely pleat top edge of petticoat. All pleats must face from center front toward center back.

Sew petticoat to waistband.

Sew center back seams together.

NECKERCHIEF:

Narrowly hem all outside edges of neckerchief. □

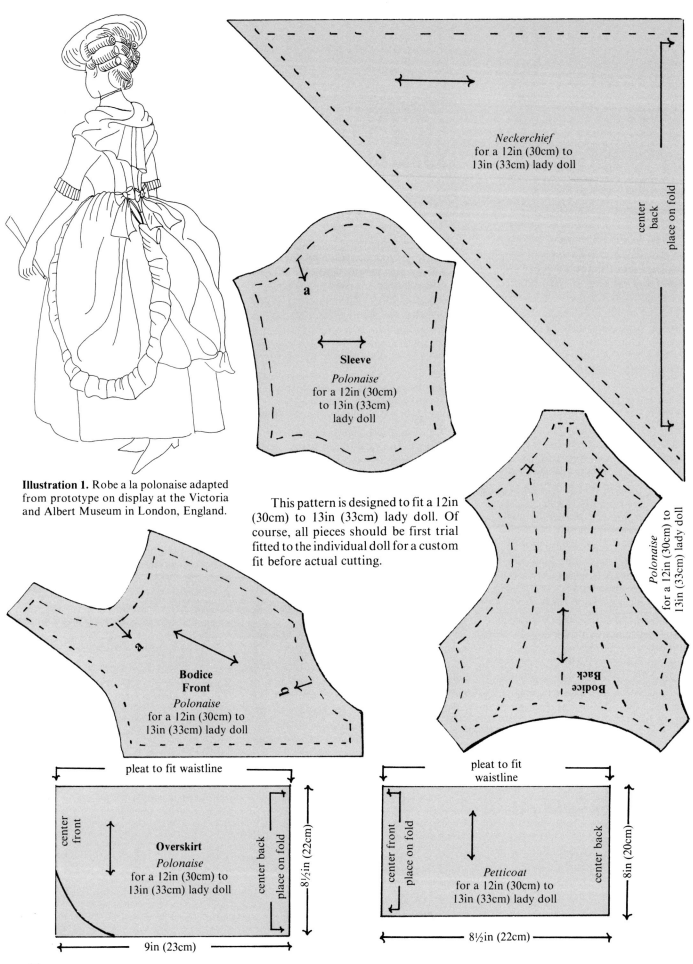

Illustration 1. Robe a la polonaise adapted from prototype on display at the Victoria and Albert Museum in London, England.

Neckerchief
for a 12in (30cm) to 13in (33cm) lady doll

center back

place on fold

Sleeve
Polonaise
for a 12in (30cm) to 13in (33cm) lady doll

a

This pattern is designed to fit a 12in (30cm) to 13in (33cm) lady doll. Of course, all pieces should be first trial fitted to the individual doll for a custom fit before actual cutting.

Bodice Front
Polonaise
for a 12in (30cm) to 13in (33cm) lady doll

a

b

Bodice Back

Polonaise
for a 12in (30cm) to 13in (33cm) lady doll

pleat to fit waistline

center front

Overskirt
Polonaise
for a 12in (30cm) to 13in (33cm) lady doll

center back

place on fold

8½in (22cm)

9in (23cm)

pleat to fit waistline

center front

place on fold

Petticoat
for a 12in (30cm) to 13in (33cm) lady doll

center back

8in (20cm)

8½in (22cm)

A Traditional English Pedlar Doll to Make

by **Barbara Pickering**

Illustration 1. A traditional English pedlar doll.

"Now Industry awakes her busy sons;
Full charged with News the breathless
   hawker runs;
Shops open, coaches roll, carts shake
   the ground,
And all the streets with passing cries
   resound."

                  (Anon.)

Reading Mary Hillier's article about English pedlar dolls (August/September 1982 **Doll Reader**®), I thought readers might like to have a pattern for this fascinating doll.

I bought a ceramic head for a 14in (36cm) to 16in (41cm) doll which had an older woman's expression, although her features were nearly all worn away. However, a little paint and paint brush soon put things right. I used sheep's wool for her hair, looking very realistic! I managed to get a pair of matching arms, although I give a pattern for making them as well.

You should put a wire frame inside the doll's body if you wish her to stand up properly. I, myself, prefer to use a doll's support stand.

After having made up the doll, do remember to check the various pattern pieces, as no dolls are alike. Some slight adjustments will inevitably have to be made to suit your particular doll. All pattern pieces are on the generous side, so they can easily be adjusted to fit your doll.

MATERIALS:
One head to suit a 14in (36cm) to 16in (41cm) doll
Sheep's wool or human hair wig
20in (51cm) by 11in (28cm) calico (body) — if you buy arms you will, of course, need less material
36in (91cm) by 21in (53cm) white cotton (drawers, shift, petticoat, apron)
1/4in (.7cm) white cotton tape (chemise, drawers)
18in (46cm) by 1in (2cm) white scalloped cotton lace (drawers)
Two small buttons (petticoats)
22in (56cm) by 11in (28cm) red flannel (under petticoat)
43in (109cm) by 20in (51cm) small patterned cotton print (dress)
7in (18cm) by 1/2in (1.3cm) off-white scalloped lace (dress collar)
Five small pearl buttons (dress)
One pair of old woolen socks, either black or dark blue (stockings)
16in (41cm) by 12in (30cm) woolen fabric (cape)
Dark blue or black bias binding (cape)
Two small dark blue or black buttons (cape)
6in (15cm) by 5in (13cm) black leather (shoes)
5in (13cm) by 3in (8cm) strong brown leather (shoe soles)
5in (13cm) by 3in (8cm) cardboard (inner shoe soles)
9in (23cm) by 7in (18cm) black felt (bonnet)

Approximately 40in (102cm) by 1/2in (1.3cm) black satin ribbon (bonnet)
Approximately 43in (109cm) by 1in (2cm) white tape (ruffle for inside bonnet)
6in (15cm) by 6in (15cm) brown silk (umbrella)
Approximately 21in (53cm) by 1/4in (.7cm) dark brown braid (edging of umbrella)
6¾in (17cm) by 1/2in (1.3cm) dowel (umbrella stick)
One small "ivory" bead, 1/4in (.7cm) diameter (umbrella knob)
Two small washers, 1/4in (.7cm) diameter (umbrella)
Sandpaper
Sanding sealer
Brown and black paint
Thin sisal (basket)
5in (13cm) by 3in (8cm) cardboard (pattern for basket)
Approximately 15in (38cm) by 9in (23cm) green felt (lining of basket)
Approximately 15in (38cm) by 3/4in (2cm) off-white cotton tape (shoulder strap of basket
Polyurethane clear varnish
Sobo glue
Filling
Machine sewing cotton

BODY: Make darts in back and front of body. Stitch both pieces together along broken lines as indicated on the pattern. Leave an opening at the neck for stuffing. Turn right side out. Stuff until it is firm and has a good shape.

ARMS: Sew all around arms along broken lines. Turn right side out. Stuff within about 1/2in (1.3cm) of the top. Sew across the top of the stuffing. Turn under raw edges and sew arms to shoulders. If you wish, you can stitch across the elbow joints so that both arms become flexible (indicated by the solid line on the pattern). Also outline the fingers with matching sewing cotton, either by machine or by hand.

LEGS: Proceed as for arms.

HEAD: Attach your head firmly to the body.

STOCKINGS: Use an old pair of dark blue or black woolen socks. To measure, wrap the material around the leg (wrong side facing you) and tack together, stretching the material tightly as you go along. Slip it off the leg and sew along tacking stitches. Cut away any surplus material, turn right side out and neaten top opening.

DRAWERS: Sew each inner leg along broken lines (French seam). The seam from groin to waist is left open. Hem each edge of crotch seam. Cut a waistband 1in (2cm) wide by the doll's waist measurement plus a little overlap. Gather top of the drawers to fit waistband. With right sides together sew waistband to top of drawers. Then turn waistband to wrong side of drawers, turn under raw edges and sew. Neaten both ends, but leave open and pull a narrow cotton tape through the waistband. Tie at the back. Adjust length of drawers, neaten hemline and sew white scalloped cotton lace to it.

CHEMISE: Stitch together shoulder and side seams (French seam) along broken lines. Make a small back opening and hem neatly. Cut a bias strip of the same material 1/2in (1.3cm) wide by neckline width. With right sides together sew strip to neckline. Turn strip to wrong side of chemise, turn raw edges under and hem. Neaten both ends but leave open to pull a narrow cotton tape through it. Tie at the back. Hem armholes. Adjust length of chemise and hem neatly. A pedlar woman's chemise was usually without lace.

RED FLANNEL AND WHITE COTTON PETTICOATS: It was customary to wear two petticoats: the first one was a lovely bright red flannel petticoat, the other a white cotton one.

Both petticoats are made in the same way. Both open at the back and are fastened with a small covered button (from the same material of the petticoat).

For the red flannel petticoat cut a piece of material measuring approximately 22in (56cm) by 10in (25cm). Cut a waistband 1in (2cm) wide by waistline measurement plus a small overlap. Mark hem fold line about 1/2in (1.3cm) from bottom edge. Then mark the first tuck fold line about 1in (2cm) above hem fold line. Repeat for second tuck fold line. Pin tucks and stitch. Always stitch from the top of the tuck, that is the side which is uppermost after pressing. Next fold the material in half and sew center back seam (French seam). Gather waistband of petticoat to fit waistband. Place right sides together and sew. Turn waistband to wrong side of petticoat, turn raw edges under and sew. Neaten and sew up both end openings. Make a small buttonhole and fasten

petticoat with a red covered button. Stitch a small pocket to the front of the petticoat to safeguard the pedlar's daily profits!

For the white cotton petticoat cut a piece of material measuring approximately 23in (58cm) by 11in (28cm). Proceed in exactly the same way as before. The red flannel petticoat should show slightly beneath the white one!

DRESS: The traditional pedlar's dress was a patterned cotton print, usually in dark colors. I used a navy blue background with tiny multi-colored flowers and green and turquoise leaves — a pattern I found just perfect for the dress.

BODICE: Sew the two bodice fronts to the back at side and shoulder seams (French seam). Make darts in front and back if necessary.

Fold the **sleeves** in half and sew along broken lines (French seam). Gather top of sleeves to fit armholes and sew sleeves into bodice.

Cut two **cuffs:** 1in (2cm) wide by wrist measurement plus a small overlap. Gather wrists to fit cuffs. Place right sides of cuffs to right sides of sleeves and sew together. Turn cuffs to wrong side, turn under raw edges and sew. Neaten and sew up both end openings. Make a small buttonhole on both cuffs and sew a pearl button on to both cuffs. Turn both sides of bodice front openings in on fold lines. Before doing so, fit the bodice to the doll to get the fold lines absolutely right. Fold under raw edges and sew. Cut a piece of the same material on the cross — about 3/4in (2cm) by neck measurement. With right sides together sew neckband to dress. Turn strip to wrong side of dress, turn under raw edges and sew. Neaten and sew up both end openings. The neckline should fit tightly. It may be necessary, therefore, to gather the neckline just slightly before you sew the bias strip on.

Make three small buttonholes on the front and fasten with three pearl buttons.

Stitch on lace collar.

SKIRT: Cut a piece of material measuring approximately 24in (61cm) by 11in (28cm). Proceed as for petticoats, but leave out the waistband. Gather top of skirt to fit bodice. With right sides together sew skirt to bodice. Finish off the front skirt opening with a small hem.

BELT: Make it from a piece of the same material measuring approximately 1¼in (3cm) by 9¼in (24cm).

With right sides together fold the material in half and sew. Turn right side out; turn under raw edges of both ends and close with neat stitches. Make a small button hole and fasten belt with a pearl button.

APRON: This is made from a piece of white cotton material, measuring approximately 11in (28cm) by 9in (23cm). Make 1/4in (.7cm) side hems and a 3/4in (2cm) bottom hem. Gather top of apron slightly to go approximately two-thirds around the waist. Cut a waistband to fit gathered top of apron and add another 8in (20cm). This will give you an adequate length to tie at the back. With right sides together, sew waistband to gathered apron top. Turn waistband to wrong side of apron; turn under raw edges and sew. Neaten and sew up both openings. Spray with starch and iron. The apron should be very crisp, indeed.

CAPE: Tradition has it that pedlar women wore red woolen capes which were often bound with a contrasting color. I found a beautiful, but rather old, red woolen skirt in my material box which was ideal for a cape.

Just cut out the pattern and bind the edges of the cape either with dark blue or black bias binding. Sew two small blue or black buttons to the front of the cape; make a thread loop in matching color and fasten the cape. Fold the cape over at the neck.

BONNET: If you have an old black velour hat, all the better. If not, black felt will do. To make the hat brim slightly stiffer, I have sewn two rows of black stitching (see pattern).

Fold the material in half and sew together the small seam indicated by the short broken lines. Insert the crown, matching points A. Then stitch black satin ribbon across the hat, leaving approximately 8in (20cm) hanging on either side for tying under the chin. Make a nice big bow and stitch to top of bonnet. I sprayed the whole bonnet with hair spray to give it more firmness.

Normally a pedlar woman would wear a starched mob cap with frills underneath her bonnet. I compromised in this respect by just lining the inside brim with a frill to frame the doll's face. For this I used approximately 42in (107cm) by 1in (2cm) white cotton tape. I pulled a gathering thread along the middle, pulled it sufficiently tight to fit the inside brim. Then I arranged the frills as evenly as possible as little box pleats. This is

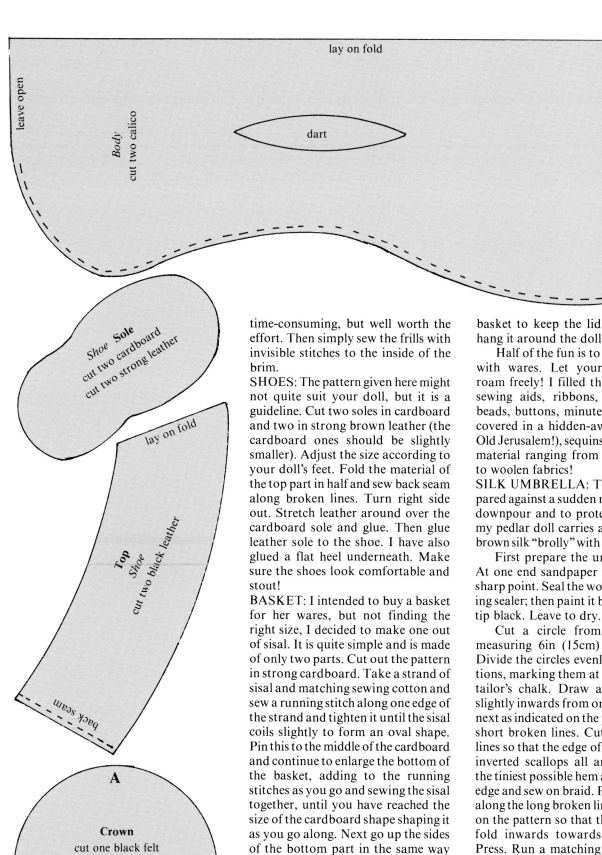

time-consuming, but well worth the effort. Then simply sew the frills with invisible stitches to the inside of the brim.

SHOES: The pattern given here might not quite suit your doll, but it is a guideline. Cut two soles in cardboard and two in strong brown leather (the cardboard ones should be slightly smaller). Adjust the size according to your doll's feet. Fold the material of the top part in half and sew back seam along broken lines. Turn right side out. Stretch leather around over the cardboard sole and glue. Then glue leather sole to the shoe. I have also glued a flat heel underneath. Make sure the shoes look comfortable and stout!

BASKET: I intended to buy a basket for her wares, but not finding the right size, I decided to make one out of sisal. It is quite simple and is made of only two parts. Cut out the pattern in strong cardboard. Take a strand of sisal and matching sewing cotton and sew a running stitch along one edge of the strand and tighten it until the sisal coils slightly to form an oval shape. Pin this to the middle of the cardboard and continue to enlarge the bottom of the basket, adding to the running stitches as you go and sewing the sisal together, until you have reached the size of the cardboard shape shaping it as you go along. Next go up the sides of the bottom part in the same way for about 3/4in (2cm).

Next make the lid. Proceed in the same way as for the bottom, but do not go upwards. Sew the lid to the basket; coat it with clear varnish to give it sturdiness. When dry, line the inside with green felt by gluing it to the sisal. Attach a tape to the lid and

basket to keep the lid open and to hang it around the doll's neck.

Half of the fun is to fill the basket with wares. Let your imagination roam freely! I filled the basket with sewing aids, ribbons, braids, lace, beads, buttons, minute scissors (discovered in a hidden-away bazaar in Old Jerusalem!), sequins, good quality material ranging from Chinese silks to woolen fabrics!

SILK UMBRELLA: To be well prepared against a sudden not infrequent downpour and to protect her wares, my pedlar doll carries a typical large brown silk "brolly" with "ivory" knob!

First prepare the umbrella stick: At one end sandpaper the stick to a sharp point. Seal the wood with sanding sealer; then paint it brown and the tip black. Leave to dry.

Cut a circle from brown silk, measuring 6in (15cm) in diameter. Divide the circles evenly into 12 sections, marking them at the edge with tailor's chalk. Draw a line curving slightly inwards from one point to the next as indicated on the pattern by the short broken lines. Cut round these lines so that the edge of the circle has inverted scallops all around. Make the tiniest possible hem all around the edge and sew on braid. Pleat the circle along the long broken lines as marked on the pattern so that these lines will fold inwards towards the handle. Press. Run a matching thread along all the points. Cut a tiny hole through the middle of the circle and slip the prepared handle down the center of pleats and out through the hole. Glue one washer to inside of material, the other to the outside. This will keep the material firmly in place. Pull up the gathering thread tightly and fasten

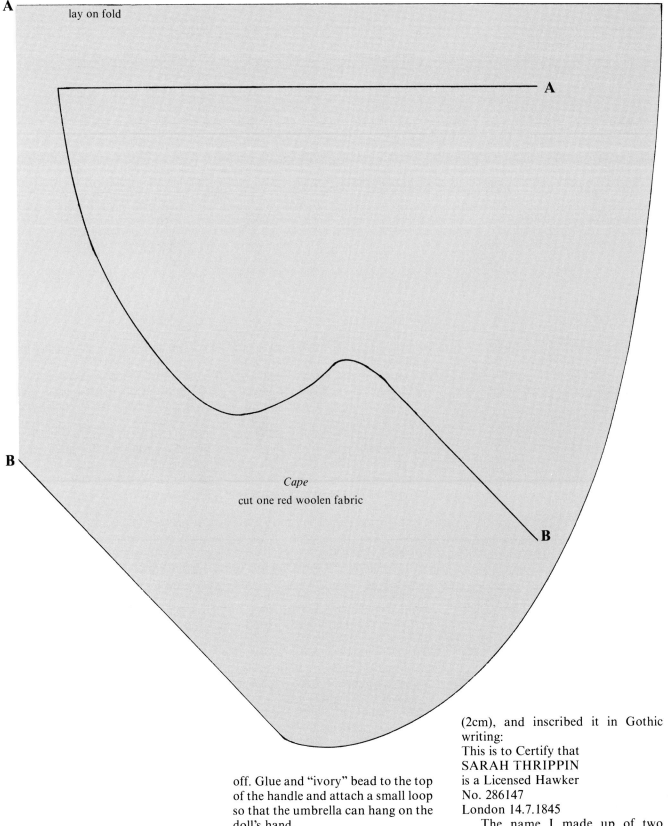

A

lay on fold

A

B

Cape
cut one red woolen fabric

B

(2cm), and inscribed it in Gothic writing:

This is to Certify that
SARAH THRIPPIN
is a Licensed Hawker
No. 286147
London 14.7.1845

off. Glue and "ivory" bead to the top of the handle and attach a small loop so that the umbrella can hang on the doll's hand.

Last but not least: In order to abide by the strict law ruling English mid-Victorian times, pedlars had to carry a license. So, naturally I made one for my doll. I cut a small piece of white cardboard, 2in (5cm) by 1in

The name I made up of two pedlars who are supposed to have roamed the English countryside, namely Sarah Thrifty and Sarah Trippin. For the numbers I used parts of my husband's and my birth dates.

HAPPY SEWING! □

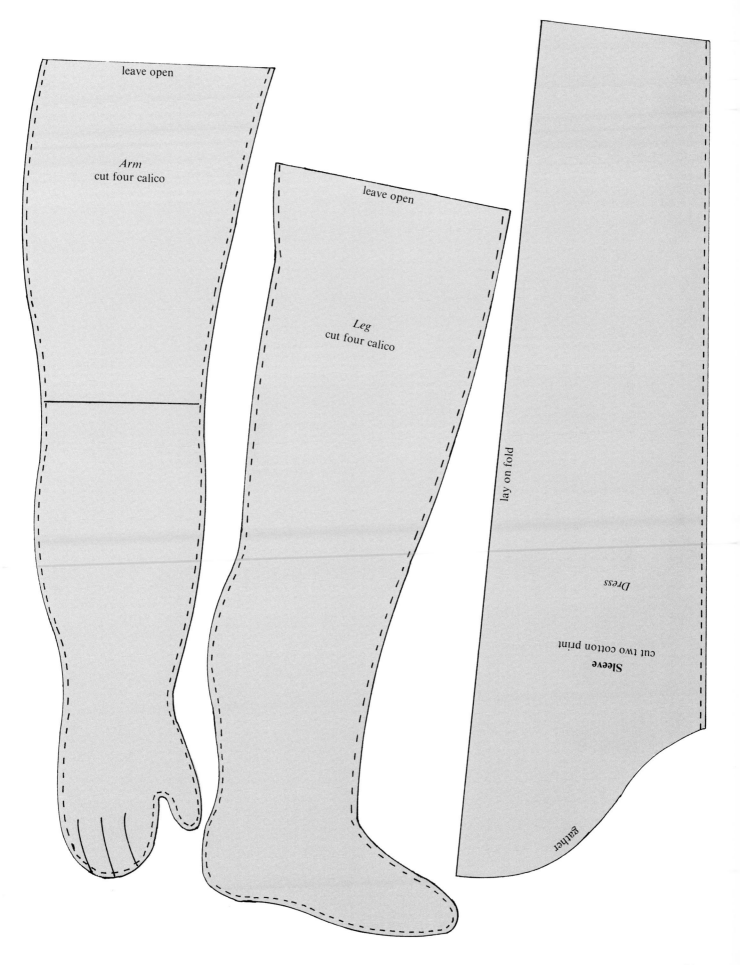

leave open

Arm
cut four calico

leave open

Leg
cut four calico

lay on fold

Dress

Sleeve
cut two cotton print

gather

gather

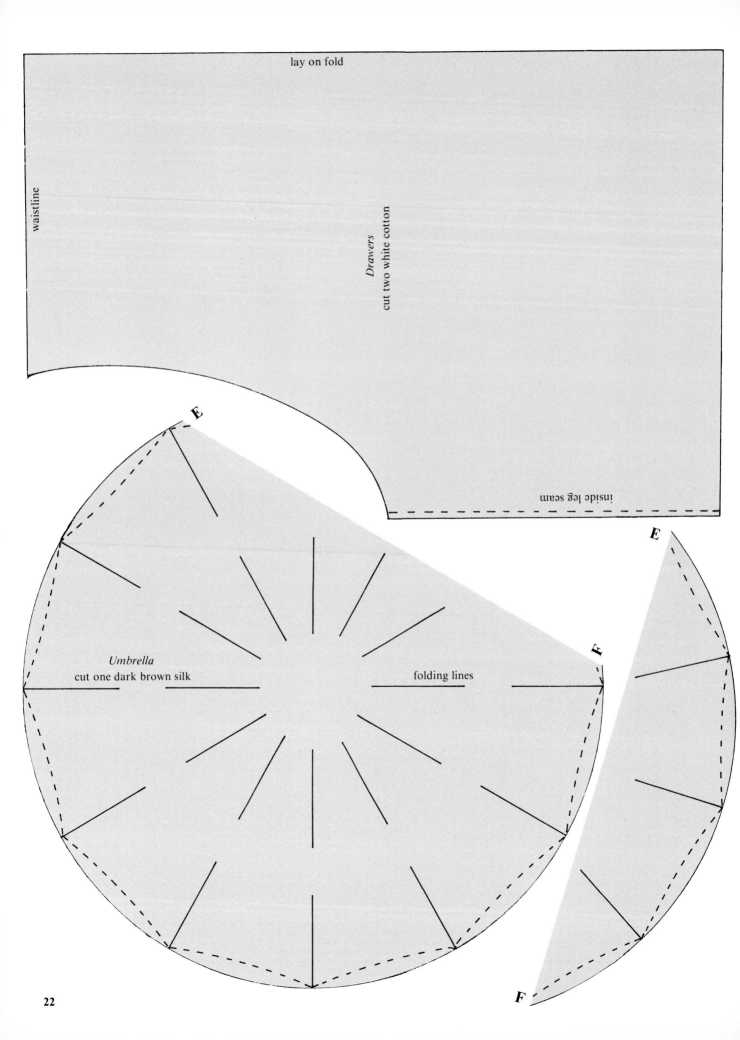

lay on fold

waistline

Drawers
cut two white cotton

inside leg seam

E

Umbrella
cut one dark brown silk

folding lines

E

F

F

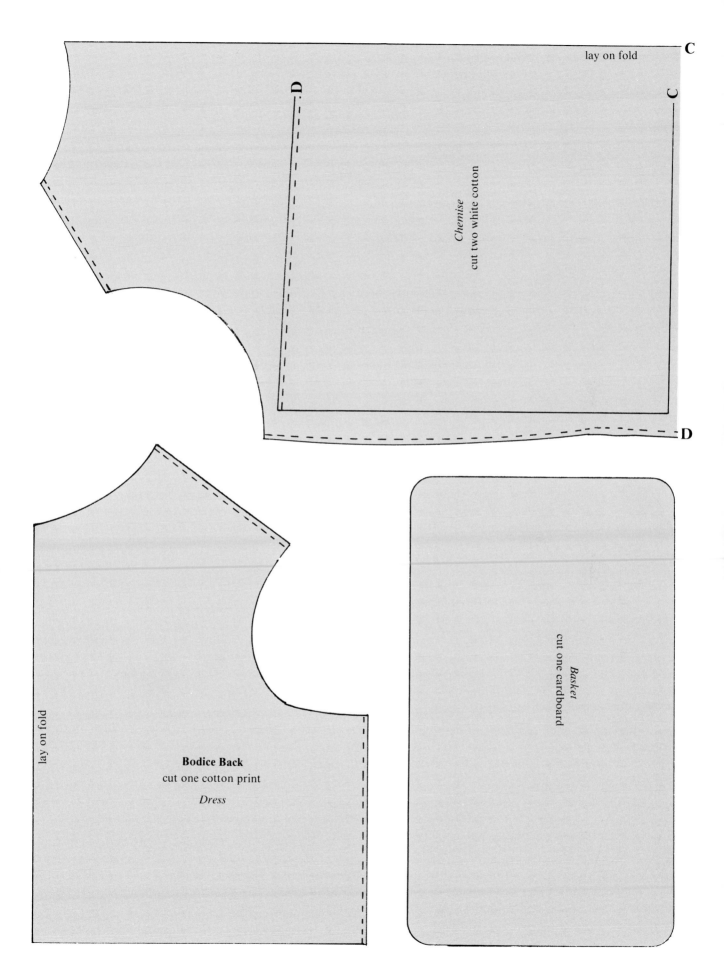

lay on fold C

C

Chemise
cut two white cotton

D

D

Bodice Back
cut one cotton print
Dress

lay on fold

Basket
cut one cardboard

23

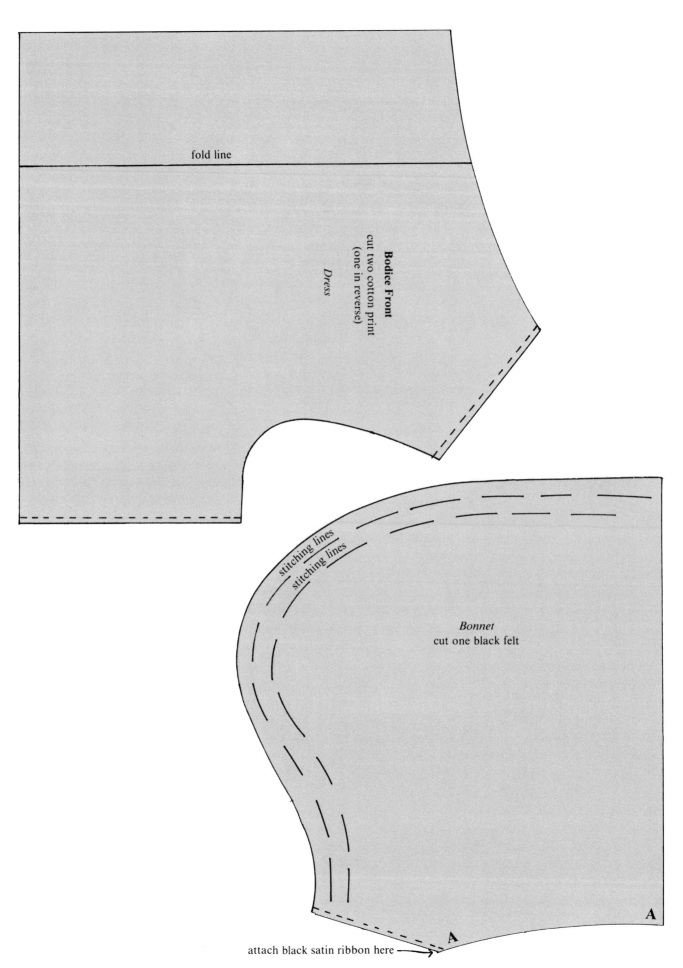

fold line

Bodice Front
cut two cotton print
(one in reverse)

Dress

stitching lines
stitching lines

Bonnet
cut one black felt

A

A

attach black satin ribbon here →

Dressing an 11½in (29cm) China Head Doll

by **Sandy Williams**

Most photographs of a "flat top" china head doll have the doll dressed in a one-piece homemade dress which seems typical of the mid to late 1800s. The low neckline is gathered into a narrow bias strip as are the sleeves. Both the bodice and the very full skirt are gathered onto the same waistband. The fabric is usually a very tiny print calico. The well-dressed women of this era wore a multitude of undergarments — quite often three or more petticoats. I like to dress my dolls in only one petticoat though, to keep down waist-line bulk.

This 11½in (29cm) doll has a china head and limbs. She is marked "C49lear" on the back of the shoulder plate. She has black molded curly hair held back from her face with two coral-tinted bows. Her cheeks, lips, eyelid and nostril markings are also coral tinted. Medium blue eyes set off her features beautifully. On her feet are plain black molded high-heeled boots. Her undressed measurements are: 6½in (16cm) chest, 5in (13cm) waist, 6in (15cm) hips, 2in (5cm) upper arm, 3½in (9cm) thigh and 5in (13cm) crotch.

The patterns are listed in order of placement on doll: open drawers, chemise, tucked petticoat (or use plain petticoat) and dress. Since the muslin bodies on china head dolls vary from doll to doll, the patterns should be used as a guide. Finish one garment **before** you measure your doll for the next garment. I like to first try out a pattern in a "pattern tracing cloth" which can be marked on, sewn on and is also semi-transparent — plus you can take the garment apart and use it as a pattern. Set your sewing machine for 10 to 12 stitches per inch. The patterns include a 1/4in (.65cm) seam allowance. Press after each sewing step. Use extra fine thread for lightweight fabrics for sewing doll clothes.

OPEN DRAWERS: 5¾in (15cm) finished length. Cut two drawer patterns from white batiste and a waistband 1in (2cm) wide by doll's waist measurement plus 1½in (4cm); I needed 1in (2cm) by 6½in (16cm). Mark the

Illustration 1. 11½in (29cm) china head doll in her dress.

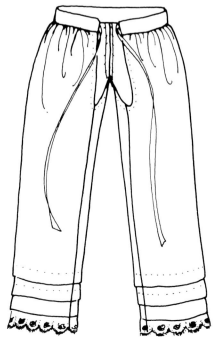

Illustration 2. Back of drawers.

two tuck fold lines; press on fold lines; stitch 3/16in (.45cm) in from fold lines to make tucks. Hem drawers 1/2in (1.3cm) and blindstitch 3/8in (.9cm) wide white lace to this edge. French seam each inner leg seam. Sew the two leg pieces together from center front waist to dot; narrowly hem each edge of crotch seam. Gather waist of drawers to fit waistband (waistband overlaps waist about 1/2in (1.3cm) on each end). Attach waistband, tucking in 1/8in (.31cm) wide white twill tape as you sew. Place drawers on doll; pull tapes; wrap tapes around doll's waist and tie in a small bow.

CHEMISE: Knee length, off-the-shoulder. Fold white batiste twice so that shoulder and center front/center back edges are on folds. Mark tucks. Sew each tuck with tiny backhand stitches; make each 1/2in (1.3cm) long; press tucks as illustrated. Gather back chemise between dots to fit doll (about 1½in [4cm] of gathers). Cut a bias strip of white batiste 3/4in (2cm) wide by the desired neckline width plus 1/2in (1.3cm) needed 3/4in (2cm) by 7in (18cm). With right sides of bias strip and chemise together, sew a 1/4in (.65cm) seam; trim to 1/8in (.31cm). Turn bias strip to wrong side of chemise and turn raw edge in 1/8in (.31cm); blindstitch closed. Hem sleeve and sew 3/8in (.9cm) wide white lace to sleeve edge. French seam side seams. Turn chemise hem up 1/2in (1.3cm) and blindstitch.

TUCKED PETTICOAT: Mid-calf length (5½in [14cm] finished length). Cut a piece of white batiste 6¾in (17cm) by 19in (48cm) and a waistband 1in (2cm) wide by waistline measurement plus 1/2in (1.3cm); I needed 1in (2cm) by 6in (15cm). Mark hem fold line 1/2in (1.3cm) from bottom edge; mark first tuck fold line 1/2in (1.3cm) above hem fold line; mark second tuck fold line 5/8in (1.6cm) above first tuck fold line (use drawer tuck lines as a guide). Follow drawers' directions for tucks, hem and lace edge. Sew a 1/4in (.65cm) center back seam to within 2in (5cm) of waistline. Press seam open; turn raw edges of center back seam and opening in and blind stitch closed. Gather waist of petticoat to fit waistband; sew together. Close petticoat with tiny button and thread loop.

Illustration 4. Petticoat.

PLAIN PETTICOAT (optional; may be used instead of tucked petticoat): Mid-calf (5½in [14cm] finished length). Cut a piece of white batiste 6¼in (16cm) by 19in (48cm) and a waistband 1in (2cm) wide by waistline measurement plus 1/2in (1.3cm). Sew a 1/4in (.65cm) center back seam to within 2in (5cm) of waistline. Press seam open, turn raw edges of center back seam and

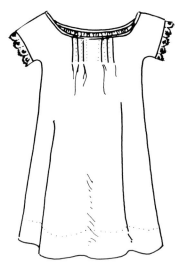

Illustration 3. Chemise.

opening in and blind stitch closed. Turn hem up 1/2in (1.3cm), tuck raw edge in and blindstitch closed. Gather waist of petticoat to fit waistband; sew together. Close petticoat with tiny button and thread loop.

DRESS: Finished skirt length is 7¼in (18cm) long. Use the dress illustration as a guide. BODICE: Fold dress fabric so that bodice shoulders and center front/center back seams are on folds. Cut out and mark all gathering symbols. Slit the bodice back center back fold line open; turn center back edges in 1/2in (1.3cm), tuck raw edges in and blindstitch closed. Gather center back, center front and shoulder neckline areas between symbols. Cut a 3/4in (2cm) by 7in (18cm) bias strip of dress fabric; adjust all neckline gathers to fit bias strip. With right sides of bias strip and bodice together, sew a 1/4in (.65cm) seam; trim seam to 1/8in (.31cm); turn bias strip to wrong side of bodice, tuck raw edge in and blindstitch closed. Gather sleeve edge between dots. Cut two bias strips 3/4in (2cm)

by 2½in (6cm). With right sides of bias strip and sleeve together, adjust gathers to fit bias strip; sew a 1/4in (.65cm) seam; trim seam to 1/8in (.31cm). Sew sleeve and bodice sides together; stitch again 1/8in (.31cm) away; trim close to second stitching. Turn sleeve bias strip to wrong side of sleeve; tuck raw edge in and blindstitch closed. Gather front bodice between stars. Cut a waistband 3/4in (2cm) by 7in (18cm). With right sides of waistband and bodice together, pin waistband to bodice with waistband ends extending 1/2in (1.3cm) beyond bodice, match center front of bodice to center front of waistband, adjust gathers to fit waistband, sew together.

DRESS SKIRT: Cut a skirt 8¼in (21cm) by 30in (76cm). With the right sides of the two 8¼in (21cm) edges together, sew a center back seam from 2in (5cm) below waist to hem. Press seam open; tuck raw edges in; blindstitch closed. Press a 3/4in (2cm) hem up; tuck raw edges in and slip stitch hem. Sew three rows of evenly spaced machine gathers within 3/8in (.9cm) of waistline edge. Pull the three gathering threads tightly to fit waistband. With right sides of waistband and skirt together (match center front of skirt to center front of waistband plus have waistband extend 1/2in [1.3cm] beyond center back skirt edges), sew a 1/4in (.65cm) seam; trim seam. Turn the 1/2in (1.3cm) waistband extensions in to wrong side of bodice. Sew 1/4in (.65cm) wide white twill tape over the raw waistline edges — the only visible raw seams inside the dress are the underarm seams. Place dress on doll overlapping center back bodice edges about 1/2in (1.3cm). Close dress with four tiny hooks and eyes or buttons and thread loops. Remove any visible gathering threads on dress. □

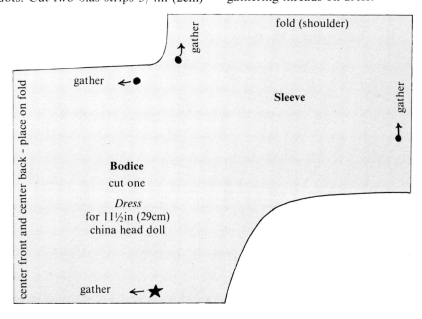

center front and center back - place on fold

gather

gather

fold (shoulder)

gather

Sleeve

gather

Bodice

cut one

Dress

for 11½in (29cm) china head doll

gather ← ★

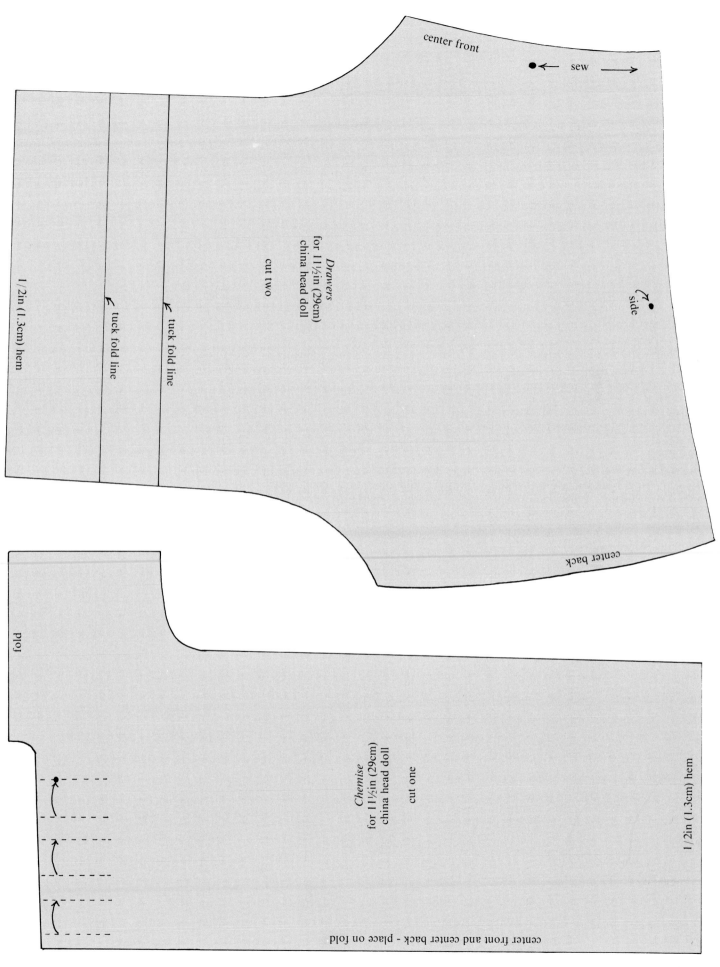

center front

sew

side

center back

1/2in (1.3cm) hem

tuck fold line

tuck fold line

Drawers
for 11½in (29cm)
china head doll

cut two

fold

Chemise
for 11½in (29cm)
china head doll

cut one

1/2in (1.3cm) hem

center front and center back - place on fold

Dress Pattern from Poupée Modèle, 15 June 1867

Submitted and translated by **Dorothy S. Coleman**
and found in the collection of the Widener Library, Harvard University

Patterns redrawn and artwork by **Sandy Williams**

From *POUPEE MODÈLE*, 15 June 1867
For Doll Number 4 (a 17 11/16in [45cm])

No. 15. Dress for doll No. 4, 17 11/16in (45cm). This dress made of woolen cloth is very simple. It is trimmed with black velvet flaps or flaps in a contrasting color to that of the dress. The flaps are held down with a pearl button or a pearl. If desired, each flap can have a narrow taffeta binding. A white border around the black velvet looks well. The flaps form pockets on each side of the skirt front. Flaps are also on the shoulders and one in the middle of the back at the neckline.

These flaps are all simply made of pieces of velvet 5/8in (1.6cm) by 3/4in (2cm) folded at the end. The belt is made in the same way. It is double thickness for strength and is not fastened with a buckle or a clasp, but with a button and a short pointed flap. (See sketches No. 15, 16 and 17 for the front and back of the dress and the belt.)

Pattern No. 18. Front of the bodice of the dress.
Pattern No. 19. Small side of bodice.
Pattern No. 20. Back of bodice.
Pattern No. 21. Sleeve.
Pattern No. 22. Skirt front.
Pattern No. 23. Side of skirt (cut two) attached to the front as indicated by the letters.
Pattern No. 24. Back of the skirt (cut two). It is pleated; all the rest of the skirt is flat. The skirt has five pieces.
Pattern No. 32. Pattern for a fanchon (kerchief) hat for a doll.
Pattern No. 33. Sketch of the fanchon hat.

Cut a piece of thin cardboard the size and shape of No. 32. Sew wire all around the edge. Cover this form by sewing straw braid in layers or with layers of pleated crepe across the back and for streamers, black or white lace is attached by sewing it flat. It is crossed without a knot under the chin. Where the streamers cross a crepe bow, folded several times, is placed and fastened with some pearls to serve as a buckle.

Pattern No. 34. Pattern for the band

from which the bow is formed.
Pattern No. 35. Sketch of the bow itself.
Pattern No. 36. Part of the lappet.

It is simply lace that one can trim. The place where this lace is sewed to the hat is covered by a folded band of crepe, see *Pattern No. 37*. Pearls, jet or crystal can ornament this band. The hat is lined with crepe. The hat can be ornamented with garlands of leaves on each side and a small bouquet at eye level. This hat can be made in any colors of crepe or in straw trimmed with whatever flowers or ribbons are desired.

ADDITIONAL INSTRUCTIONS

Doll Number 4 is a lady or girl doll - Number 4 denoting a 14in (36cm) to 17½in (44cm) doll.

Before you cut out this pattern, measure your doll and compare these

No. 15 Front of Dress

No. 33 Fanchon Hat

No. 16 Back of Dress

No. 17 Belt

No. 35 Bow Sketch

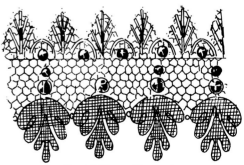

No. 36 Part of Lappet

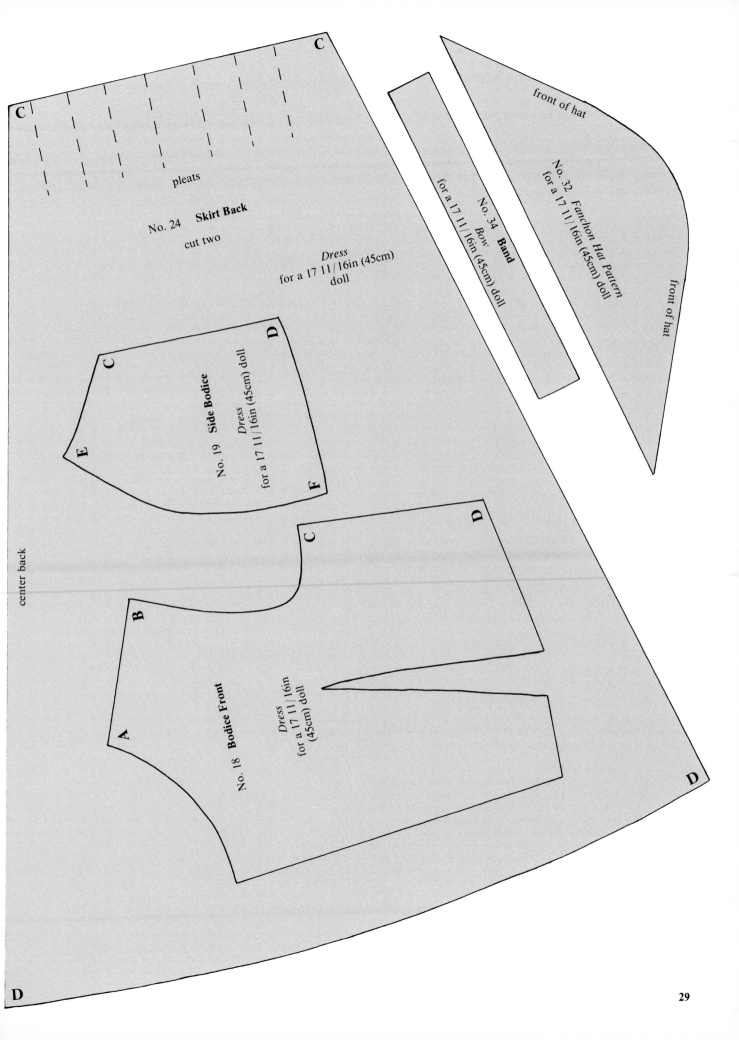

C

C

pleats

No. 24   **Skirt Back**

cut two

Dress
for a 17 11/16in (45cm)
doll

D

C

E

No. 19   **Side Bodice**

Dress
for a 17 11/16in (45cm) doll

F

center back

C

D

B

A

No. 18   **Bodice Front**

Dress
for a 17 11/16in
(45cm) doll

D

D

front of hat

No. 32   *Fanchon Hat Pattern*
for a 17 11/16in (45cm) doll

front of hat

No. 34   **Band**
Bow
for a 17 11/16in (45cm) doll

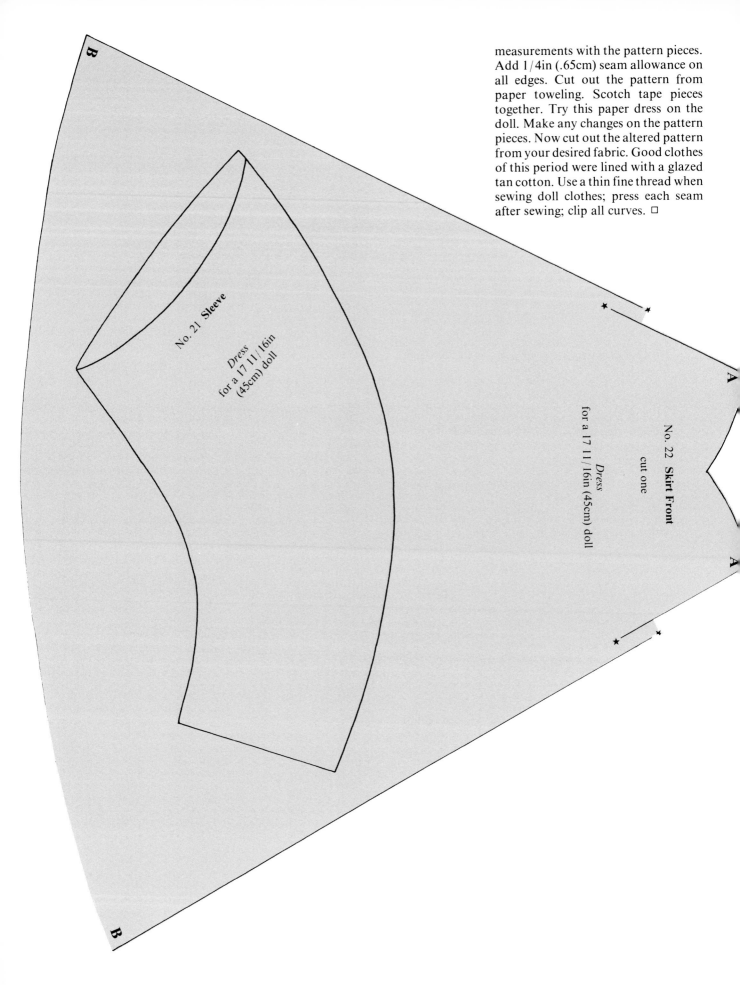

measurements with the pattern pieces. Add 1/4in (.65cm) seam allowance on all edges. Cut out the pattern from paper toweling. Scotch tape pieces together. Try this paper dress on the doll. Make any changes on the pattern pieces. Now cut out the altered pattern from your desired fabric. Good clothes of this period were lined with a glazed tan cotton. Use a thin fine thread when sewing doll clothes; press each seam after sewing; clip all curves. □

No. 21 **Sleeve**

Dress
for a 17 11/16in
(45cm) doll

No. 22 **Skirt Front**

cut one

Dress
for a 17 11/16in (45cm) doll

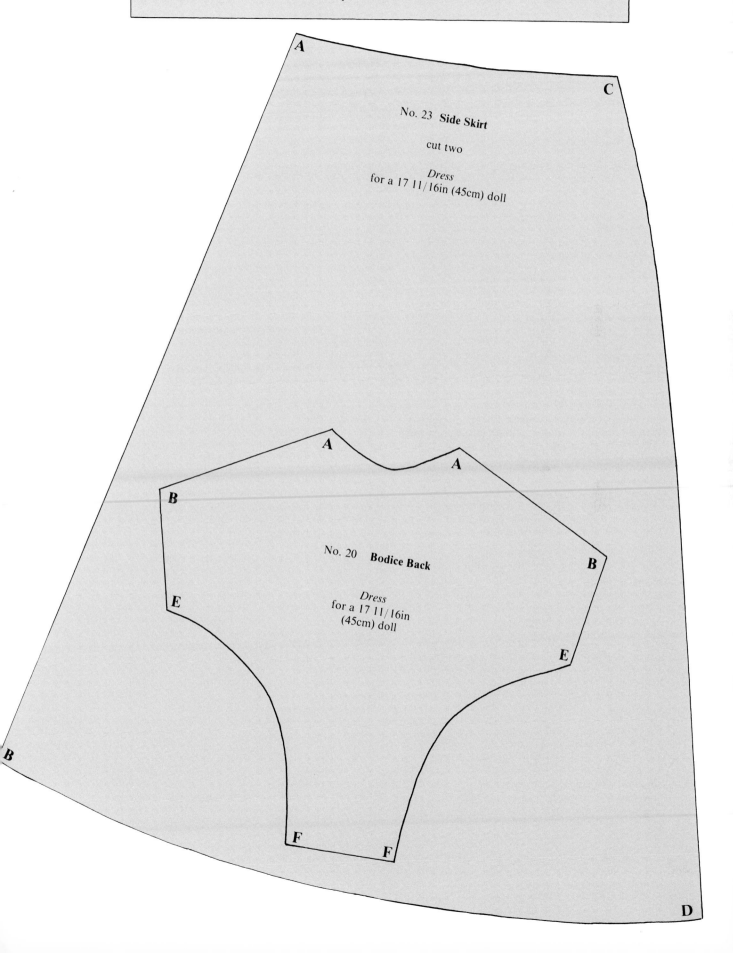

No. 37   Fold crepe three times to this size — for hat

A

C

No. 23 **Side Skirt**

cut two

Dress
for a 17 11/16in (45cm) doll

A

A

B

B

No. 20 **Bodice Back**

Dress
for a 17 11/16in
(45cm) doll

E

E

B

F

F

D

Pattern from Poupée Modèle, August 1867

Submitted and translated by **Dorothy S. Coleman**
and found in the collection of the Widener Library, Harvard University.

Patterns redrawn and artwork by **Sandy Williams**

Patterns for dolls' clothes from the August 1867 issue of *La Poupée Modèle*, a French publication for little girls, are for a skirt, two Bretonne jackets, a mule (bedroom slipper) and a pendant. They will fit a doll size 2, that is 14in (36cm) to 15½in (39cm) tall, except for the mule which fits a doll size number 4, 17½in (44cm) tall. The skirt is made in the same way as the skirt from the article "Dress Pattern from *Poupée Modèle*, 15 June 1867" for a size number 4 doll (see pages 28-31).

Pattern No. 18. Sketch of the skirt and a plain short jacket. Pearl gray wool is suggested as a possible fabric, but other colors and materials could be used.

Pattern No. 19. Pattern for the front of the skirt.

Pattern No. 20. Pattern for the side of the skirt. Two of these pieces are needed, one on each side.

Pattern No. 21. Pattern for the back of the skirt. Cut two.

Pattern No. 22. Pattern for the ornamentation around the bottom of the skirt. This is a Greek design made with narrow red and black braid. Three pieces of braid are placed in the lower sections and fastened at the top with a large steel bead as shown.

Two jacket designs are given. The plain one shown in *Pattern No. 18* is trimmed with braid matching that on the skirt. It is also suggested that it could be bound around the edges with black ribbon and the braid trimming placed on that.

Pattern No. 28. A sketch of a fancy version of the Bretonne jacket with pinked edges, pockets, an escutcheon and embroidery trim. The patterns for this jacket could be used for the

plainer jacket also by negating the pinking around the edges.

Pattern No. 23. Pattern for one of the fronts of the jacket. Two fronts are required.

Pattern No. 24. Pattern for the back of the jacket.

Pattern No. 25. Pattern for the sleeve of the jacket. Four of these pieces would be needed, two for each sleeve.

Pattern No. 26. Pattern for jacket pockets showing embroidery on them. Cut two. The framing is done with a chain stitch. The placing of the two pockets on the jacket is shown in *Pattern No. 28.*

Pattern No. 27. Pattern for the escutcheon which is a pinked rectangle having a male figure embroidered on it, with a red chain stitch frame for the figure. It was noted that if this jacket were made for a larger doll, size number 4, 17½in (44cm) tall, there should be a second frame of green and brown around the red frame. The directions for the male figure were as follows:

The embroidery is done with horizontal stitches of varying lengths. The hat is made of three black silk stitches of varying lengths. The hat is made of three black silk stitches, the face of three pink silk stitches, the middle one being a little longer to indicate the nose. On the top pink stitch, put two tiny black stitches to indicate the eyes. The body and the arms are made of brown silk stitches in varying lengths. The trousers are yellow silk stitches; the stockings are red silk stitches and two black silk stitches form each of the feet. The reader is assured that this figure is "very easy and a pleasure to embroider."

Tunisian Mule for doll size number 4 17½in (44cm)

Pattern No. 35. Sketch of mule.

Pattern No. 36. Pattern for covering the toe part of the mule. It is to be made in red, green or blue velvet or other cloth in one of these colors. It is trimmed with embroidery and a white parchment or paper motif. The parchment is glued onto the velvet and held in place by red or gold threads. If desired the parchment can be replaced by soutache braid. The rest of the trimming consists of red or gold thread embroidery and gold spangles. The mule is bound around the edge with red, blue or green ribbon and sewed onto the sole.

Pattern No. 37. Pattern for the sole which is made of leather or cardboard

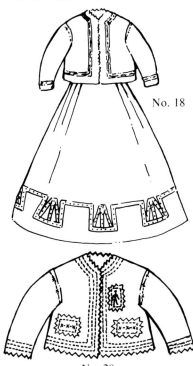

No. 18

No. 28

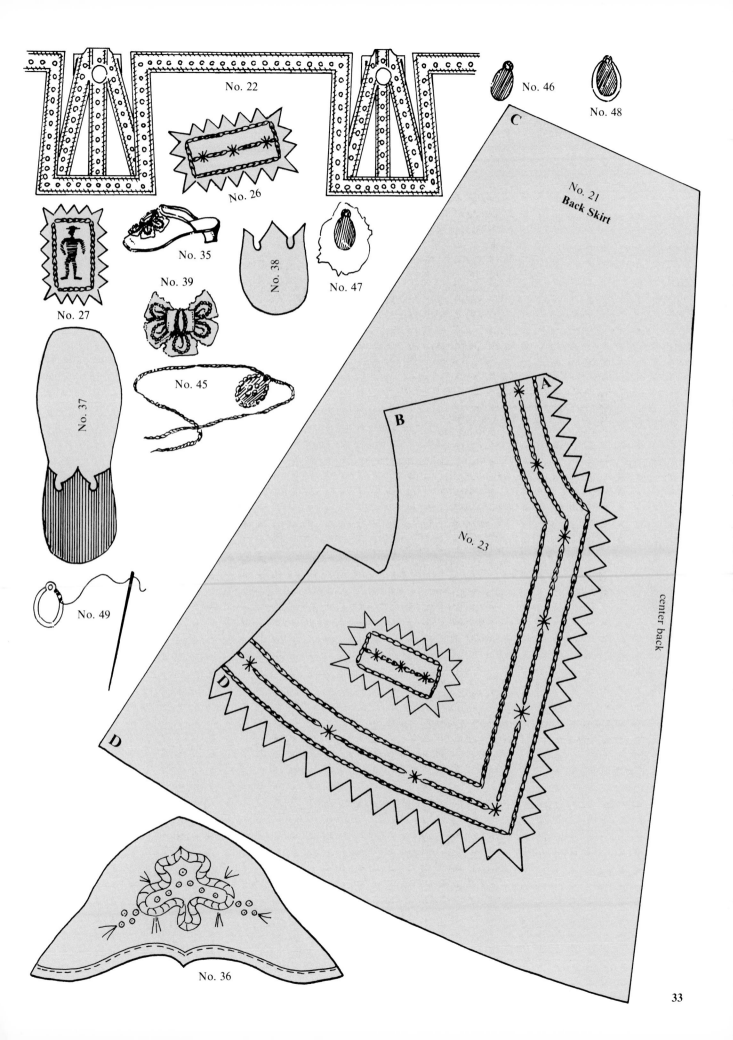

No. 22

No. 46

No. 48

No. 26

No. 35

No. 38

No. 47

No. 27

No. 39

No. 37

No. 45

No. 49

C

No. 21
Back Skirt

B

A

No. 23

D

D

center back

No. 36

33

covered with white kid on the inside. *Pattern No. 38.* Pattern for a motif cut out of kid or reddish brown paper which is glued onto the part of the sole (*Pattern No. 37*) indicated by parallel lines. (Also see *Pattern No. 35.*)

If one wishes to simplify the making of this mule, it can be made of fabric or morocco leather and trimmed with the bow shown as *Pattern No. 39.*

Pattern No. 39. Bow for the mule is made of five folds of satin ribbon held by a sixth fold on which gold beads are affixed to simulate a buckle. The color of the ribbon matches the color of the mule. On each of the folds

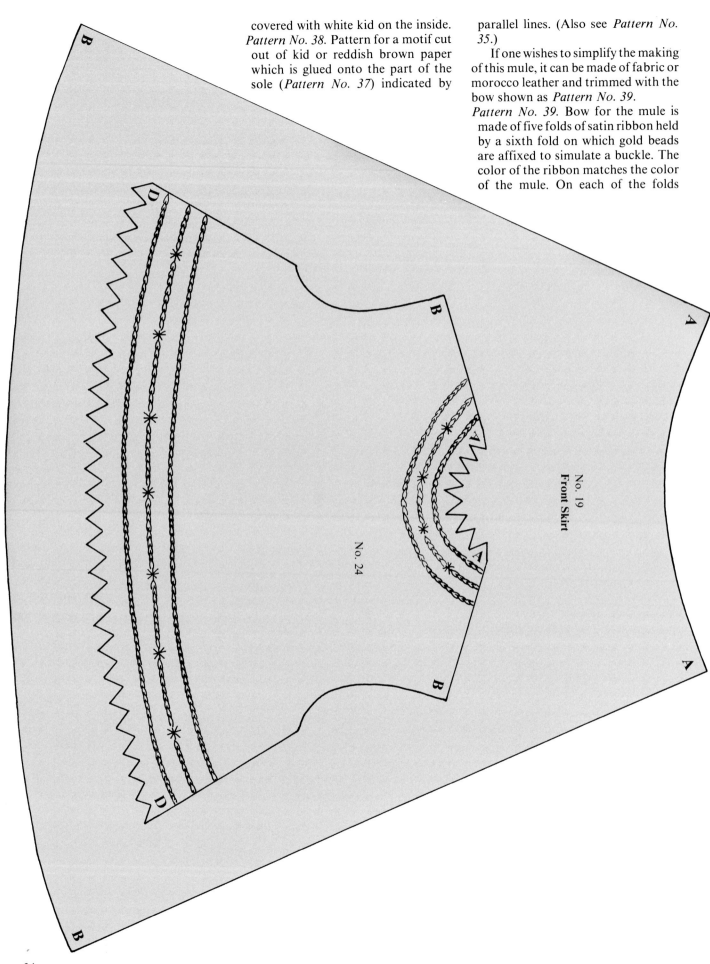

either gold embroidery twist or gold beads form a three-fourths circlet. No mention is made for the heel of the mule other than showing it in *Pattern No. 35*.

A Gold Pendant or Medallion for a doll

Pattern No. 45. Sketch of the pendant.

Pattern No. 46. Pattern for pendant made of gold-colored metallic paper. The original suggestion was to use the paper from wrappings of wax candles but today we could best use gold paper wrappings from candy. Two identical pieces should be cut from the pattern.

Pattern No. 47. Shows how the gold paper is glued to the piece of calico.

Pattern No. 48. Shows the calico forming the edges of the pendant.

Pattern No. 49. Shows the two parts of the pendant being sewn together so that the gold paper appears on both sides. Beads cover the edge and trim the center as shown in *Pattern No. 45*. A cord is used to tie the pendant onto the neck of the doll. □

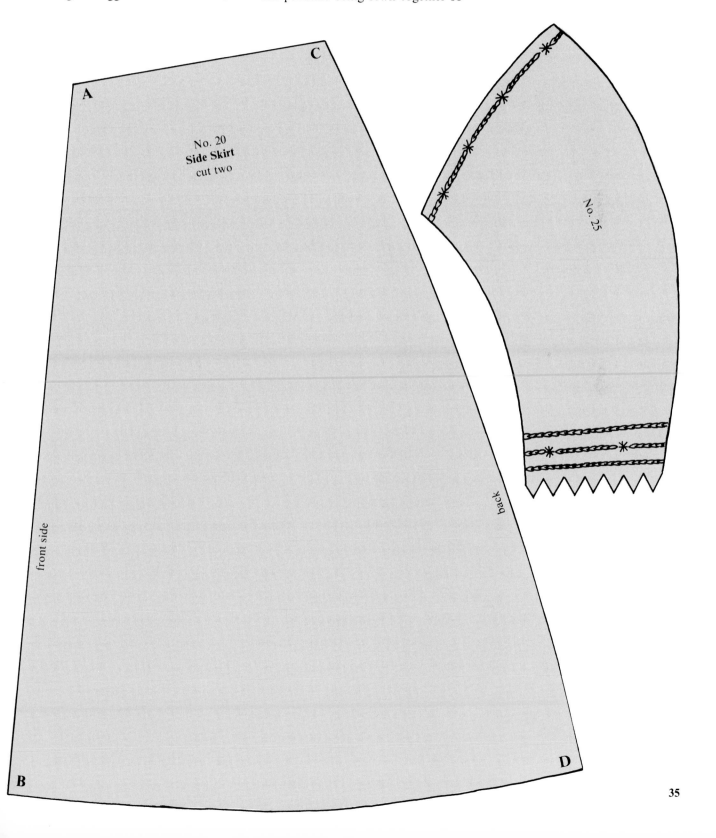

No. 20
Side Skirt
cut two

front side

No. 25

back

Boy Doll's Suit

by **Dorothy S. Coleman**

Pattern from *La Poupée Modèle* July 1881
Patterns redrawn and artwork by **Sandy Williams**

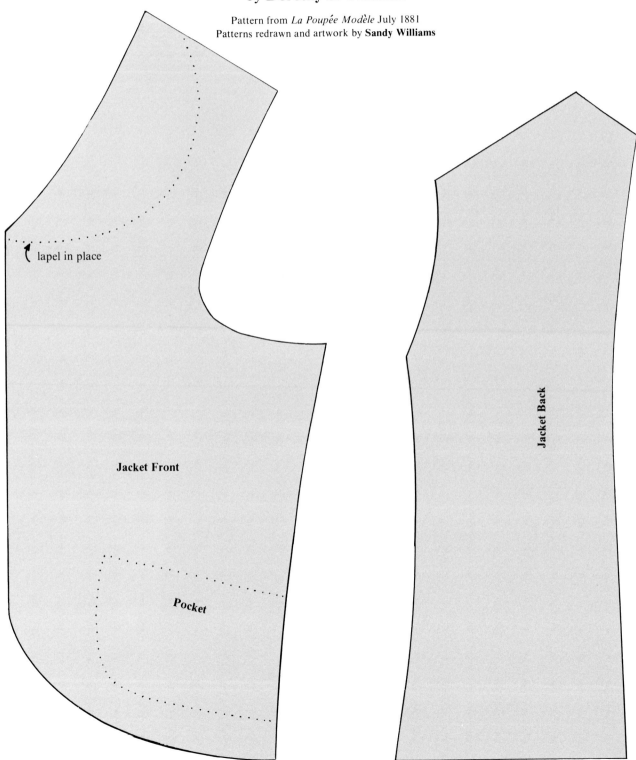

lapel in place

Jacket Front

Pocket

Jacket Back

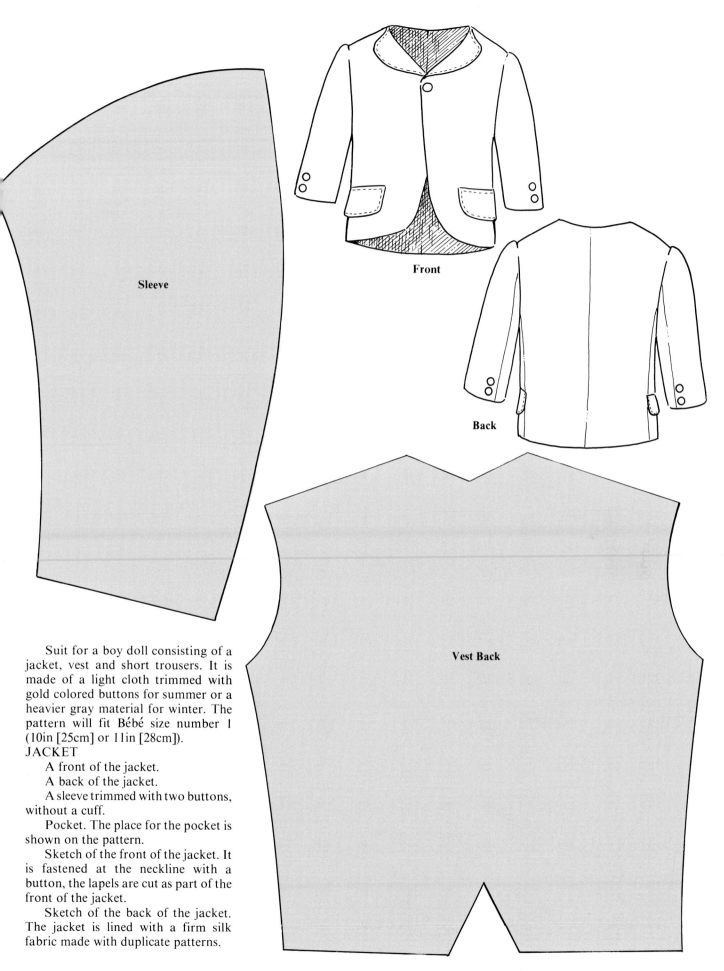

Sleeve

Front

Back

Vest Back

Suit for a boy doll consisting of a jacket, vest and short trousers. It is made of a light cloth trimmed with gold colored buttons for summer or a heavier gray material for winter. The pattern will fit Bébé size number 1 (10in [25cm] or 11in [28cm]).

JACKET

A front of the jacket.

A back of the jacket.

A sleeve trimmed with two buttons, without a cuff.

Pocket. The place for the pocket is shown on the pattern.

Sketch of the front of the jacket. It is fastened at the neckline with a button, the lapels are cut as part of the front of the jacket.

Sketch of the back of the jacket. The jacket is lined with a firm silk fabric made with duplicate patterns.

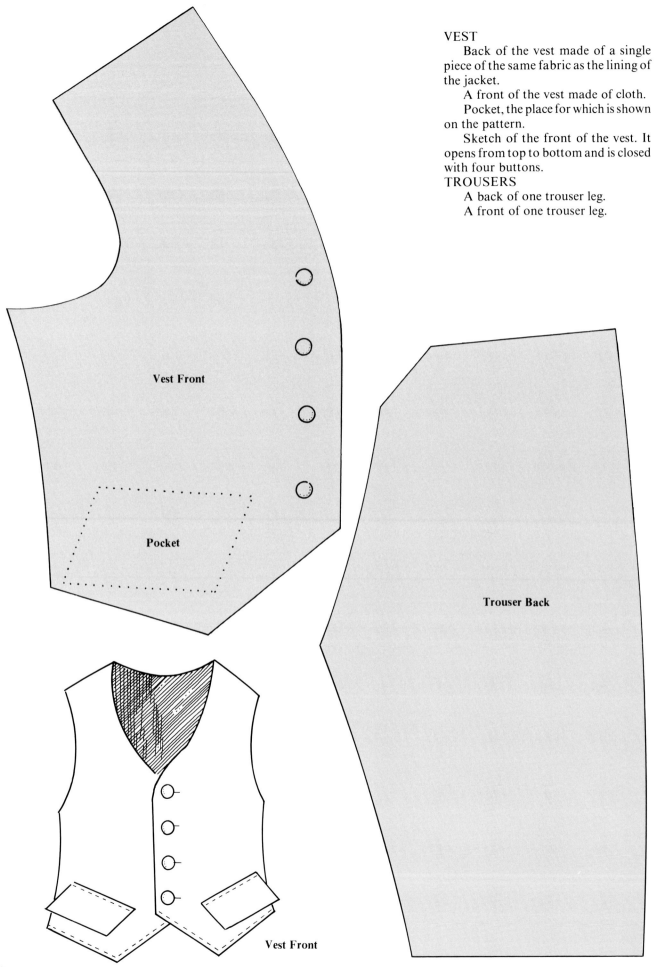

VEST

Back of the vest made of a single piece of the same fabric as the lining of the jacket.

A front of the vest made of cloth.

Pocket, the place for which is shown on the pattern.

Sketch of the front of the vest. It opens from top to bottom and is closed with four buttons.

TROUSERS

A back of one trouser leg.

A front of one trouser leg.

Vest Front

Pocket

Trouser Back

Vest Front

Sketch of the trousers. The legs are trimmed with three buttons. The trousers are made of the same fabric as the rest of the outfit and can be lined with a light calico. The two legs are joined in the rear to form a belt. The front remains open. The exterior seams of the trousers, the turn of the jacket, the lapels, the pockets are all sewn with silk.

This charming costume came from Madame Lavallée, 21 rue de Choiseul. It can be made easily and will give variety to your playing with dolls. □

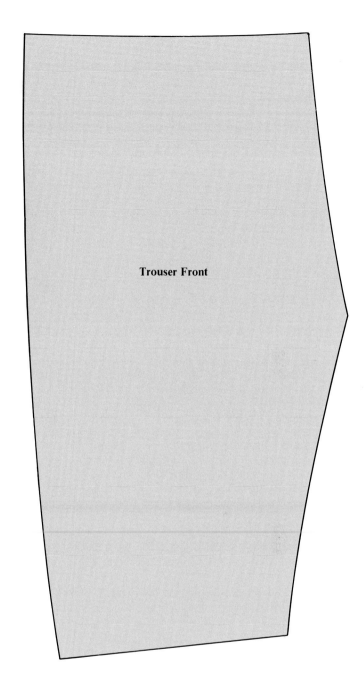

Trouser Front

Trousers

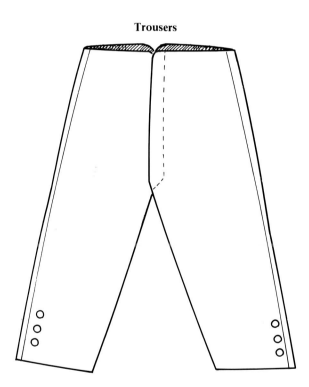

Dressing A Tiny Bisque Doll

by **Sandy Williams**

From the top of her honey-blonde hair to the bottom of her brown two-strap shoes, she measures a mere 4¾in (12cm). This little charmer is jointed at her shoulders and hips and is marked on her back: "7547//3/0//GERMANY." Bright pink cheeks, red lips, blue glass stationary eyes and honey-blonde eyebrows offset her long honey-blonde mohair wig. She also has molded medium-pink ribbed socks. Her undressed measurements are 3⅛in (8cm) chest, 3in (8cm) waist, 3½in (9cm) hips, 2in (5cm) thighs and 2½in (6cm) crotch.

She is wearing a sleeveless medium-blue china silk dress. Self-fabric cording edges the armholes and bodice. Narrow lace frames the low V-pointed bodice and armholes. Tiny jet beads are sewn down the center front bodice. Underneath her dress she wears a white batiste drawers/petticoat combination which is trimmed with lace around the drawers hem and petticoat hem. When sewing for tiny dolls, use thin, tightly woven natural fabrics and trims that drape well and trim scaled down to the doll's size.

First measure and fit your doll with the drawers/petticoat combination and then measure and fit the dress to the doll over her underwear. Since a doll's measurements will vary from doll to doll, the patterns should be used as a guide. I like to first try out a pattern in a "pattern tracing cloth" which can be marked on, sewn on and is also semi-transparent — plus you can take the garment apart and use it as a pattern. Since the garments are so small, I sewed the outfits by hand. Sew with tiny running stitches and occasionally take one backstitch to lock the stitches. The patterns include a 3/16in (.45cm) seam allowance unless otherwise stated in the directions. Carefully lay out all patterns on the straight of grain. Silk is not difficult to sew with — just take a few precautions and you will be rewarded with beautiful results: use a dry iron on a low setting, use fine sharp needles for hand sewing and use silk or extra-fine thread.

MATERIALS:

1/4yd (.23m) of china silk or suitable fine closely woven fabric.

1/4yd (.23m) of 100 percent cotton white batiste, matching silk or extra-fine thread for lightweight fabrics.

1yd (.91m) of 1/4in (.65cm) to 3/8in (.9cm) wide fine white cotton lace.

Six tiny jet beads for buttons.

15in (38cm) of baby yarn for cording.

A blunt (tapestry) needle.

Fine sharp hand sewing needles.

DRAWERS/PETTICOAT COMBINATION:

From the white batiste, cut out two drawers, one petticoat and one waistband. Press up a 1/8in (.31cm) hem on the right side of each drawers. Lay lace over the hem just covering the raw hem edge; blindstitch lace drawers. With right sides of drawers together, sew the center front crotch together; then sew the center back crotch together from the dot to crotch point. Narrowly hem the center back opening. Match front crotch to the back crotch, sew leg opening closed. Trim crotch and leg seams and turn the drawers right side out. Turn up the hem and sew lace to the petticoat hem following the directions for the drawers. With right sides of petticoat together, sew center back edges together from dot to hem. Narrowly hem center back opening. Turn petticoat right side out. Pin drawers petticoat right side out. Pin drawers to petticoat at waistline, matching center back and center points together. The petticoat will be fuller at the waistline than the drawers — as you gather the drawers and petticoat waistlines together, distribute the extra fullness of the petticoat evenly on the drawers. Pull the gathering thread of the drawer/petticoat to fit the waistband. Sew the waistband on using 3/16in (.45cm) seams on each edge. Place underwear on the doll and sew waistband closed with tiny concealed stitches. Sewing the drawers and petticoat on the same waistband eliminates

a hook and eye and helps to reduce unnecessary bulk on a small doll.

DRESS: BODICE:

With a pencil, lightly trace all pattern lines (cutting, sewing and center front bodice) of the front and back bodice on the batiste. Lay the marked batiste (lining) on the wrong side of a piece of silk; pin together. With tiny running stitches, first baste the batiste and silk together just inside the cutting lines, then baste the sewing lines and the center front bodice line. Cut out the pattern pieces on the penciled cutting lines and treat as one piece of fabric from now on. Sew the shoulders together of the front and back bodice; press seams open; overcast shoulder seam edges to bodice lining, taking care not to sew through to the silk bodice. Turn right center back bodice seam to wrong side of bodice, tuck raw edge in and sew to bodice lining. Cut a strip of silk bias tape 3/4in (2cm) by 15in (38cm). Fold bias strip in half lengthwise; with tiny running stitches, sew 1/8in (.31cm) in from fold the entire length of tape. With the blunt needle threaded with the baby yarn, gently draw yarn through cording. Lay cording just above the 3/16in (.45cm) seam allowance on one armscye. With tiny stitches sew the cording to the armscye seam; start and stop the armscye seam at the two points where the armscye seam meets the two side seams — have the ends of the cording extend 3/8in (.9cm). Trim armscye seam. Sew side seams together; press open and overcast seam edges to bodice lining. Press bias tape to inside of bodice. Open each end of cording and cut yarn even with side seam to reduce bulk. The bias tape has two raw edges — trim the inner edge close to the armscye stitches; tuck the outer raw edge of bias tape in and stitch to bodice lining — it is helpful to insert the handle of a wooden spoon into armhole; repeat with other armscye and side seam. Starting at the right center back neck edge (extend cording edge 3/8in [.9cm] beyond bodice), sew cording to neckline, left back bodice edge and waistline, ending at the right center back waist edge. To finish sewing the cording, follow the cording armscye directions except trim and notch all points of the bodice to keep the points sharp.

SKIRT: Turn hem up 1/2in (1.3cm), press, tuck raw edge in, and sew hem. Mark center front point of skirt at waist and hem, starting at one side of center front point, mark and baste pleats toward center front points; press. Repeat with other side of skirt. Pin pleated skirt around doll's petticoat waistband (placing center front of skirt waistline at center front of petticoat wasitband). Place bodice on doll, pinning center front point of bodice waistline to center front of skirt (pull bodice down front of skirt — it will extend below skirt's natural waistline), continue pinning skirt to bodice adjusting pleats where necessary. Make sure the hem is even on doll. Sew skirt waistline to bodice in the groove between the cording and the bodice. Overcast skirt waistline seam to bodice lining — trim excess skirt seam at bodice center front point. Sew skirt center back opening seam from dot to hem; turn raw edges of skirt opening in and sew. On the wrong side of bodice, sew narrow lace around the sewing line of armscye cording; repeat with other armscye. Using the illustration as a guide, sew lace to the bodice starting at each neck back opening, bringing the lace to a point at waistline and then below and just tucked under the cording ending at the center back skirt opening. Repeat with the other side of dress. Evenly space and sew the six tiny jet beads down the center front of the bodice.

Remove all basting threads. Place dress on doll. To further eliminate unnecessary bulk on the doll, either sew the back opening closed with tiny stitches or fasten with concealed straight silk pins. □

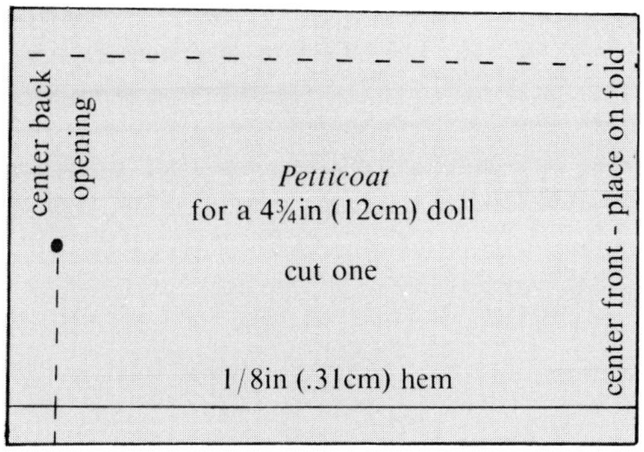

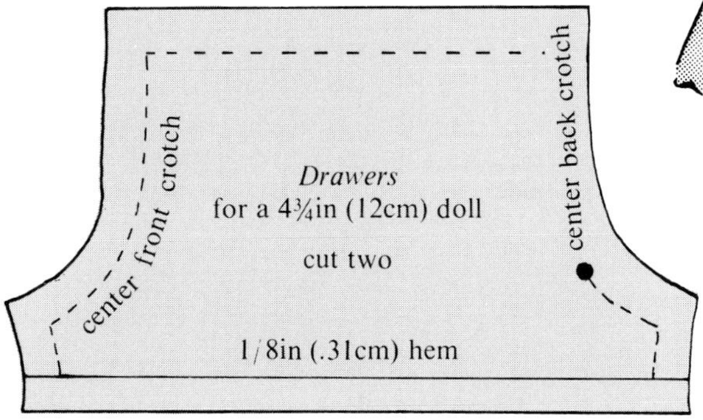

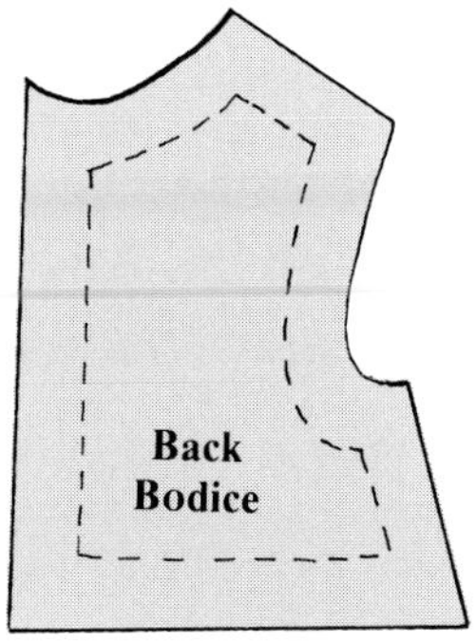

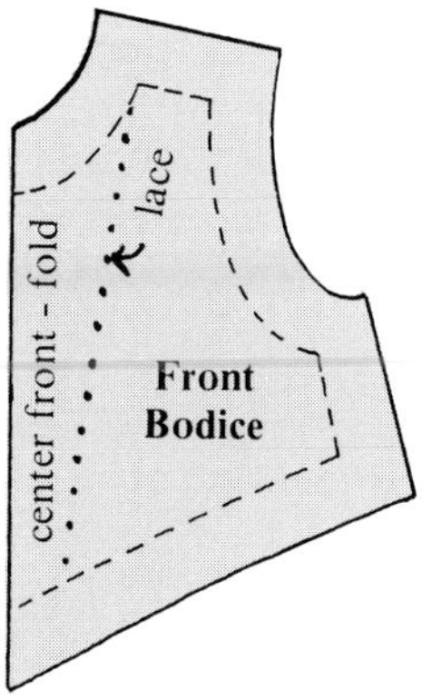

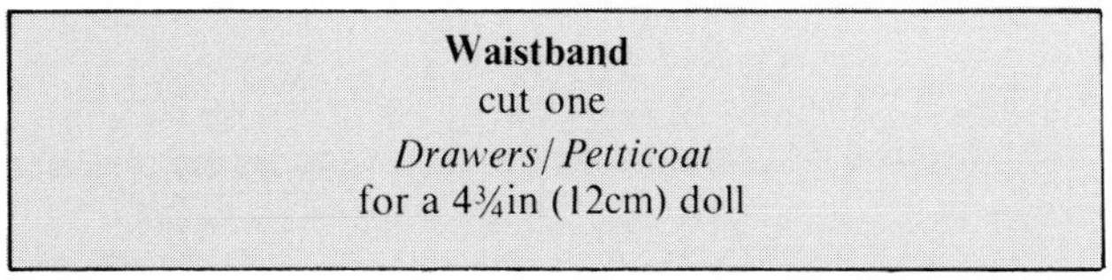

Illustration 1. 4¾in (12cm) doll wearing her sleeveless dress. She is marked on her back: "7547// 3/0//GERMANY."

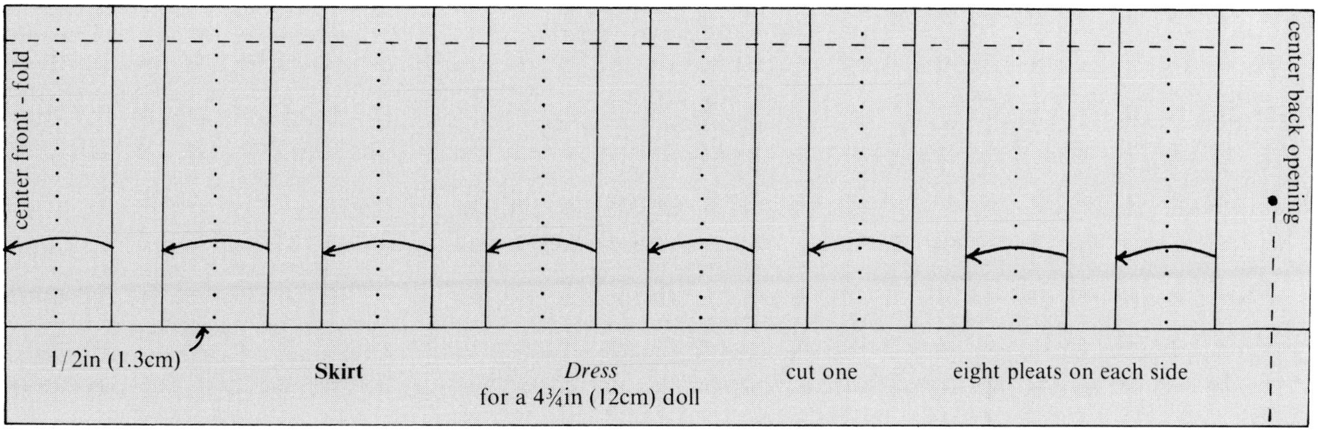

Petticoat
for a 4¾in (12cm) doll
cut one

center back opening

center front - place on fold

1/8in (.31cm) hem

Drawers
for a 4¾in (12cm) doll
cut two

center front crotch

center back crotch

1/8in (.31cm) hem

Back Bodice

Front Bodice

center front - fold

lace

Waistband
cut one
Drawers/Petticoat
for a 4¾in (12cm) doll

center front - fold

center back opening

1/2in (1.3cm)

Skirt

Dress
for a 4¾in (12cm) doll

cut one

eight pleats on each side

A Little German Schoolgirl,

Part I

by **Donna Miska**
Photographs by **Joe Miska**

Recently I had the opportunity to view an all-original 24in (61cm) Armand Marseille 390 schoolgirl wearing an outfit that had been hand-made for her in Germany. The doll belonged to an elderly lady who had brought the doll with her from Germany when she came to live in the United States.

I wanted to make a copy of the A.M.'s clothing and I just happened to have a beautiful 24in (61cm) doll marked "Special" by A. Wislizenus with blue sleep eyes and her original Waltershausen mohair wig. She also had no clothes. I designed the schoolgirl outfit to fit my own doll; if your doll is smaller you will have to cut the pattern down. If your doll needs a wig, I would suggest that you try to match the short "bob" haircut shown on the original A.M. because it is more fitting for the 1920s era.

The Armand Marseille doll had ordinary muslin underwear, pantaloons trimmed with lace and a half-slip buttoned on the side. I did not feel it necessary to reprint the underwear pattern here because any underwear pattern for a German doll (1910 to 1920) would be suitable. The original doll did not wear a camisole but I did put one on mine.

I tried to match the fabrics used on the original doll, however, I was not able to duplicate them exactly. I needed old fabrics so I went to the nearest thrift shop. I needed black wool for the doll's coat and found it in an old skirt. The red-orange cotton needed for the doll dress was harder to find because there are so many polyesters and other man-made materials on the market now days. Eventually I found an old housedress that worked all right although the original had more texture.

Illustration 1. 24in (61cm) Armand Marseille 390 wearing what appears to be her original hand-made outfit. The doll originally belonged to an elderly lady who had brought the doll with her from Germany when she came to the United States to live. The doll carries a leather book case that holds miniature school books written in German. The book case may have been a backpack.

An old white dust ruffle became the underwear and I bought an old pair of children's socks from which to make the doll's socks. It does not do to mix old and new materials when making an outfit for an old doll, new material is too bright and crisp and often does not hang right. I had some old black crepe for the coat lining. The three black buttons and black braided trim edging the coat front and neck opening were bought at a flea market. The only thing I could not buy old was the blue and white felt needed for the hat. That I had to buy new at a fabric shop.

I took the old clothing apart, hand washed all the pieces, then line dried and ironed them. Always iron wool with a clean damp pressing cloth. I have known of collectors who worry about using wool on their dolls for fear that it will attract moths. First of all, if you wash wool before you sew it up it will repel moths fairly well. For added protection you can always make up little pouches just big enough for a mothball and sew or pin these to the inside of the garment. I also put a mothball under the hat of any doll that has a mohair wig and have never had any moth damage.

The dress, seen in **Illustration 2,** has long set-in sleeves with cuffs, a high waistline and a scalloped hemline. I used medium blue embroidery floss (marked 8m DMC 25 Mouline Special, made in France, cotton) for all embroidery on the dress yoke and hemline. The dress front yoke has a self lining at the lower front edge for the embroidery and is topstitched to the skirt front. The collar is made in two sections with a separation in the back. The dress opening is in the front. **Note:** I allowed just a little of the slip to peek from below the dress hemline.

DIRECTIONS FOR THE DRESS:
1. Sew front and back shoulders together.
2. Sew sleeve into armhole opening. Gather wrist opening to cuff. (Fold cuff piece into thirds lengthwise to create an interfacing.)
3. Sew yoke lining to the bottom of two front dress top pieces, turn right side out and press.

Illustration 2. 24in (61cm) Wislizenus doll marked "Special" wearing a copy of the dress worn by the AM 390 shown in **Illustration 1.** Note the embroidery work at the yoke and hemline.

Illustration 3.

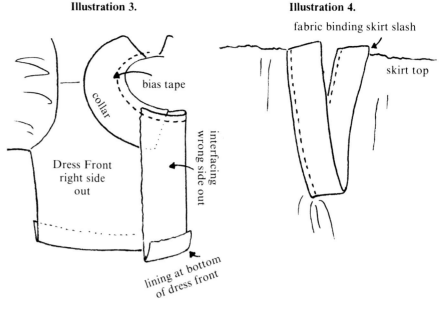

collar

bias tape

Dress Front right side out

interfacing wrong side out

lining at bottom of dress front

Illustration 4.

fabric binding skirt slash

skirt top

Illustration 5.

fold inside, press

skirt top

Illustration 6.

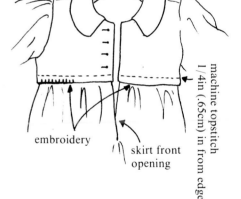

embroidery

skirt front opening

machine topstitch 1/4in (.65cm) in from edge

4. Sew collar pieces together, turn right side out, press and sew to dress neck opening. Leave 3/8in (.9cm) gap in back.

5. Fold dress interfacing for neck opening inside out against front of dress and stitch collar and neck opening interfacing the bias to finish inside neck opening. Turn neck opening right side out and press. Hand-stitch lower edge of bias tape in place along inside neck band. See **Illustration 3.**

6. For skirt front, cut one piece of fabric 28in (71cm) wide by 15in (38cm) long. At center top of skirt cut a slash 3½in (9cm) deep for the center front opening. Do not cut slash less than 3½in (9cm) or you will have trouble getting the finished dress on the doll.

7. Bind this slash opening with a strip of fabric 7¼in (18cm) long by 2in (5cm) wide (folded in half lengthwise). See **Illustration 4.**

8. Fold the left side flap of skirt opening under and press. See **Illustration 5.**

9. With right sides facing out, pin dress front top to the dress front skirt, matching neck opening and skirt opening. Gather skirt to fit exact width of dress top. Dress top will overlap skirt top and is topstitched to skirt front 1/4in (.65cm) in from finished lower edge of dress top. This leaves a 1/4in (.65cm) exposed edge on dress front for embroidery. See **Illustration 6.**

10. Cut fabric for dress skirt back 28in (71cm) wide by 15in (38cm) long and gather to dress back in a conventional manner. There is no embroidery on the back of the dress top.

11. Turn dress inside out and sew both sides of dress together in two long seams running from the cuff all the way to the skirt bottom. Try to match underarm seams as you go.

12. Turn up 3in (8cm) hem wrong side out and pin in place. With cloth marker or soft pencil draw scalloped edge (sample section included in pattern) all around skirt hemline 4/16in (.6cm) up from bottom edge.

13. Machine sew along scallop edge and trim with scissors. Turn hem to the inside and press.

14. Finish dress with four white buttons and four bound buttonholes at the neck and embroider designs on the dress yoke and hemline. Details for embroidery are shown in **Illustration 8.** □

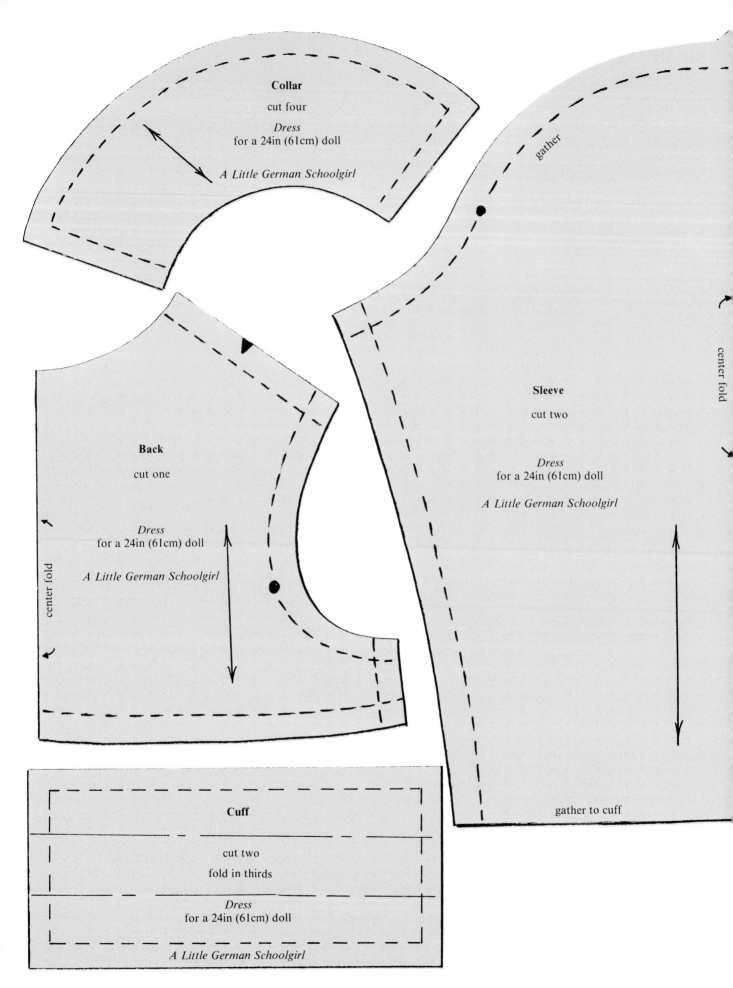

Collar

cut four

Dress
for a 24in (61cm) doll

A Little German Schoolgirl

gather

center fold

Sleeve

cut two

Dress
for a 24in (61cm) doll

A Little German Schoolgirl

gather to cuff

Back

cut one

Dress
for a 24in (61cm) doll

A Little German Schoolgirl

center fold

Cuff

cut two

fold in thirds

Dress
for a 24in (61cm) doll

A Little German Schoolgirl

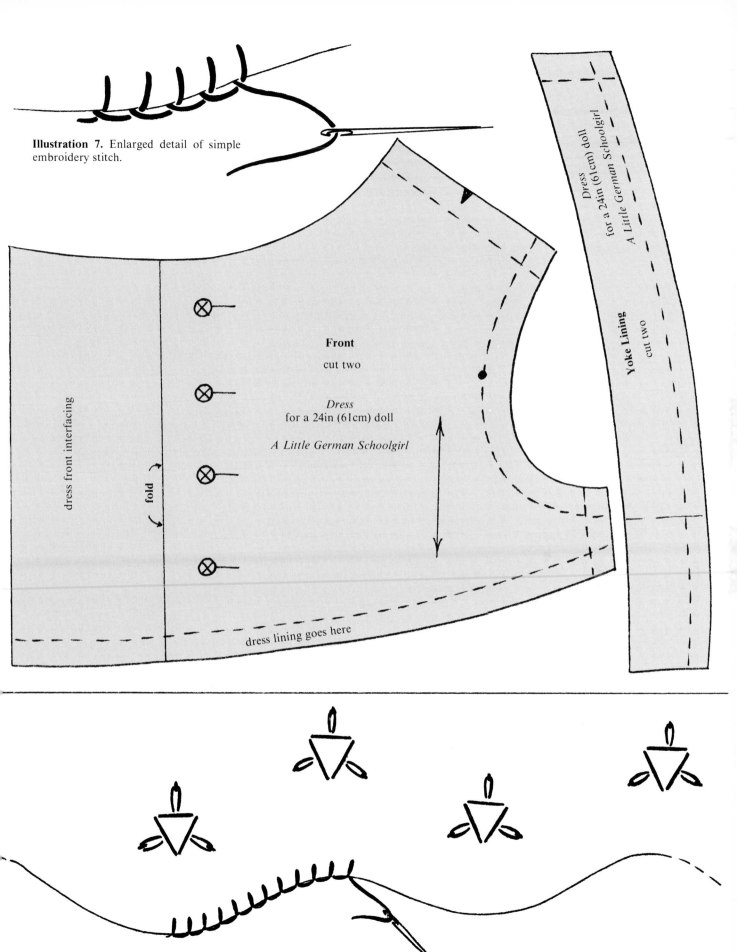

Illustration 7. Enlarged detail of simple embroidery stitch.

Front

cut two

Dress
for a 24in (61cm) doll

A Little German Schoolgirl

dress front interfacing

fold

dress lining goes here

Dress
for a 24in (61cm) doll
A Little German Schoolgirl

Yoke Lining
cut two

Illustration 8. Actual size detail of embroidered design on skirt hem.

A Little German Schoolgirl,
Part II

by **Donna Miska**
Photographs by **Joe Miska**

In the first part of this article the pattern for the dress seen on a 24in (61cm) Armand Marseille 390 schoolgirl was given. The pattern for the hat and coat is given here along with directions for making the doll's accessories.

The original doll wore brown leather tie shoes and carried a 3in (8cm) by 4in (10cm) brown leather schoolbook case. I did not buy brown leather shoes for my doll; instead I bought white leather and dyed them myself. This gave a much more antique look to the shoes and the color was a perfect match with the original doll shoes. Also, the old-looking dyed shoes were more in keeping with my doll's clothing which was made from old fabrics. Leather shoe dye can be bought from most shoe repair shops. Just follow the directions and I am sure you will be pleased with the results. (Leather dyes come in a choice of colors, so you may custom color your doll shoes to match the outfits!) I dyed the entire shoe, soles and ties included. The dye is quite thin, almost like an ink, so I just dipped the ties into the bottle. After the shoes were completely dry I polished them with brown shoe polish. Of course, you could simply buy brown leather shoes; they would be a little darker than the original antique shoes but they would do.

It is easy to make doll socks from children's old socks. Simply turn the socks inside out, slip the cuff part only over your doll's foot, pull snug and pin the back and along the bottom of the doll's foot. Remove the sock, being careful not to loosen your pins, and sew the back and bottom seams on the machine. I sew twice along the seam so it will not pull apart when the sock is stretched over the doll's foot. I usually use the cuff of the sock because it will not unravel, however, I have used the lower parts of socks as well and never had any trouble. Children's old socks work well because the fabric is not too thick. Unless you are dressing a very large doll, you can get at least two doll socks from one child's sock. See **Illustration 11.**

For the doll's schoolbook case I used a doll's old leather suitcase bought in an antique shop years ago. I tied this to my doll's hand with a brown ribbon. However, a case could be constructed using lightweight real or imitation leather (perhaps from an old pocketbook). You could either glue the leather around a block of wood or cardboard form for the effect of a book case, or you could build a case that would really hold miniature books (see **Illustration 12**). If you do not want to make your own carrying case, check your local department store for key cases or small wallets with snap closures. Some of these are just the right size and color. Just glue on leather or ribbon straps and tie to your doll's hand. Make the straps long enough and you have a shoulder bag or backpack.

DIRECTIONS FOR COAT:

Fits 24in (61cm) doll. Materials used: black wool, black crepe, black edge trim 1/2in (1.3cm) wide by 52in (132cm) long, three 1/2in (1.3cm) diameter black shank buttons.

1. Sew center back seams together, press flat (use damp pressing cloth).
2. Sew shoulder seams, press flat.
3. Sew in sleeves, gather slightly. Clip along curved seams to ease fit.
4. With right sides facing, sew both sides together in long continuous seams. Try to match armhole seams as you go. Press side seams flat.
5. Turn coat right side out and slip on doll. Fold sleeve hem under and

Illustration 9. 24in (61cm) Wislizenus doll marked "Special" wearing a copy of the black wool coat, red dress and blue hat originally worn by an AM 390.

with black single thread baste in place.

6. Using coat pattern, cut lining from black crepe or other lightweight fabric. Sew together exactly the same as for coat (see steps 1 through 4.)
7. With right sides facing, pin lining to coat (matching shoulders), then sew in one long seam up front opening, around neck opening, and down the other front opening. If there is extra fabric in the lining, make a tuck at center back.
8. Turn right side out and press coat front and neck opening flat.
9. Slip lining sleeve inside coat sleeve, turn up lining and hand-sew to coat sleeve.
10. Sewing by hand, add decorative black braid or trim to front opening and around neck opening.
11. Turn up coat hem, pin, press and sew by hand. Coat should be slightly shorter than finished dress.

Illustration 10. Close-up of the doll's hat showing the unusual blue and white pattern on the crown.

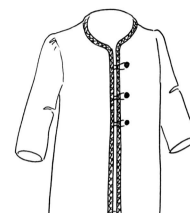

Illustration 12. Basic type of book bag, shown here as a backpack, used by German schoolchildren. Could close with a snap, button or buckle.

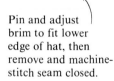

Illustration 13. The finished coat.

Illustration 14.

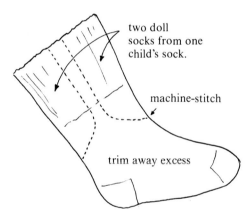

two doll socks from one child's sock.

machine-stitch

trim away excess

Illustration 11. Making the doll socks.

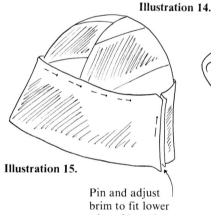

Illustration 15.

Pin and adjust brim to fit lower edge of hat, then remove and machine-stitch seam closed.

Illustration 16.

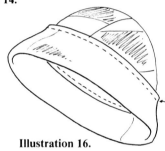

Machine-stitch brim to hat, then turn up brim and tack in place.

12. Turn lining hem and sew by hand. Lining hem should hang free and not be attached to coat. Check to be sure it does not hang below coat.

13. Using a chain stitch or lightweight black cord, make three loops for buttonholes on edge of coat right front. Sew three black shank buttons directly opposite on left side. Coat lapels come just together in the front and do not overlap. See **Illustration 13** for finished coat.

DIRECTIONS FOR HAT:

Fits 11in (28cm) to 11½in (29cm) circumference doll head, slightly larger with wig. Materials used: One 9in (23cm) by 11in (28cm) white wool felt square. Two 9in (23cm) by 11in (28cm) light blue wool felt squares.

1. Cut two strips of white felt 2in (5cm) by 11in (28cm).

2. Cut one strip of blue felt 2in (5cm) by 11in (28cm).

3. Sew the three strips together lengthwise, alternating white, blue, white (see **Illustration 14**) using 1/4in (.65cm) seams. Lightly press seams open with a damp pressing cloth. Test this on a scrap first because sometimes felt deforms when damp-pressed.

4. Place hat pattern at an angle across blue and white strips (as indicated on pattern). Felt has no fabric nap and can be used in any direction.

5. Cut out four hat sections and sew together. Trim the lower edge with scissors so it is even and set aside.

6. For the hat brim you will need a strip of blue felt 4in (10cm) wide by 18in (46cm) long. If you are using felt blocks as I did, you will have to sew two pieces together to get the

desired length. Again, lightly press seams open.

7. Pin the hat brim around the lower edge of the hat to determine the exact length needed for the brim. Pin and sew seam and trim excess fabric. (See **Illustration 15**.)

8. Fold brim lengthwise, right sides facing out, pin and sew to lower edge of hat. Felt does not ravel and there is no need for bulky turned-under seams, so...topstitch hat and brim together. (See **Illustration 16**.)

9. Fold brim up and tack in a few places.

Your little German schoolgirl is finished. I hope you enjoy yours as much as I enjoy mine. □

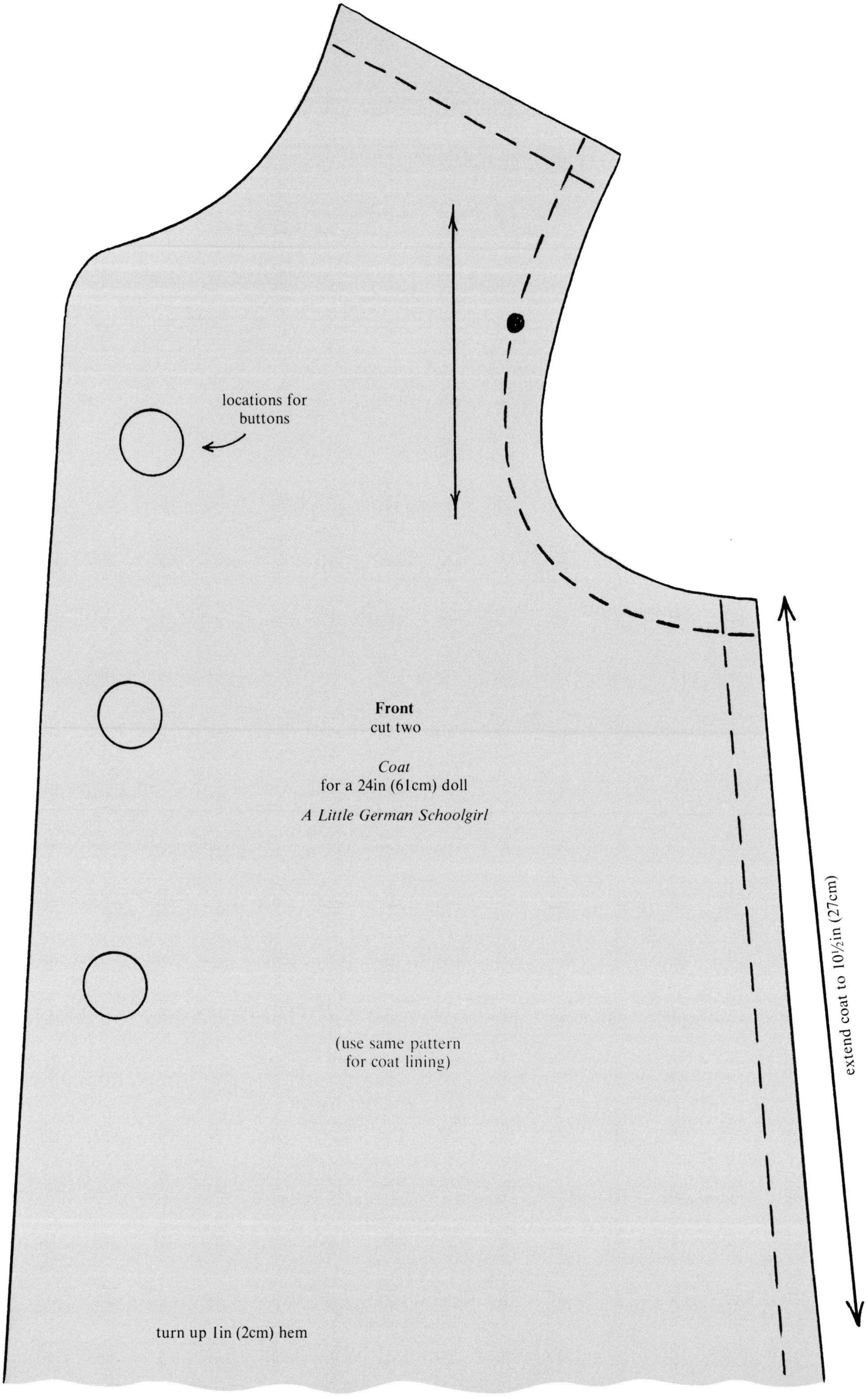

locations for
buttons

Front
cut two

Coat
for a 24in (61cm) doll

A Little German Schoolgirl

(use same pattern
for coat lining)

extend coat to 10½in (27cm)

turn up 1in (2cm) hem

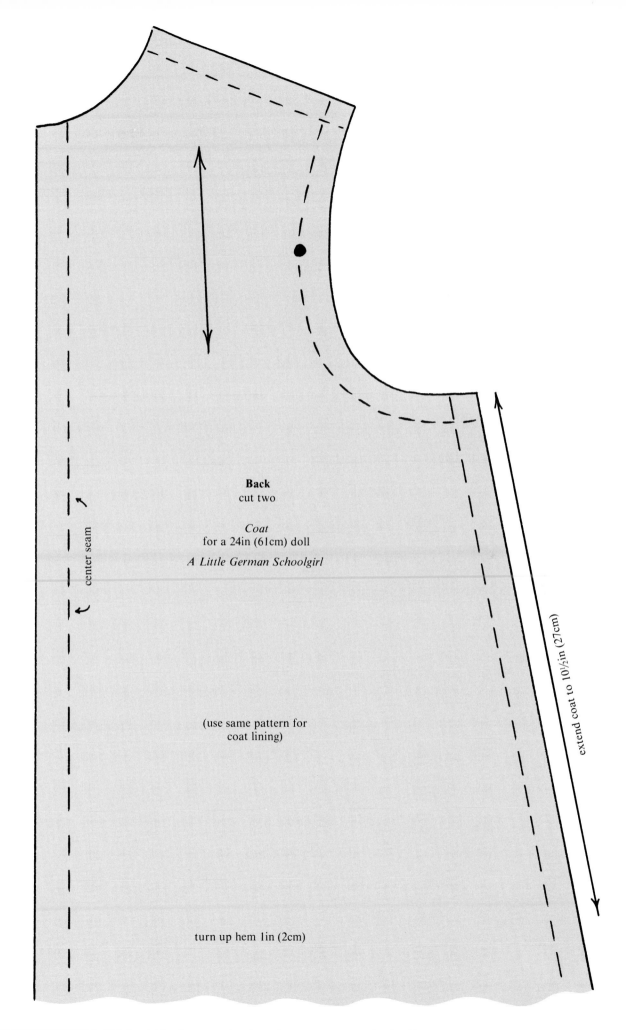

Back
cut two

Coat
for a 24in (61cm) doll

A Little German Schoolgirl

(use same pattern for
coat lining)

center seam

extend coat to 10½in (27cm)

turn up hem 1in (2cm)

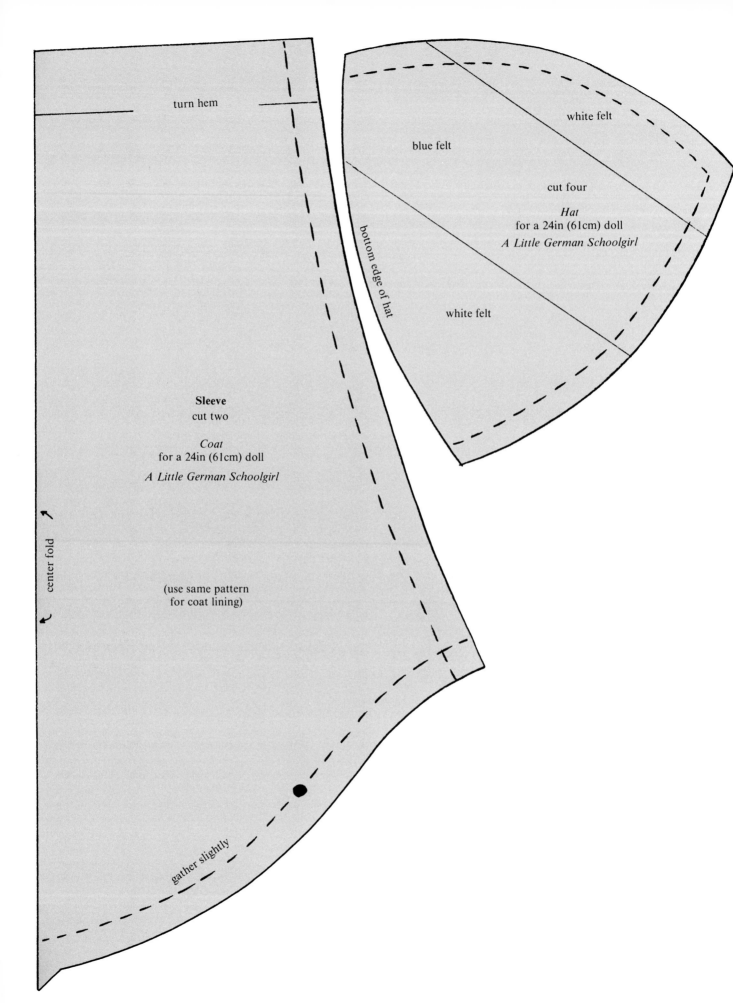

turn hem

Sleeve
cut two

Coat
for a 24in (61cm) doll
A Little German Schoolgirl

center fold

(use same pattern
for coat lining)

gather slightly

blue felt

white felt

cut four

Hat
for a 24in (61cm) doll
A Little German Schoolgirl

bottom edge of hat

white felt

A Ball Gown of the 1890s

by **Brenda Paske**

Illustration 1. Striped silk ball gown in the style of 1894 for a 32in (81cm) doll.

Illustration 2. Close-up showing details of the hair and jewelry.

The 1890s marked not only the end of a century, but the end of a way of life. The old aristocratic order of wealth and privilege was soon to be swept away forever. It was the final era of overwhelming glitter and extravagance in fashionable dress.

This gown was created to be typical (though not a copy) of an evening dress in 1894.

The sleeves are the well-known balloon-shaped gigot sleeves. In 1894 and 1895 they were at the absolute maximum circumference. Perhaps this was to make up for the lack of bustle or crinoline skirt support for the first time in 80 years.

The bosom is heavy (and well padded), a distinctive feature of this era. The skirt falls into generous pleats in the back and a front panel of velvet matches the sleeves. Velvet sleeves that harmonized or even contrasted with the fabric of the dress were fashionable at this time. In fact, colors in general were often quite pronounced, almost unladylike.

Beads and sequins were popular and trim both the skirt and bodice of the dress, as well as the peacock feather fan.

Long gloves, beaded or with lace insets were popular accessories. There was a great variety of fans, sequined,

lace and feather but all were enormous and exaggerated. The "dog-collar" necklace is, of course, instantly recognizable as the style of the day.

Most people think of the "Gibson Girl" puffed hairdo as belonging to this period; however, it is still a little early for it. The hair is swept up in a little topknot at the back and the forehead is softened with crimped bangs.

The perky bow headdress is also quite typical, although the projections could just as easily be feathers or jeweled ornaments.

Illustrations 3 and **4** give an idea of the layers of underwear appropriate

Illustration 3. Top layer of underwear. A black satin corset and pink silk petticoat.

Illustration 4. Bottom layer of underwear. Wide drawers and camisole to match the petticoat, stockings held up with elastic garters, shoes match the dress.

for this period costume. The boring bundle of virginal white Victorian underthings has given way to a scanty (by comparison) froth of slightly racy underwear.

The corset is still a necessity (and so is artificial padding!) but there is only one petticoat. Dainty embroidered stockings that reached above the knee came into vogue during this period.

Illustrations 5 and **6** show the bodice pattern full scale for a 32in (81cm) doll. All edges are faced and the whole thing is stiffly interlined so that the proper wrinkle-free shape will be maintained. It closes center back with hooks and eyes.

The sleeve and skirt patterns in **Illustrations 7** and **8** are quite simple by comparison. The outer edge of the sleeve is gathered to fit the armhole. Some stiffening or support may be needed at the shoulder if the fabric is limp. The bottom of the sleeve is gathered into a band which is turned in and tacked invisibly into place.

The skirt is mounted into a waistband with the opening to one side of the front panel. The skirt will fall naturally into folds at the back, but you may wish to tack them into place at the waist to preserve their symmetry. There is a stiff facing around the hem to make the skirt stand out.

Illustration 9 shows the basis of the skirt trim. It is a simple strip of organdy twice the length of the edge to be decorated. It has a wavy gathering line and is overlaid with sequins and beads.

The dress is really fairly simple to make, if time consuming. The only difficulty lies in fitting the bodice to your particular doll. Most dolls do not have the right proportions and a little judicious pading may be required. □

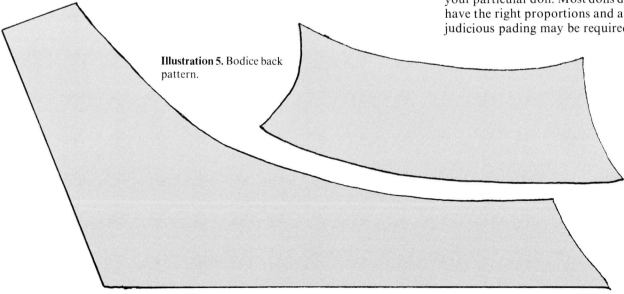

Illustration 5. Bodice back pattern.

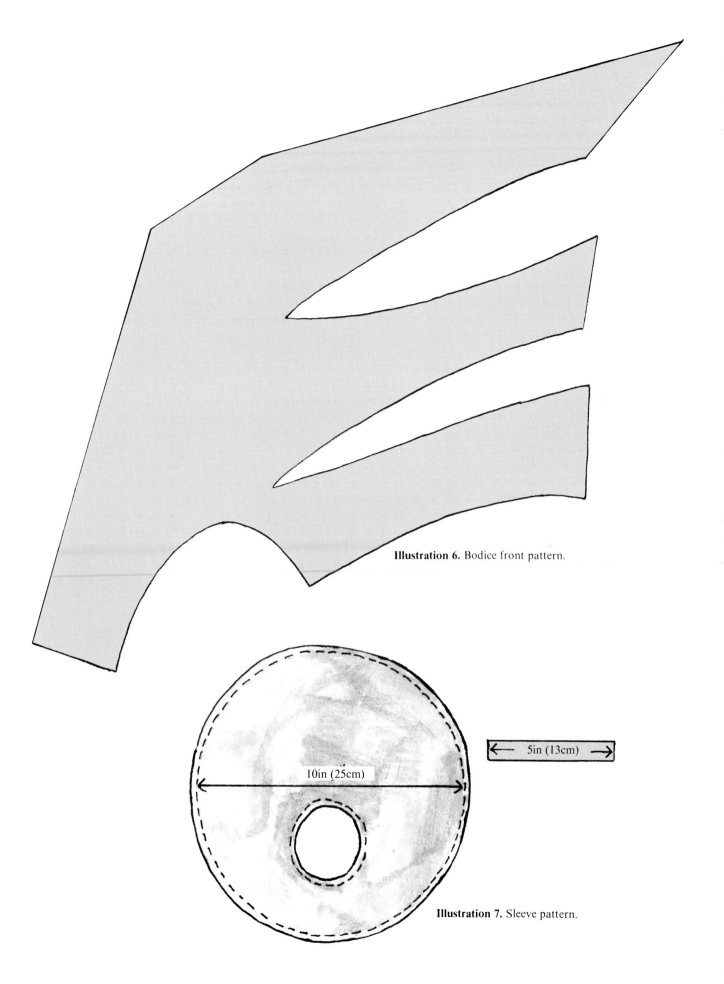

Illustration 6. Bodice front pattern.

10in (25cm)

5in (13cm)

Illustration 7. Sleeve pattern.

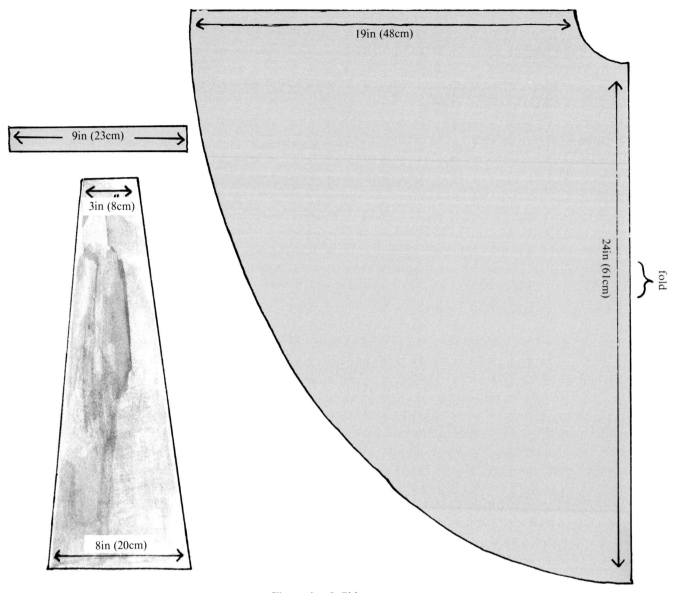

Illustration 8. Skirt pattern.

Illustration 9. Trim base.

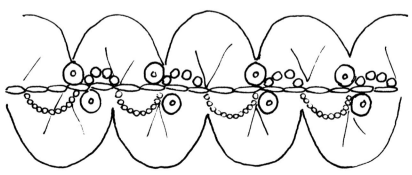

Illustration 10. Trim with sequins and beads.

Armand Marseille Baby Dressed in Early 1860s Style

by Barbara Pickering

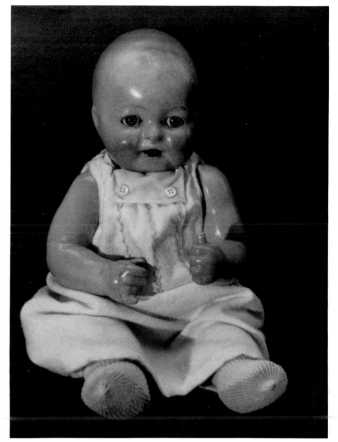

Illustration 1. 13in (33cm) baby doll whose head was probably made by Armand Marseille, shown wearing her early 1860s style dress and bonnet.

RIGHT: Illustration 2. 13in (33cm) baby doll whose head was probably made by Armand Marseille, shown wearing her barrow coat.

The 13in (33cm) baby doll shown here was given to me by a friend when she had a clear-out some time ago. As the doll was unfamiliar to me, I sent a photograph to Patricia N. Schoonmaker who identified her as a possible *Baby Gloria,* circa 1920. Colemans' *The Collector's Encyclopedia of Dolls* states that the bisque head was probably made by Armand Marseille. It has blue glass sleep eyes, an open mouth with two upper teeth, composition arms, a soft body and legs.

The doll was dressed in a very unbecoming crocheted pink dress. I immediately thought she deserved better than that and decided, in spite of purists saying the doll should be dressed in early 1920s style, to make all the pretty clothes a baby in early 1860 used to wear. They are so much richer in every way. And after all, the clothes could have been handed down from generation to generation....

The baby clothes consist of:

a PILCH which is worn over a diaper. It is made of red flannel with the top band in white calico. The leg holes are trimmed with white cotton lace. It is fastened with four linen-covered buttons;

a SHIRT made of very fine white cotton. It is fastened on the shoulders with two small buttons and edged with very narrow lace. It has flaps at the front and back of the neck. These fold over the neck of the

white flannel BARROW COAT and keep it clean. It is fastened to it with buttons. The barrow coat has a back opening, three pleats at the front and two pleats at the back. All pleats are embroidered in pink with feather stitching. The back opening is fastened with drawstrings. On top of the barrow coat the baby wears

a fine white linen PETTICOAT. It is fastened at the neck and waist with drawstrings. The hem has three tucks;

white little cotton SOCKS;

the DRESS is made from fine white lawn. It has a front panel of lace, and the bottom is decorated with eight narrow tucks and two slightly wider tucks.

Finally, the baby's wardrobe would be incomplete without a BONNET made of broderie anglaise and edged with lace.

INSTRUCTIONS FOR SEWING:
Check and try all pattern pieces as no dolls are alike. Some slight adjustments may have to be made to fit your particular doll. All pattern pieces I have given here are on the generous side so that they can easily be adjusted.

MATERIALS:
11½in (29cm) by 9in (23cm) red flannel (pilch)
Approximately 11in (28cm) by 1in (2cm) calico (waistband of pilch)
Approximately 22in (56cm) by 1/4in (.65cm) white cotton lace (edging of leg holes)
Four small white linen-covered buttons

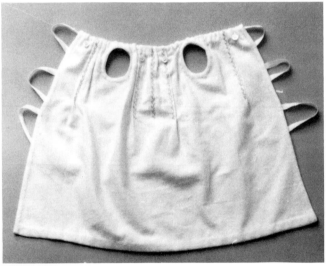

TOP TO BOTTOM: Illustration 3. Top, left to right: petticoat, barrow coat. Bottom, left to right: pilch, socks and shirt.

Illustration 4. The barrow coat opened up.

Illustration 5. The dress and bonnet.

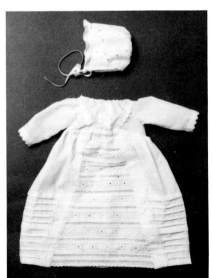

13in (33cm) by 7½in (19cm) fine white cotton (shirt)

26in (66cm) by 1/4in (.65cm) white lace (edging of shoulder straps and armholes)

Two small buttons

14in (36cm) by 11½in (29cm) white flannel (barrow coat)

Pink embroidery cotton (for feather stitching)

25in (63cm) by 14in (36cm) fine white linen (petticoat)

26in (66cm) by 19in (48cm) fine white lawn (dress)

10in (25cm) by 9in (23cm) white lace (front panel of dress)

Approximately 26in (66cm) by 1/2in (1.3cm) white lace (edging of sleeves, across shoulders front and back)

Approximately 2½in (6cm) by 1in (2cm) white lace (decoration of front bodice)

Approximately 13½in (34cm) by 1/8in (.31cm) white lace (neckline)

White thin cotton socks (baby's socks)

Roll of narrow white cotton tape (drawstrings)

8in (20cm) by 6in (15cm) broderie anglaise (bonnet)

Approximately 7in (18cm) by 1/4in (.65cm) white cotton, cut on the cross (neckband of bonnet)

Small length of narrow white satin ribbon (to tie bonnet)

Approximately 12in (30cm) by 3/4in (2cm) white lace (brim)

PILCH: Turn under raw edges of front openings and sew. Cut a calico waistband, approximately 11in (28cm) by 1in (2cm) to fit waist of pilch. With right sides together; sew waistband to pilch top. Turn waistband to wrong side of pilch, turn under raw edges and sew. Neaten edges of both leg holes and sew on lace. Make four small buttonholes as marked on the pattern. Cover four small buttons with linen and sew into place.

SHIRT: Sew the two side seams (French seam). Next, insert the two underarm pieces, matching points A and B. Turn under raw edges of shoulder straps, flaps and hem and sew. Sew very narrow lace around armholes and shoulder straps. Make six small buttonholes as marked on the pattern. Sew two small buttons to front of shoulder straps.

BARROW COAT: Make five pleats altogether: three at the front, two at the back. Cut a narrow strip of the same material on the cross, long enough to go round each armhole. With right sides together; sew the strip to the armholes. Turn strip to wrong side of barrow coat; turn under raw edges and sew. Turn under raw edges of back opening and neckline and sew. Adjust hemline and sew. Sew on four drawstrings as marked on the pattern and pull a drawstring through neckline. Sew on four small buttons corresponding to the buttonholes of the shirt. Finally embroider the five pleats with feather stitching as follows: Bring the needle out at the top center; hold the thread down with the left thumb; insert the needle a little to the right on the same level and take a small stitch down the center; keeping the thread under the needle point. Next, insert the needle a little to the left on the same level and take a stitch to center, keeping the

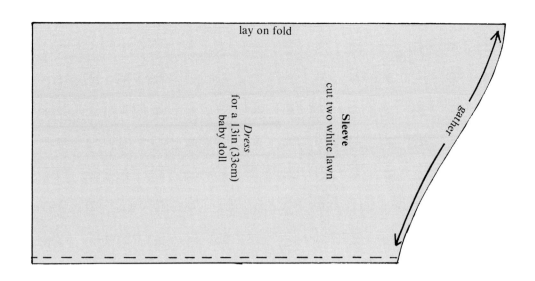

lay on fold

Dress
for a 13in (33cm)
baby doll

Sleeve
cut two white lawn

gather

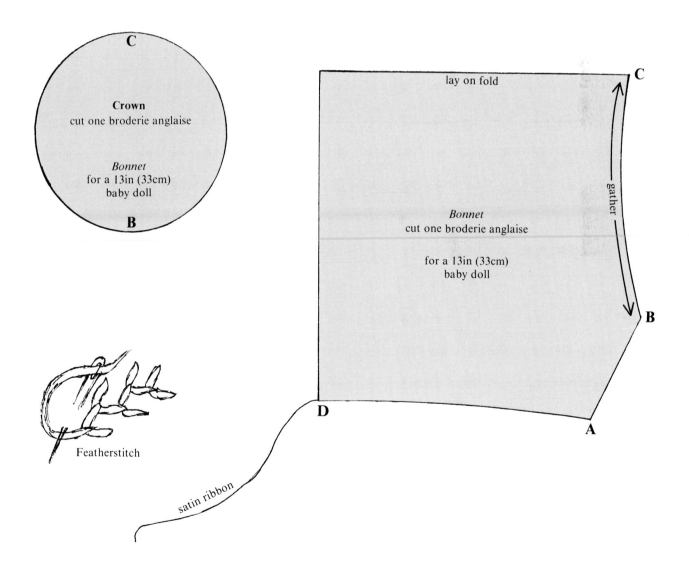

Crown
cut one broderie anglaise

Bonnet
for a 13in (33cm)
baby doll

C

B

lay on fold

C

Bonnet
cut one broderie anglaise

for a 13in (33cm)
baby doll

gather

B

D

A

Featherstitch

satin ribbon

Neckband cut one white cotton

fold

Bonnet
for a 13in (33cm) baby doll

D

A

D

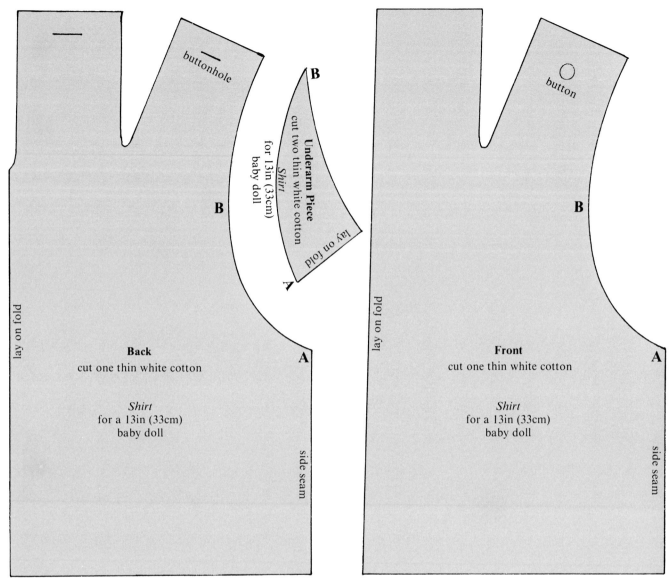

Pattern labels within the figure:

buttonhole

B

B

Underarm Piece
cut two thin white cotton
Shirt
for 13in (33cm)
baby doll
lay on fold

A

button

B

lay on fold

Back
cut one thin white cotton

Shirt
for a 13in (33cm)
baby doll

side seam

A

lay on fold

Front
cut one thin white cotton

Shirt
for a 13in (33cm)
baby doll

side seam

A

---

thread under the needle point. Work these two movements alternately (see sketch).

PETTICOAT: Face the armholes in exactly the same way as for the barrow coat. Next, make the tucks. Mark hem fold line about 1/2in (1.3cm) from the bottom edge. Turn under raw edges and sew hemline. Then mark the first tuck fold line about 1in (2cm) above hem fold line. Repeat for second and third tuck, that is the side which is uppermost after pressing. Then gather the lower part to fit the upper part of the petticoat. Before stitching the two parts together, adjust the length. Only then sew the lower part to the upper part (right sides together). Turn under raw edges of back opening and neckline and sew. Pull a drawstring through the neckline and sew two drawstrings to the waistline as marked on the pattern.

SOCKS: To measure, wrap the material around the leg (wrong side facing you) and tack together, stretch-ing the material tightly as you go along. Slip it off the leg and sew along tacking stitches. Cut away any surplus material. Turn right sides out and neaten top opening. Pull a medium thick cotton thread through the top, long enough to tie it into a bow.

DRESS: Start with the BODICE. With right sides together, fold sleeves in half and sew along broken lines (French seam). Gather top of sleeves to fit armholes and sew sleeves into armholes.

SKIRT: Proceed in exactly the same way as for the petticoat. Make four narrow tucks (each measuring about 1/8in [.31cm]), then slightly wider one (approximately 1/4in [.65cm], four more narrow ones lastly another wider one. Then fold the material in half and sew center back seam (French seam) from A to B. Gather top of skirt to fit the bodice. Pin provisionally to the bodice, making sure that 4in (10cm) of the material in

the front is without gathers, that is, straight. Remove skirt from bodice. Now pin, tack and sew the lace panel to the ungathered front part of the skirt. Then cut off the skirt material behind the lace panel, leaving just enough material on each side to neaten all edges. This may be an unorthodox way of inserting a lace panel, but it is easy and saves you time in fiddling around to match the tucks evenly on either side of the lace panel.

Having completed the skirt and adjusted the length, sew it, with right sides together, to the bodice. Turn under raw edges of back opening and sew. Turn under raw edges of neckline and sew. Adjust sleeve length, turn under raw edges and sew. Sew lace round the neckline and sleeves, to the front of the bodice, right across and down both shoulders to the waistline. Pull a drawstring through the neckline and sew two drawstrings to the back of the dress at waistline.

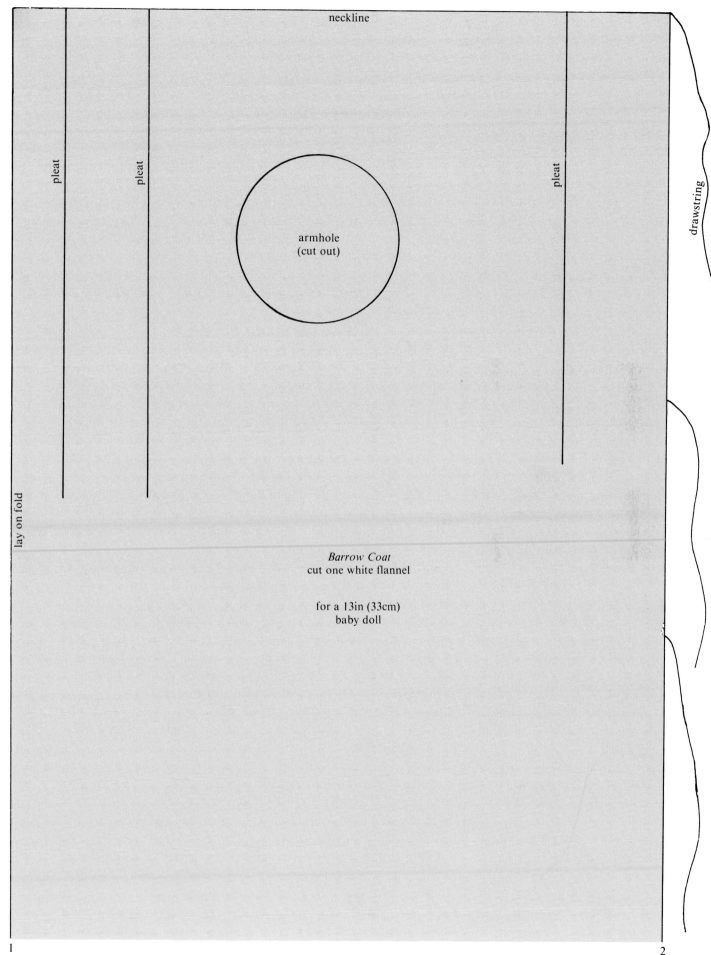

neckline

pleat

pleat

pleat

drawstring

lay on fold

armhole
(cut out)

Barrow Coat
cut one white flannel

for a 13in (33cm)
baby doll

1

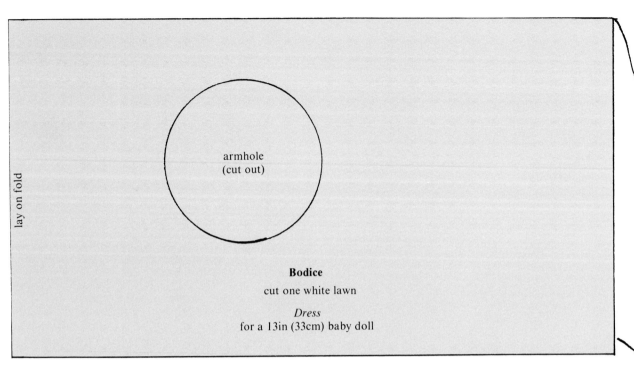

lay on fold

armhole
(cut out)

drawstring

Bodice

cut one white lawn

Dress
for a 13in (33cm) baby doll

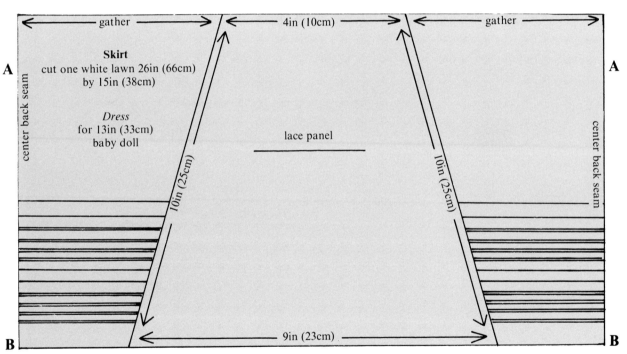

gather · 4in (10cm) · gather

A · A

center back seam

Skirt
cut one white lawn 26in (66cm)
by 15in (38cm)

Dress
for 13in (33cm)
baby doll

10in (25cm) · 10in (25cm)

lace panel

center back seam

B · 9in (23cm) · B

1 · 2

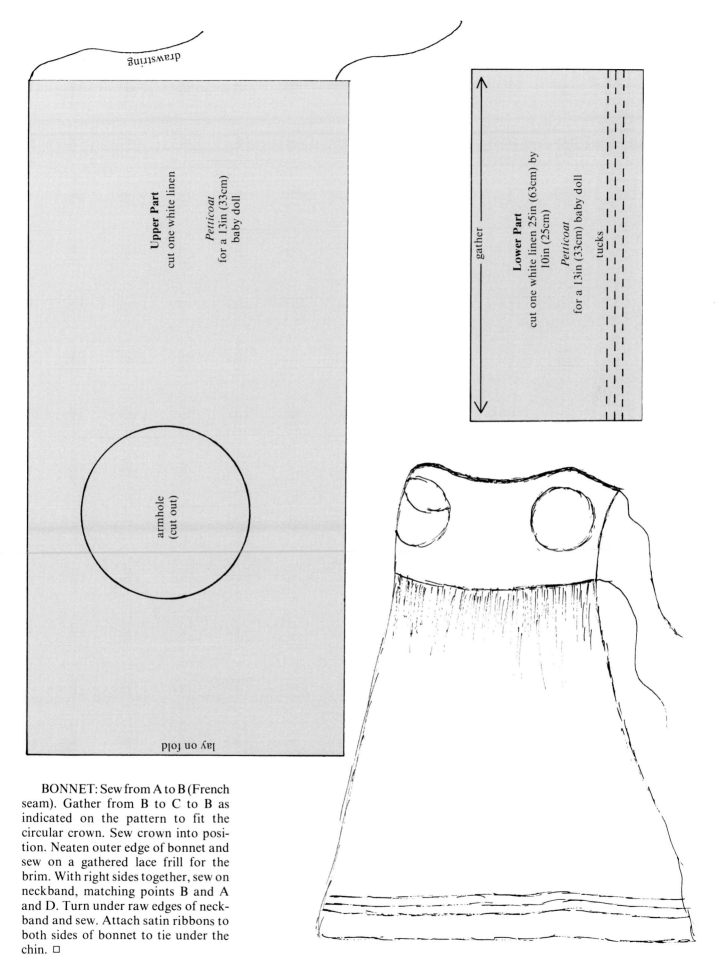

Upper Part
cut one white linen

Petticoat
for a 13in (33cm)
baby doll

armhole
(cut out)

drawstring

lay on fold

Lower Part
cut one white linen 25in (63cm) by
10in (25cm)

Petticoat
for a 13in (33cm) baby doll

gather

tucks

BONNET: Sew from A to B (French seam). Gather from B to C to B as indicated on the pattern to fit the circular crown. Sew crown into position. Neaten outer edge of bonnet and sew on a gathered lace frill for the brim. With right sides together, sew on neckband, matching points B and A and D. Turn under raw edges of neckband and sew. Attach satin ribbons to both sides of bonnet to tie under the chin. □

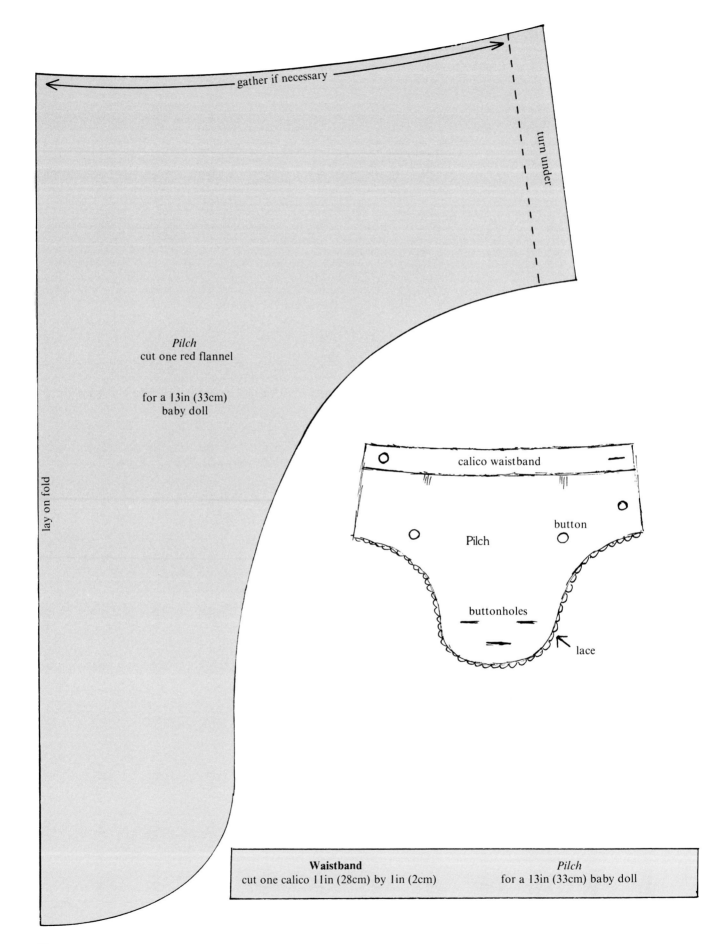

gather if necessary

turn under

Pilch
cut one red flannel

for a 13in (33cm)
baby doll

lay on fold

calico waistband

button

Pilch

buttonholes

lace

Waistband
cut one calico 11in (28cm) by 1in (2cm)

Pilch
for a 13in (33cm) baby doll

Kate Greenaway Outfit for a 14in (36cm) doll

by **Virginia Cross**

Illustration 1. An Alexander doll in a striped dress of white voile with rose and moss green flowers, Version One.

Kate Greenaway is said to have "dressed the children of the world." It is one of fashion's charming whimseys that the biggest influence on children's clothing of all time was neither a designer nor a highly visible celebrity, but a shy Victorian who wrote and illustrated children's books; and the fashions she drew were not of her invention or even of her own time, but were resurrected from the previous century because the illustrator found both the values and styles of that time more appealing than her own.

Kate Greenaway was born in 1846 to hardworking middle-class parents. Her father was a wood engraver and her mother ran a fancy goods store. Young Kate studied at the Art Department of South Kensington in England and had her first exhibit, a series of drawings on wood blocks, in 1868. Later she began to illustrate articles for children's periodicals and the *Illustrated London News*. As her popularity increased, she moved on to children's novels and eventually her own books, and a line of greeting cards that were a great commercial success.

Her best known works are probably the illustrations of *Under The Window, The Marigold Garden, The Pied Piper of Hamlin* and *Kate Greenaway's Book of Games.*

Greenaway's work has always received mixed reviews. Her drawings have been sometimes criticized for being saccharine and superficial. She always defended her art, however, by claiming therapeutic value for innocence and beauty. Her drawings extolled children and nature, and while they are not profound, they have a delicate charm and elegance that has endured. Kate Greenaway's belief in the values of her art is supported; her books are still in print today.

The cottages, country lanes and gardens of rural England were the England Greenaway loved, and though she lived in a time of increasing industrialization, she chose not to portray it. Her mannerly and rather sexless children romp through flowery meadows and pour tea in quaint brick-walled gardens. Village streets are calm and empty enough for a child to ride a hobby horse there. There is not a railroad, crowded city scene, iron bridge, factory of smokestack to be found. In short, Greenaway was as much a victim of galloping nostalgia as we are today!

Just as she preferred the way of life and the landscape of an earlier century, Greenaway also found greater charm and simplicity in the clothing of that time. The styles she drew were derived from the children's fashions of about 1800 to 1815. Even the soft fabrics and gentle colors in Greenaway's illustrations belong to the earlier period rather than to the richer, more brilliant, even gaudy tastes of the Victorians.

Kate Greenaway's influence on little girls' fashions was enormous. The high waisted dresses with puffy sleeves and gently gathered skirts are true classics. Laura Ashley's country English styles and fabrics are grown-up derivatives of the style. (It is interesting to note that the major influence has been in feminine styles. The "Lord Fauntleroy" suits for boys have enjoyed periodic, brief revivals but have never really caught on, presumably because only mothers and aunties like them. Little boys detest them.) Toys, greeting cards and wrapping paper decorated with Greenaway style children sell very well. A fascinating irony is that the most commercial, most relentlessly merchandised tot of our time, *Miss Strawberry Shortcake*, is a direct descendant of the children who played in Kate Greenaway's simple and distinctly uncommercial English gardens.

Greenaway children are consistantly middle-class. They are well clothed, but not formally. They sometimes engage in light domestic tasks, but never anything truly dirty or enslaving. For watering the flowers, they will sometimes protect their dress with a pinafore apron. (It always puzzled me why a dark play dress was protected by a white apron, but that seems to have been the style.) This very middle-classness makes the clothes wonderfully translatable to doll clothes. The appropriate fabrics are small in scale and soft, and the simple lines are very becoming to miniature bodies.

When sewing for your doll, it is fun to copy the delicacy of the drawings in your fabric selection, but it would be a mistake to limit yourself to pastels. Greenaway's children are also clad in a soft brick red, moss green, or even a gentle brown. The trick to using the deeper shades is to make sure they are gentle, not harsh or brilliant. Greenaway's art was mostly watercolors, and if you picture the same color first as it would appear in an oil painting, and then in a watercolor print, you will have the right idea of how to choose.

Pastel wallpaper type floral prints are, of course, suitable, as is simple, pure white. A white dress and mobcap with the single accent of a colored ribbon sash would be authentic and elegant. Polka dots both large and small, and candy striped fabrics would also be good choices. You will rarely see rich formal fabrics like velvet or taffeta used for anything but coats and cloaks in Greenaway illustrations. The dresses are soft and gently flowing. Batiste, voile, lightweight muslin and other fine cottons are good. I have used

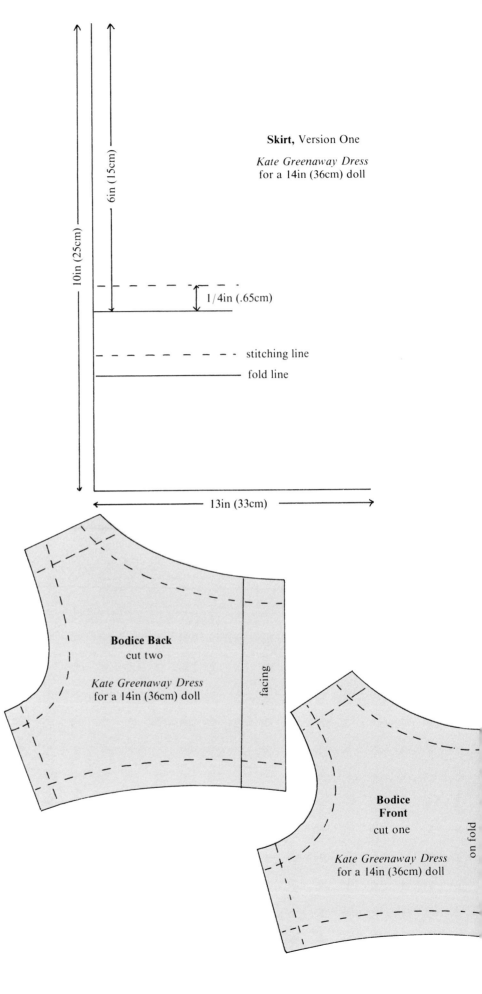

Skirt, Version One

Kate Greenaway Dress
for a 14in (36cm) doll

10in (25cm)

6in (15cm)

1/4in (.65cm)

— stitching line

— fold line

13in (33cm)

Bodice Back
cut two

Kate Greenaway Dress
for a 14in (36cm) doll

facing

Bodice Front
cut one

Kate Greenaway Dress
for a 14in (36cm) doll

on fold

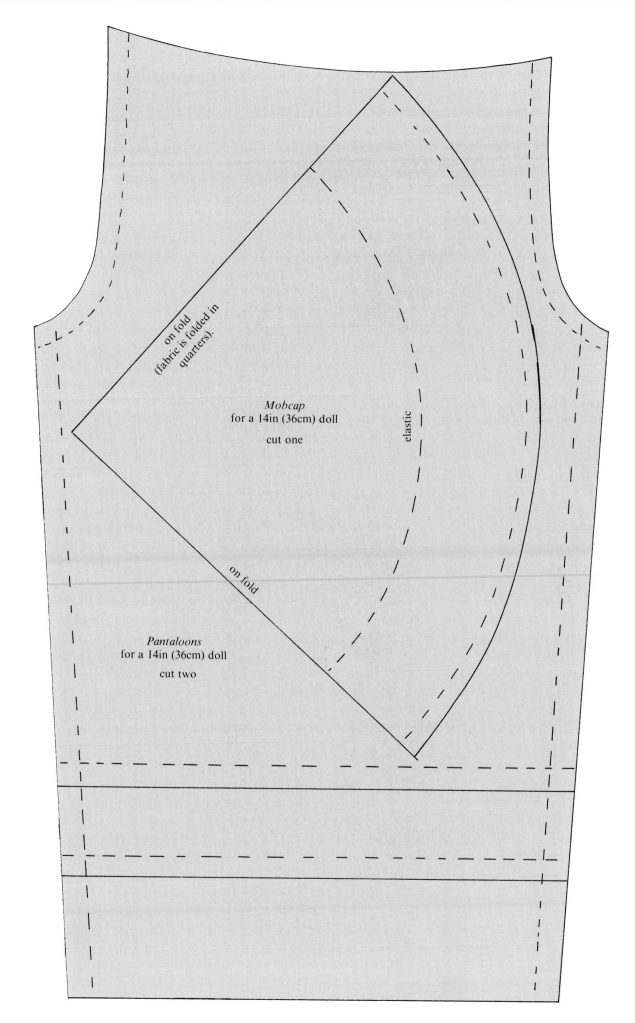

on fold
(fabric is folded in quarters).

elastic

Mobcap
for a 14in (36cm) doll

cut one

on fold

Pantaloons
for a 14in (36cm) doll

cut two

Illustration 2. An Alexander doll in a floral print dress, Version Two.

a white muslin for the pantaloons, petticoat and mobcap. The striped dress (**Illustration 1**) is of blue and voile with rose and moss green flowers, and the floral print (**Illustration 2**) is a pale green and white cotton calico.

PANTALOONS

Make tucks in legs as shown.

Sew center front seam.

Sew center back seam to notch.

Turn under raw edges above notch on each side and sew down.

Turn waist under 1/2in (1.3cm) and sew down, 1/4in (.7cm) from fold to form casing.

Hem leg edges and trim with lace.

Sew crotch seam.

With large needle, run narrow ribbon or string through casing at waist. Pantaloons are tied at waist.

PETTICOAT

Cut piece of fabric 7¼in (18cm) by 12in (30cm).

Sew short ends of fabric, right sides together, leaving top 2½in (6cm) open.

Turn under raw edges and finish waist as in pantaloons.

Hem skirt and add lace trim.

I might add here, I do like some of the results of drawstring waists for doll clothes, for avoiding bulk at the waist. Put the doll's dress on first. If there is a sash or belt, make it as tight as you can. Next put on her petticoat, tying drawstring rather loosely, so that it rides just below the waist; then do the same with the pantaloons. It seems to me elastic always wants to congregate at the narrowest point, which is the doll's waist, of course. The drawstrings allow the bulk to be staggered so that the only fabric around the actual waist is the dress. This is particularly desirable for some period fashions when you want a tiny waist and huge skirts, but even in these slightly empire styles, I think it gives a cleaner line.

MOBCAP

Turn outer edge under 1/4in (.7cm) and sew.

Cut elastic to fit snugly around doll's head. Sew, stretching as you go, to dotted line 1¼in (3cm) from edge.

If desired, tack ribbon on right side to elastic sewing line (not shown) and tie bow in front.

STRIPED DRESS

Since I have used a sheer fabric for the dress, I lined the bodice. The petticoat makes lining the skirt unnecessary. Cut sleeves and bodice front and back in lining fabric also. Batiste or fine muslin both make good linings.

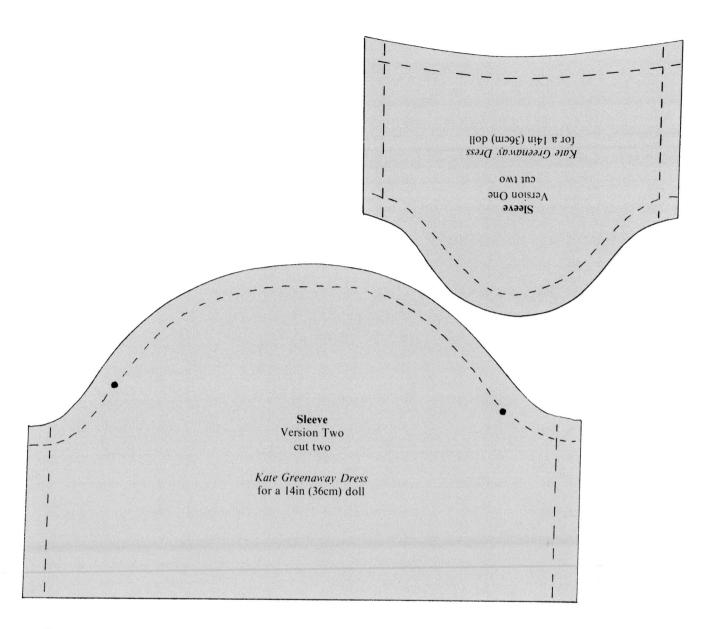

Sleeve
Version One
cut two

Kate Greenaway Dress
for a 14in (36cm) doll

Sleeve
Version Two
cut two

Kate Greenaway Dress
for a 14in (36cm) doll

Sew shoulder seams in dress and lining bodices, respectively.

Sew dress unit to lining around neckline, right sides together. Clip curve, turn and press.

Sew lace to neck edge. I like to use a flat lace rather than the kind that is pre-gathered on a tricot edge. Run a gathering thread along top edge; pull up gathers to desired fullness. Stitch in place on right side of neckline with tiny zigzag stitch.

Gather lace for sleeves as you did for neck. Pin gathered edge to sleeve edge, right sides together and baste.

Sew linings to sleeves at bottom edge, right sides together, turn and press. Lace edge will be enclosed in seam.

Sew sleeves to armholes, easing between dots. Pin and sew carefully, as you are working with four layers of fabrics.

Sew underarm seam from waist to sleeve edge.

Cut upper skirt piece 6½in (16cm) by 13in (33cm). Gather to waist.

Cut lower skirt 13in (33cm) by 4½in (11cm), with stripes running perpendicular to stripes in upper skirt.

Sew lower skirt to upper. Sew center back seam, leaving open 2in (5cm) below waist seam, using 1/2in (1.3cm) seam allownce for this seam only. Turn under facing from neck to waist and stitch. Close with snaps.

To finish skirt, turn dress wrong side out. Fold lower skirt up approximately in half; fold raw edge under and pin in place at seam joining upper and lower skirt pieces. Hem by hand. No raw edge will show at skirt.

DRESS VARIATION

With the heavier calico, lining is optional. If you choose not to line, simply turn raw edge under at neckline after sewing shoulder seams and stitch.

Follow general sequence of first dress except: Gather sleeve between dots before sewing sleeves to armhole. Turn under sleeve edges 1/2in (1.3cm) to form casing for elastic. Pull elastic up to fit doll's arms and fasten at ends. You can do this in one step with sewing the side seams, as long as you are careful to hang on to the ends of the elastic while you are working.

Cut skirt piece 10in (25cm) by 13in (33cm). Make tucks as shown in diagram, and finish dress as in first version.

These outfits will fit all 14in (36cm) hard plastic or composition dolls with slender bodies, such as Madame Alexander's *Wendy Ann* or *Margaret, Sweet Sue,* R & B *Nanette, Toni* and *Mary Hoyer.* The model in the illustrations is a Madame Alexander doll with the *Margaret* face. □

Cinderella and Fairy Godmother Costumes for *Ginny* and *Jill*

by Lauren Welker

Vogue Dolls were the undisputed "fashion leaders in doll society" during the 1950s. The construction of their clothing was both simple and ingenious. They used quality fabrics and trims to dress their charming dolls.

While one can never hope to exactly duplicate vintage doll clothing, one can approximate it. The same fabrics and trims may no longer be available to us. Indeed, even colors go in and out of fashion and, in any given season, certain colors may be impossible to find. It is with this in mind that I offer these patterns. My best advice is to sew to please yourself and have fun. The pleasure in creating something lovely is its own reward.

These patterns will also fit other similar-size dolls. The *Ginny* pattern will fit all the Madame Alexander 8in (20cm) dolls from the 1950s on. It will also fit the newer international *Ginny* dolls because they still have the chubby toddler shape. The *Jill* pattern will fit other 10½in (27cm) high-heeled dolls like *Little Miss Revlon, Jan* and *Cissette.*

GENERAL INSTRUCTIONS: 1/4in (.65cm) seams are allowed. For a neat finish, sew each seam a second time close to the first seam, then trim away excess allowance. Remember not to choose fabrics that will be too bulky. Commercially made clothing was gathered at the waist by a special machine. Since we home sewers do not have this machine, clothing made with a sewn-in slip can become too bulky at the waistline. Eliminate bulk by gathering the slip on a separate waistband.
BRAID LOOP-EDGE TRIM: This was a common finish for Vogue and other doll clothing. Sew your braid loop-edge trim with the loop edge facing toward the garment (on the right side). Press the trim over toward the back of the garment so that only the loop edge shows on the right side. Topstitch through the garment and trim. Finished edge will look like
Illustration 1.

GINNY CINDERELLA INSTRUCTIONS:
SUGGESTED FABRICS AND TRIMS: *Ginny* Cinderella bodice and panniers should be cut from a silky-textured pastel fabric in a shade like baby blue, with a matching rose bouquet. An organdy fabric of white dotted with silver might be used for the skirt. Silver loop-edge trim should be used for the neck edge, panniers and hem. Add a silver braid bow to the rose bouquet on the bodice.

Sew bodice neckline as per "braid loop-edge trim" instructions.

Fold sleeve ruffle and press. Gather along the long raw edge. Right sides together, baste in place at the armhole, adjusting the gathers evenly. Sew in place, press and topstitch. Do other sleeve the same.

Sew the side seams. Be sure that the sleeve ruffles meet evenly.

Sew loop-edge trim to the panniers. Turn and press but do **not** topstitch.

Mark skirt for panniers using the dotted edge of the pattern for a guide. If you use hand basting to mark your line, it will not leave a mark on the fabric.

Lay the trimmed edges of the panniers along the marked lines. Topstitch in place. The gathering edge will extend above the skirt. It is supposed to. The extra fabric is what makes the panniers "puff up."

Use the braid loop-edge finish along the bottom of the skirt.

Press over the center backs of the skirt from the top edge to about halfway down. Adjust the panniers so that the top edges of the panniers match the top edge of the skirt. Run a row of gathering stitches through both layers.

Gather the skirt and baste it to the bodice adjusting the gathers evenly. Sew firmly in place.

Sew halfway up the center back of the skirt. Add a small hook and eye at the waist. Baste the silver bow and rose bouquet to the waist.

JILL FAIRY GODMOTHER INSTRUCTIONS:

SUGGESTED FABRICS AND TRIMS: The skirt should be made of a silky-textured fabric in a vivid shade like fuchsia. The apron and bodice should be cut from a light blue organdy with gold dots or a similar dainty fabric. Gold loop-edge trim should be used for the neck, sleeves, apron and hem.

Sew the bodice darts. Press.

Use the braid loop-edge finish at the neck and sleeve edges. (Cap sleeves are part of the bodice. There is not a separate pattern piece.)

Sew the side seams, being careful to match the sleeve edges. Press.

Use the braid loop-edge finish around the curved edge of the apron but do **not** topstitch.

Lay the apron over the skirt, matching the center fronts. Topstitch in place around the trimmed edge.

Use the braid loop-edge trim finish at the bottom edge of the skirt.

Press over the center backs from the top about halfway down.

Gather the top edge of the skirt, treating the skirt and apron as one piece.

Baste the skirt to the bodice, adjusting the gathers evenly as you go. Machine stitch.

Sew halfway up the center back of the skirt. Add a small hook and eye at the waist.

ACCESSORIES:
Both dolls should have slips of stiff organdy cut the same size as their respective skirts. Gather each slip to its waistband. Hem each so that it does not stick out below the costume. Add a row of gathered netting around the outside of each slip.

Cinderella should have a hair ribbon to match her dress. The Fairy Godmother should have a "magic wand." One can be made by pasting a cardboard star to a toothpick. Paint the wand gold, adding some glitter to the star. If desired, make a cone-shaped hat from felt. Trim with narrow ribbons. □

Apron

cut one

Fairy Godmother Costume
for a 10½in (27cm) doll

cut skirt fabric
6¾in (17cm) by 20in (51cm)
cut slip as above

fold

gather

Pannier

cut two

Cinderella Costume
for an 8in (20cm) doll

fold

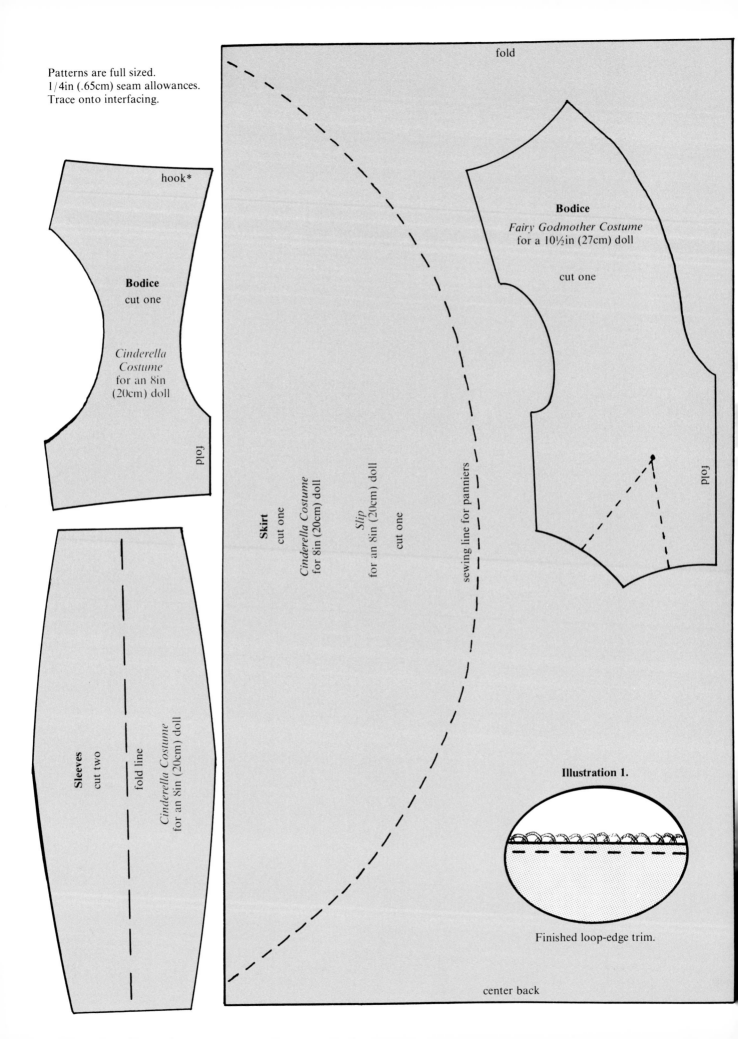

Patterns are full sized.
1/4in (.65cm) seam allowances.
Trace onto interfacing.

Bodice
cut one

Cinderella Costume for an 8in (20cm) doll

hook*

fold

Sleeves
cut two

fold line

Cinderella Costume for an 8in (20cm) doll

Skirt
cut one

Cinderella Costume for 8in (20cm) doll

Slip for an 8in (20cm) doll

cut one

sewing line for panniers

fold

Bodice

Fairy Godmother Costume for a 10½in (27cm) doll

cut one

fold

Illustration 1.

Finished loop-edge trim.

center back

A Party Dress for Tiny 8in (20cm) *Betsy McCall*®

by **Lauren Welker**

Illustration 2. View B of the dress for *Betsy McCall.*

Illustration 1. *Betsy McCall* wearing the dress, View A.

Trim allowances, turn and press. Cut two pieces of lace 2¾in (7cm) long. Gather and sew to the outside of the bodice along the sleeve edges. You may either whipstitch the lace in place or sew by machine. Cut a 9in (23cm) piece of lace for the neck/back edge. Gather and pin in place, adjusting the gathers to the neck edge and letting the lace lay flat along the center back edges. For the neatest finish, whipstitch the lace in place. Sew a piece of lace along the bottom of the bodice front. Most of the lace should lay above the 1/4in (.65cm) seam allowance so it will show on the finished bodice. Right sides together, sew the side seams being sure to catch the raw edges of the lace. Turn and press.

SKIRT: Press the first tuck. Be sure to keep it even. Sew the tuck in place keeping your line of stitching about 1/8in (.31cm) from the fold. Press the second tuck keeping it an even distance from the first. Sew. Repeat for third tuck. Press the tucks down and the hem up. Sew a row of lace about 1/4in (.65cm) from the lowest tuck, catching the hem allowance as you sew. Sew a second row of lace along the hemline. Press over the center back seam allowances and sew. Run a row of gathering stitches along the top.

ASSEMBLING: Pin the skirt to the bodice matching the center fronts and adjusting the gathers evenly. Sew. Make a second row of stitching about 1/8in (.31cm) away from the first; then trim away the excess seam allowance. Sew ribbon rosettes in place (see illustration).

SLIP: Join top and bottom slip at the waist matching center fronts. Sew again about 1/8in (.31cm) away from

the original stitching line. Trim away excess seam allowance. Press the raw edge toward the wrong side all the way around the slip. Sew. By hand, tack the slip to the dress at the side seams and center backs. Add a snap at the center back waist sewing through both the dress and slip. Add other snaps if needed.

PANTIES: Clip and press over the seam allowances around each leg. Sew. Sew one side seam and press open. Press down the seam allowance at the waist. Apply 1/8in (.31cm) elastic to the waist stretching the elastic as you sew and firmly catching the seam allowance and panty. Sew remaining side seam.

VIEW B: This is a simplified version of the same dress pattern. It eliminates the ruffled lace, tucks and slip. You need soft cotton (either solid or a small print), baby rickrack and enough ribbon for a sash.

Cut one bodice and one bodice lining. Clip bodice at the triangles to mark the cap sleeves. Cut one skirt the same width as the pattern piece but 3/4in (2cm) shorter because you are eliminating the tucks.

Assemble like dress A but ignore the instructions for the tucks and lace. Before attaching the bodice to the skirt, add rickrack around the neck/back edge of the bodice and add rickrack along the bottom skirt as desired. When finished add a ribbon sash around the waist. □

Betsy McCall® is a registered trademark of the McCall Corp.

VIEW A: To make this dress you will need nylon or organdy, 3/8in (.9cm) or 1/2in (1.3cm) lace, silk or lining fabric for the slip, 1/8in (.31cm) elastic for the panties, three ribbon rosettes and snaps. This pattern has 1/4in (.65cm) seam allowances. Always use a straight foot rather than a zigzag foot when working on tiny garments.

Cut out your pattern pieces. Using the bodice pattern cut a lining from either the same fabric or a small piece of tulle. I prefer the tulle for very sheer fabric. Mark the cap sleeves, hem and tucks by making a small clip at each triangle.

BODICE: Right sides together, sew the sleeve edges from clip to clip. Sew up one center back, around the neck and down the opposite center back.

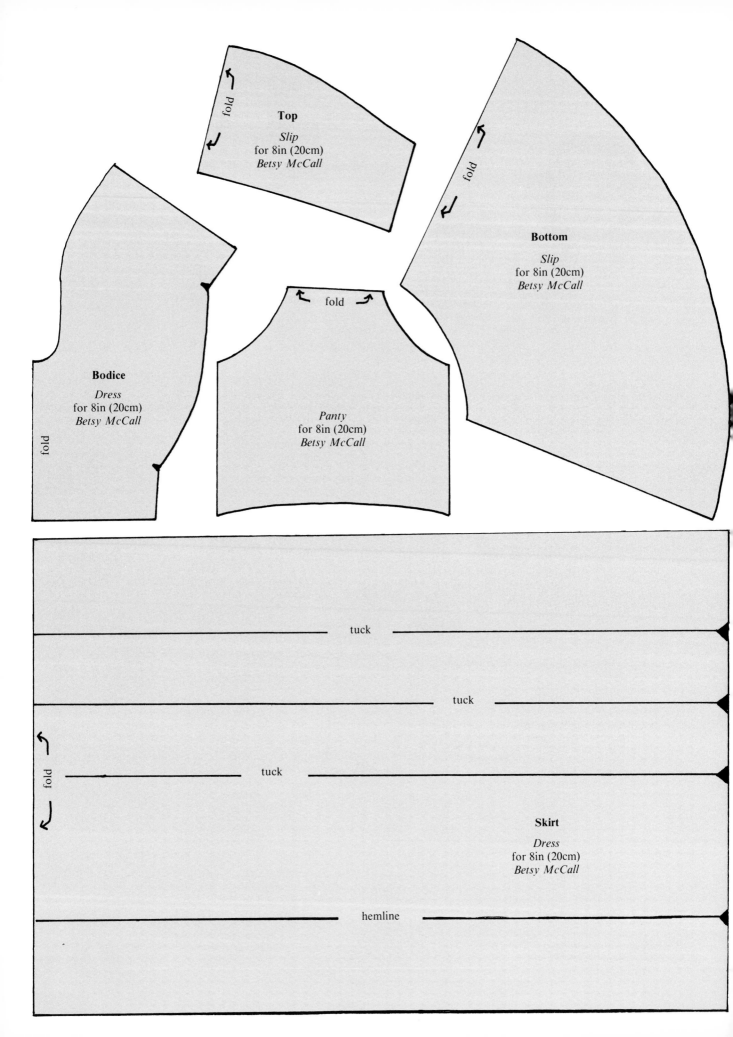

Top

Slip
for 8in (20cm)
Betsy McCall

fold

Bottom

Slip
for 8in (20cm)
Betsy McCall

fold

Bodice

Dress
for 8in (20cm)
Betsy McCall

fold

fold

Panty
for 8in (20cm)
Betsy McCall

tuck

tuck

tuck

fold

Skirt

Dress
for 8in (20cm)
Betsy McCall

hemline

Crocheted Dress and Bonnet for a 12in (30cm) *Bye-Lo Baby*, Head Circumference 9in (23cm)

by **Pat Nelson**

Photographs by the **Author**

Illustration 1. Crocheted dress and bonnet with cape collar on the *Bye-Lo Baby.*

Illustration 2. Crocheted dress, booties and bonnet without the cape collar.

The *Bye-Lo Baby* is given life through the medium of crocheted clothes made especially for her/him, and those seeing the dressed doll are spellbound! The delicate thread used brings out the utmost in appearance and presentation, then with the addition of dainty pastel ribbons strung through inserts of the dress and tied in bows, the doll is exquisite!

A small doll was chosen for the clothes made, but with care, the pattern can be adjusted to fit other dolls by increasing length in areas needed, and increasing stitches.

It is important to remember NOT to use bulky yarns as some do in baby clothes. Bedspread type thread number 30 is ideal for 12in (30cm) dolls, but number 40 may be used. Number 12 crochet hook must be used, and makes a larger dress. Experimenting with various needles and thread will aid you in making other doll clothes.

The bonnet and cape collar is unique, and frames the doll's face in elegance, with collar flowing like a cape. Made longer, it would be delightful as a christening cape the length of the dress. It could be lined, too, with a soft satin.

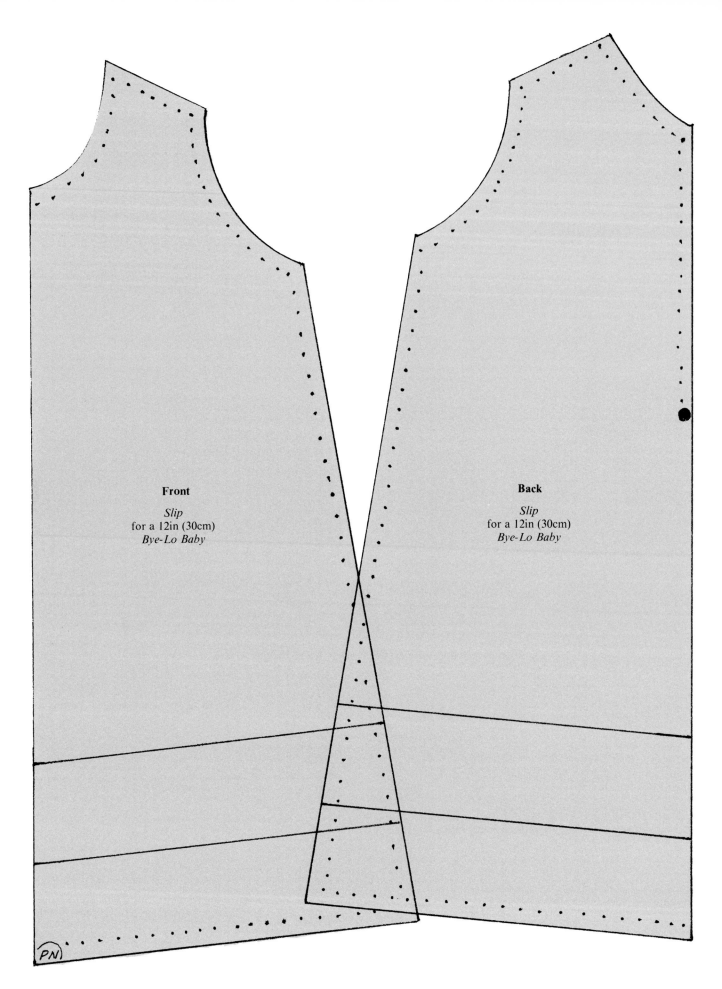

Front

Slip
for a 12in (30cm)
Bye-Lo Baby

Back

Slip
for a 12in (30cm)
Bye-Lo Baby

PN

MATERIALS REQUIRED:
Two balls size 30 white thread.
Size 12 crochet hook.

BODICE:
Work is accomplished by working each part in sections, left back, front and right back. When brought together when finished, they form the armhole.

INSTRUCTIONS: Ch 90 sts to be the neckline of the baby dress.

Row 1: Turn and make 1 dc in fourth st from end of ch, 1 dc in each st across. Ch 2, turn.

Row 2: 1 hdc in each st across, ch 2, turn.

Row 3: *1 hdc in next 4 sts, 2 hdc in next st, * repeat across. Ch 2, turn.

Row 4: *1 hdc in next 4 sts, 2 hdc in next st, * repeat across. Ch 2, turn.

Row 5: Make 1 hdc in each st, ch 2, turn.

Rows 6, 7, 8, 9, 10, 11 and 12: Repeat Row 5. *Cut* thread. (This forms the yoke of the dress.)

Row 13: Make loop on thread, attach to one side of yoke. Ch 2, make 1 hdc in each st for 19 sts. Ch 2, turn.

Rows 14, 15, 16, 17, 18, 19, 20: Repeat Row 13, *cut thread.* (Completes one back section of bodice.)

Row 21: (Front bodice) Leaving 10 sts free for armhole, make a loop and attach thread to the 11th st; ch 2, then make 1 hdc in each st across front only, for 25 sts, ch 2, turn.

Rows 22, 23, 24, 25, 26, 27, 28: Make 1 hdc in each st across bodice front, *cut* thread. (This completes front bodice.)

Row 29: Make a thread loop, attach to end of back yoke of third section of bodice, ch 2 and make 1 hdc in each st across OMITTING 10 sts for armhole. Ch 2, turn.

Rows 30, 31, 32, 33, 34, 35, 36: Repeat Row 29, making 1 hdc in each st to finish final or third section of bodice. Ch 2, turn.

Row 37: Make 1 hdc in each st from back end, working toward armhole section. Chain 10 for armhole, join to front bodice with 1 hdc and continue to next armhole section; chain 10 again, make 1 hdc in back bodice section, continuing to end with 1 hdc in each st to end. (This attaches the three sections together to form the front and back bodice.) Ch 2, turn.

Row 38: Make 1 hdc in each st, and 10 hdcs in each bottom armhole section, continuing with 1 hdc to opposite end. Ch 3, turn.

Row 39: (Ribbon row insert) Skip 1 st, make 1 dc in every second st across to end. Ribbon will be run in and out of each bar section for waist. Ch 2, turn.

Row 40: Make 1 dc and 2 dcs in each st across, repeating to end. Join ends with slip st and secure. (This completes bodice without sleeves.)

Row 41: Start skirt at back with increased sts to begin skirt, ch 2, * 1 dc in next st, 2 dc in next st * repeating to end, join, and slip st to next row.

Row 42: Ch 6, 1 dc in second st, *ch 6, 1 dc in second st*, repeat to last loop. Ch 3, starting next row.

Row 43: Repeat Row 42, making as many rows as desired for length of dress skirt. Dress skirt must cover length of slip.

Row 44: Finish bottom of skirt with a tiny shell stitch as follows: Starting with one loop in skirt bottom, sc in ch, make another sc and increase by making 2 dcs, 2 scs and join to next loop. Repeat to end, join and secure thread; cut. Hide thread end between stitches above skirt.

SLEEVES:
Row 1: Make loop on crochet hook, join to underarm section where 10 sts were made, ch 2, 1 hdc in next 10 sts, and 1 dc in each st around, join ch 2 (50 sts).

Row 2: 1 dc in each st around (50 sts), join, ch 2, turn.

Rows 3, 4, 5, 6, 7: Repeat Row 2, making 1 dc in each st, join, ch 6.

Row 8: Chain 6 begins a slight puff in sleeve in an open mesh to match dress skirt. Make 1 sc in second st, * ch 6, 1 sc in second st* repeat around sleeve to end, ch 3, 1 trc in first sc.

Rows 9, 10, 11, 12, 13, 14: Repeat ch 6, 1 sc in second st (7 rows total).

Row 15: Ch 2, make 2 hdc in each chain loop around, join to ch 2.

Row 16: 1 hdc in each st around, join to ch 2.

Row 17: (Decrease slightly) * 1 hdc in first st, pick up an extra st with next hdc * repeating to end. Join, ch 2.

Row 18: (Decreasing continued) *1 hdc in first st, pick up an extra st with next hdc * repeating to end, decreasing to give a puffed effect in chain work. Join, ch 3.

Row 19: (Ribbon insert row) Make 1 dc in second st, *ch 1, skip 1 st and dc in next st *. Repeat to end , join. Ch 2.

Row 20: 1 hdc in each st around, join, ch 2 (Sleeve opening should be the size of a quarter in circumference.)

Row 21: 1 hdc in each st around, join.

Row 22: Ch 6 and sc in 2nd st, *ch 6, slip 1 st and sc in next st* repeat to end, join.

Rows 23, 24: Repeat same as Row 22.

Row 25: Trim edge for sleeve: In each ch 6 loop at end, make 1 sc, 1 hdc, 2 dc, 1 hdc and sc, repeat for each loop to end, join, secure knot, cut thread. Hide thread ending in sts. (Edge is a dainty shell effect to set off dress. Use this edging at neckline too.)

Make second sleeve same way.

BABY BONNET/ CAPE COMBINATION:
Crown: ch 10, join.

Row 1: Ch 3, make 19 dc in ring (20 sts).

Row 2: Ch 3, *2 dc in next st, 1 dc in following st*, repeat around, join, ch 3.

Row 3: *1 dc in next 4 sts, 2 dc in following st*, repeat around, join, ch 3.

Row 4: *2 dc in next st, 1 dc in following st*, repeat around, join, ch 3.

Row 5: *1 dc in next 4 sts, 2 dcs in following st*, join, ch 6, begin open mesh with chain sts.

Row 6: With ch on end, skip 1 st and sc in next st. Ch 3, 1 trc in last st. Leave 8 sts free for back of neck.

Row 7: Ch 6, sc in next ch loop, repeating across. End with ch 3, 1 trc in last loop, turn.

Rows 8, 9, 10, 11, 12, 13, 14: Repeat Row 7.

Row 15: Make 2 hdc in each chain loop around, join to first hdc, ch 2.

Row 16: Make 1 hdc in next 50 sts (counting is important), ch 1, turn.

Rows 17, 18, 19, 20: Make 1 hdc in each of 50 sts, ch 1, turn. (This ends bonnet; you may secure thread st, and cut thread if only bonnet is desired. Continue with cape for a collar effect on dress.) Edging for bonnet brim given at end of cape instructions.

Row 21: Beginning of cape collar — ch 2, make 1 dc in same st as ch. *Ch 1, skip 1 st, and make 2 dc in following st*. Repeat 25 times.

Row 22: Ch 3, turn, *1 dc in next 2 sts, 2 dc in next st*, repeat around, ch 3, turn.

Row 23: 1 dc in next 4 sts, *2 dc in next st, 2 dc in next 5 sts, 2 dc in next st* repeating around, ch 3, turn.

Row 24: *Make 1 dc in next 2 sts, 2 dc in following st*, repeating around, ch 3, turn.

Rows 25, 26, 27, 28: Repeat instructions of Row 24.

Trim for edge of cape: 1 sc, 1 hdc, 3 dc, 1 hdc, 1 sc in each chain loop around. Secure thread st, cut thread, hide thread ends in sts.

Trim for Bonnet Brim: With loop of thread on hook, begin on one side of bonnet where the chain st begins (fifth row of brim). Ch 6, make 1 sc in next loop, repeat this across to other side of bonnet cape. Make two rows of same sts. In last row, in each ch loop, make 1 sc, 1 hdc, 2 dcs, 1 hdc, 1 sc, repeating across. Secure end, cut thread, hide thread ends.

Note: Finished garments are lightly pressed. Trims on bonnet, sleeves and edgings are spray starched before ironing. Be careful not to scorch. Thread *ribbons* of soft colors in areas indicated for ribbon. On sleeves, bow is tied in center; dress waist is tied in back after back bodice is sewn with light stitches and four to five pearls sewn in to look like buttons. On bonnet at nape of neck with bow to face front, allow for tieing bow and streamers 8in (20cm) long. Allow streamers to hang in waist back too. Booties are tied with bows at front ankle.

BOOTIES FOR BABY: Since *Bye-Lo Baby* dolls have cloth curved feet/legs, fit as you crochet, (adding or subtracting stitches given). Crochet a chain the length of the foot, then sc on each side of the chain. Join each row, make six rows, decreasing at heel section of each row for fit.

Row 7: Chain mesh sts begin, *ch 6, skip 1 st and sc in following st. Repeat around, join, ch 2.

Rows 8, 9, 10: Repeat Row 7 for a total of four rows.

Row 11: Make 2 hdc in each ch loop around, join.

Row 12: **Ribbon Row:** Ch 3, skip 1 st, dc in next st, ch 1, skip 1 st and dc in next st*, repeat around ankle, join.

Row 13: Make 1 hdc in each st around, join.

Row 14: Ch 2, make 1 hdc in each st around, join.

Rows 15, 16: *Ch 6, skip 1 st, sc in next st*, repeat around, join.

Trim for Top of Bootie: In each chain loop, make 1 sc, 1 hdc, 2 dc, 1 hdc and 1 sc. Complete around with this shell stitch, join and tie off end. Hide thread inside sts. Run ribbon through openings in bootie, tie bows in front. Make small bows, 1/2in (1.3cm) loops each side, with 1½in (4cm) tied ends. Dress yor doll. (Remember to iron and spray starch edges.)

Baby diaper is folded flannel to fit, pinned each side. Slip pattern is given, make of lightweight white material.

Slip for Crocheted Dress for 12in (30cm) Doll Bye-Lo Baby

MATERIALS NEEDED:

White handkerchief material
1½yd (1.36m) 1/4in (.65cm) white satin ribbon
White number 30 crochet thread
Number 12 crochet needle
White sewing thread
Sharp cutting scissors

INSTRUCTIONS: On FOLD, cut each pattern piece given, one each.

a. Cut center back of slip to dot.

b. Sew satin ribbon on lines indicated at bottom of slip (two).

c. Sew shoulder seams, then make a machine-stitch 1/8in (.31cm) around neckline and armholes. Sew down back opening too. Sew side seams, and make a machine-stitch on slip bottom, same as neckline and armholes. This will be a staystitch for crochet needlework.

d. *Crocheted Edges:* Crochet a buttonhole stitch by making 2 scs in each st around armholes, neckline and back, and slip bottom. Then make four rows of shell trim at slip bottom as follows: Ch 2, make two rows of hdc in each st around. Join. Ch 6, skip 1 st, sc in next st*. Repeat around, join. (Make four rows.) In last row of chain loops, make *1 sc, 1 hdc, 2 dc, 1 hdc and 1 sc*. Repeat for each row, join. When finished, cut thread, hide ends in sts. □

A Coat for a Dolls' House Man

by **Jane Thompson**

A few years ago a handsome gentleman 7in (18cm) tall came to live in my dolls' house. He had a splendid handlebar moustache and was marked "448 - 8/0" on the back of his bisque shoulders, but I almost turned him away because his coat was in tatters. He certainly could not join the fashionable ladies at dinner in such a state of dishevelment!

His striped gray trousers, white linen shirt front and black bow tie looked elegant with his high black molded-bisque boots, but his coat was beyond repair. Fortunately, the remnants of his original black felt coat proved to be sufficient to make a

pattern for an accurate replacement, and I was able to restore him to respectability. The ladies were delighted!

To make the coat as shown in the illustration, cut the pattern pieces from black felt and assemble as follows:

1. On the wrong side, stitch shoulder seams, top seam of sleeves to armholes, underarm seams and side seams.
2. Turn sleeves right side out.
3. Sew buttons or beads in place on outside of left front.
4. Put coat on doll and glue collar to coat along edge of neck.
5. Glue to tack edge of left front over edge of right front. □

Illustration 1. 7in (18cm) bisque-head doll house man with molded moustache. Marked: "448 - 8/0".

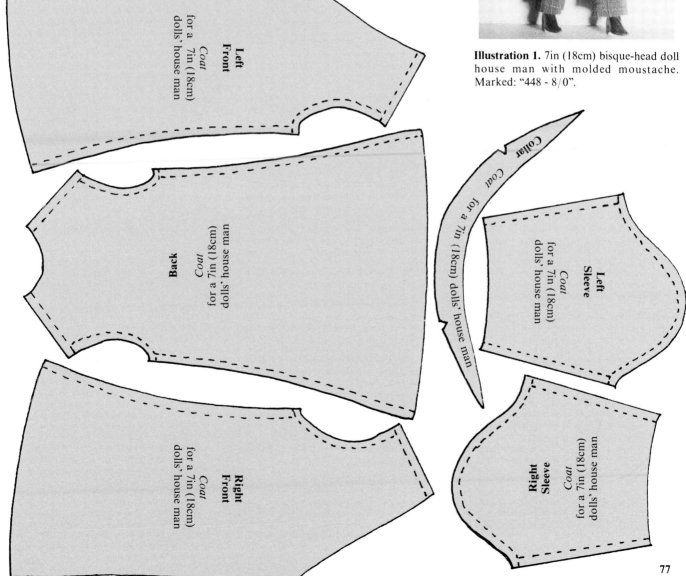

Pattern Drafting for Antique Doll Clothing for dolls under 8in (20cm)

by **Dorothy Noell De Campus [Kern]**

Most doll collections of any collectors who aspire to have a well-rounded assortment will have at least one or more dolls which fall under 8in (20cm) in size. Very likely the doll will be sans its original outfit, and supplying an authentic well-fitting replacement can sometimes frustrate even veteran doll dressers. The difficulty lies in the dolls' very smallness. Pattern drafting must be exact and precise, allowing just enough for ease, and no more. Dolls so tiny are easily overwhelmed by too much bulk.

First of all, before we consider the actual drafting of the patterns, a very brief discussion of the proper fabrics and trimmings would be in place. As a basic rule of thumb, use only the finest fabrics possible, keeping the scale of the pattern and weave especially in mind. Laces should be as delicate and narrow as you can obtain. You will find that the narrow 1/4in (.65cm) Val laces will shrink considerably in width and overall scale of pattern if you soak the lace in very hot water for a few minutes, squeeze nearly dry with a terry cloth towel, and then iron carefully. Tiny flat-back beads work well for buttons, as do the tiniest pearl buttons. Braids and ribbons should be thin and fine, so as not to appear too stiff, and the narrower the better. Pure silk 1/8in (.31cm) baby ribbon is wonderful for these little dolls; it drapes very gracefully and is quite easy to manipulate.

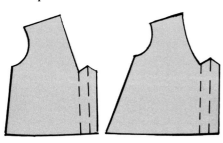

Illustration 1.

Paper toweling works very well for use in making the patterns. Tissue paper shreds and is not durable, while the paper towels are strong, can easily be drawn upon with a ball-point pen, have limited qualities of drapability and are fairly easy to manipulate.

Before starting the measurement taking, study the *proportions* of your doll. Most dolls which are under 8in (20cm) in size are the all-bisque type. These dolls generally have rather short thick necks, large abdomens and thick thighs. You may find it necessary to alter, for instance, the traditional cut of a sailor blouse, and have to widen it considerably at the waist to account for the oversized abdomen. (See **Illustration 1.**) If you make knickers, as an example, for a sailor boy, you might have to make slight gathers at the knees and waist, rather than the tailored straight leg style, because of those thick thighs and large abdomen! Also on many styles of boys' blouses, not just the sailor style, you will find it impossible to make a pullover style because the head is just too big in circumference for it to pass over, or the arms may not be able to be manipulated enough to accommodate this style. An opening down the front will be necessary.

When taking measurements for dolls this tiny, it is necessary to be very accurate! This just cannot be over stressed. Find a tape measure no more than 1/4in (.65cm) in width. (Mine is from West Germany.) Note the dolls' measurements on a piece of paper to which you can refer as you draw and cut; fit on the doll, and then re-draw and re-cut until the pattern fits.

The following is a good scale when allowing extra for ease:
Around neck: 1/8in (.31cm) to 1/4in (.65cm) extra.
Around armhole: 1/2in (1.3cm) extra.
Around waist: 1/4in (.65cm) extra.

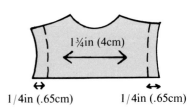

Illustration 2.

Around knee: 1/4in (.65cm) extra.
Around elbow: 1/4in (.65cm) extra.
Around hips: 1/4in (.65cm) extra.
From waist to knees for boy's knickers: approximately 1/2in (1.3cm) extra.
Shoulder to shoulder: 1/4in (.65cm) extra.
Shoulder to wrist: 1/4in (.65cm) to 1/2in (1.3cm) extra.

These are extra amounts to allow above and beyond the actual measurements and style of the costume, when drafting the pattern. For instance, if you are making a simple cotton dress hanging from a yoke for a girl doll, and the width from shoulder to shoulder is 1½in (4cm), add 1/2in (1.3cm) for

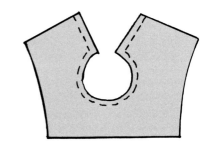

Illustration 3.

seam allowances (1/4in [.65cm] is taken at each armhole seam), and then 1/4in (.65cm) more for ease of movement. (See **Illustration 2.**) If you are making a sailor blouse for either a boy or girl doll, and you want it slightly gathered on a drawstring about the waist, and the doll's waist is 5in (13cm), allow 7in (18cm) for around the waist, add 1/4in

(.65cm) each side seam, and then allow about 1/2in (1.3cm) more; you can always take in too much fullness, but cannot create extra! Waistbands on knickers and skirts should allow 1/4in (.65cm) extra for ease, beyond the "lap" allowance.

When you draft the neck size, especially on something as close-fitting as a yoke or bodice with a "jewel" neckline, it should be *exactly* the circumference of the neck, plus *only* 1/8in (.31cm) to 1/4in (.65cm) more, for ease. Next add for shoulder seams, the turn under finish for the front or back closure and the lap for the closure. Then add a 1/4in (.65cm) seam allowance all around the neck edge, for when you bind the edge and turn the bias facing strip; or you can use the method of cutting two yokes or bodices, sewing together the neck and closure edges (see **Illustration 3**) and then inverting. This is my favorite method, as it gives a clean-cut neat-fitting neckline.

If you make wrist or elbow cuffs or bands, remember they must be big enough to pass over the hand circumference which is usually a fraction larger than the wrist. Knee bands should be drafted with the calf in mind, not the knee!

It is best to draft a pattern to the exact measurements of the doll, then add hems, seam allowances (1/4in [.65cm] seams are very good for sewing and can be trimmed narrower after stitching, if necessary), extra for laps at closures and allowance for ease. Viewed this way, drafting a pattern is actually a rather scientific procedure; if you know the correct cut of the garment, and follow these rules, you cannot go wrong!

Be careful about how much extra you allow for gathering a dress skirt into a bodice or yoke, knickers into a waistband, sleeves into armholes and cuffs and so on. Too much is far worse than too little, on a small doll! A costume slightly on the snug side is at least trim looking; a too full skirt, over full sleeves or knickers, can destroy hours of effort to produce a pleasing costume. The weight and sheerness of the fabric greatly influence how much extra to allow; it is a matter of personal judgment. There can be no hard and fast rule. As always, if in doubt, add a little extra; you can take in extra bulk, if there is any.

One last hint: the simpler the style, the better. If you want detail, for instance, in a girl's dress, then execute fine embroidery, minute pin tucks and be sure any gathering or pleating you do is fine and perfect, rather than ruffles, too much lace and detail in the cut of the style. You will also find it necessary to sew many seams by hand. Leave the straight seams only for the machine! Cut your patterns out in fine cotton first, sew together with large stitches, adjust for a perfect fit and then take apart for your final pattern pieces.

Sailor styles have been mentioned quite often here because they so admirably suit these tiny dolls. Not only were they one of the most popular styles when the dolls were made, but they offer enough variety of detail and style to allow the doll modiste to be creative, yet when well made, the garments never overwhelm the doll. Also, sailor hats are very easy to make, and perched at a jaunty angle, can add just the right note of piquancy! When making underclothing, keep them simple and close-fitting so that when taking your measurements over it for the costume itself, you will have added very little extra bulk.

The ultimate test in making well-fitting and attractive clothing for these charming "miniature" dolls is in having the patience to attend to nitty-gritty details. If you make up your mind to do this, you cannot help but create charming costumes. □

DOLL DRESSING:
COSTUMING AIDS:

The Fashionable Bride, 1330 to 1930
  by Brenda Paske
Beautiful Brides, 1892 to 1908
  by Lyn Alexander & Janice Miller
A Fashionable Wardrobe, 1836 to 1853
  by Brenda Paske
Costume Guide for 1837 Day Dress
  by Kathleen Songal
Fancy Needlework, 1900 to 1930
  by Lyn Alexander
For New Arrivals From Storktown
  by Lyn Alexander
On Dressing the Schoenhut Doll
  by Ruth H. Zimmerman
Miniature Sewing Techniques
  by Lauren Welker

The Fashionable Bride, 1330 to 1930

by **Brenda Paske**

Illustration 1. From a miniature, circa 1340. Pink silk dress lined with yellow; sleeves have short hanging tippets and the neckline is heavily embroidered; silvery-blue underdress with long tightly-buttoned sleeves. Clothing at this time was extremely tight-fitting. A dress might be made from 12 or 14 shaped pieces. The overdress is long and trails on the floor, but there is no train as such. The crown was simply another item of jewelry at this time and did not necessarily designate royal rank.

Illustration 2. From a miniature, circa 1470. The dress is of rich red and gold brocade in a "pomegranate" pattern, trimmed and lined with brown fur. The dress has a very long round train, striped "fill-in" at the neck and a wide blue belt buckled in the back; deep blue underdress, probably with very short sleeves; red and gold hennin with trailing veil. The veil is a fashionable accessory, *not* a bridal veil.

Illustration 3. From a German painting, 1525. Red velvet dress trimmed with bands of gold brocade. The skirt is cartridge pleated, a very popular treatment in Germany during this period. The sleeves are slashes, another popular form of decoration; very sheer gathered partlet with embroidered collar. Enormous and heavy gold chains were a favorite item of jewelry, although to the modern eye they are quite clumsy.

A wedding was always a perfect occasion for a fine new dress, and if the bride was wealthy the dress was of the latest fashion and as elaborate as possible.

Until 1600 red was a popular color for young brides; obviously it had different connotations than those it has today! Thereafter white was the color of choice, although it did not become the only proper bridal color until the 19th century.

Brides often wore their hair loose until the start of the 17th century. Again, this rule was not absolute. For instance the bride in **Illustration 2** is wearing a tall hennin and not showing so much as a single hair. In fact, there were few conventions in wedding attire until the 19th century.

Gloves were worn or carried from the start of the 18th century, but this was more because they were a part of formal dress than a special wedding accessory. From 1820 on the veil became a traditional part of bridal attire where it endures until this day. The bouquet was carried only after 1880. Before then a tiny handkerchief or Bible was carried in the hand. □

Illustration 5. Dutch, circa 1640. Two-piece "jacket" dress of white brocade with a pink, green and gold floral design; black lace scarf in hair, pale pink and aqua feathers. This was a great age for lace and the bride wears a matching set of cuffs, collar and neckerchief. A pearl choker and matching earrings were favorite items of jewelry.

Illustration 4. From a French engraving, circa 1600. Queen's farthingale gown trimmed with braid and embroidery. The bodice is a replica of the masculine doublet. The skirt has the typical ruffle to soften the hard line at the top of the farthingale. Flaps hang from the shoulder wings. Some form of oversleeve was common at this time and several different pairs might be made to match one dress. There is a moderate ruff supported by a wire framework — almost a piece of jewelry. The rest of the jewelry is really quite unostentatious compared to the usual parure of tiara, collar, bracelets, brooches and belt.

Illustration 6. French, circa 1696. Heavy brocade gown with mantle. The front of the bodice is plastered with large jeweled brooches, a pair of which also loop up the overskirt. There are ruffled lace sleeves and the wide neck of the dress is adorned with a matching flat lace collar.

Illustration 7. French, circa 1740. Silver and white brocade dress laced across the front (the neckerchief conceals most of the lacing). The sleeves have deep pleated cuffs. It is probably a sacque dress, with a loose flowing back. The gathered chemise sleeves have double lace ruffles and show beneath the sleeves of the dress.

Illustration 8. Existing gown, circa 1775, in an English museum but believed to be French. Shown with a hair style from an engraving of a French Bride. The dress is trimmed with self-puffings, and tassels, a favorite treatment of the period. It is a formal pannier style, wide from side to side and narrow from front to back.

Illustration 9. Fashion plate, circa 1820. Empire high-waisted dress trimmed with puffings and satin roses. The trims are three-dimensional, a characteristic of formal dresses at this time. Long elbow-length gloves are worn. This is the first appearance of the bridal veil.

Illustration 10. Fashion plate, circa 1832. Very wide sleeves with lace ruffle at the shoulder; large white roses finish the sleeves; ruched trim decorates the neck, wrists, sides of the head and the overskirt. The underskirt is trimmed with tiers of lace, probably one in the front where it shows! There is a lace frill around the topknot.

Illustration 11. Fashion plate, 1848. Low necked dress with long tight sleeves; lace cape, lace ruffles on skirt, and wide satin bows. At this time skirts were supported by a multitude of stiffened and starched petticoats.

Illustration 12. Godey's fashion plate, 1865. Widest possible crinoline dress trimmed with heavy cord, satin folds and chenille ball fringe. A modest neckline in wedding dress becomes common from this period on, low necks are reserved for evening dress. The skirt is supported by a cage crinoline.

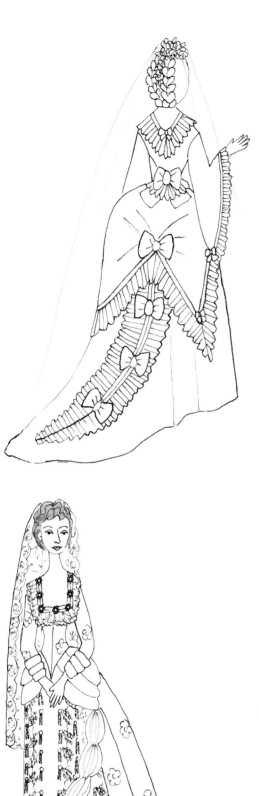

Illustration 13. *Englishwomen's Domestic Magazine*, 1869. A relatively restrained bustle dress with large satin bows and pleated frills; "pannier" overskirt, high neck and wide sleeves.

Illustration 15. Fashion plate, 1885. Bustle dress of white satin with ruffled lace petticoat. The bodice is long and the bustle projects abruptly, in complete contrast to the bustle dresses of the late 1860s and early 1870s.

Illustration 14. Existing dress, circa 1882. Rich brocade patterned with gold flowers; plain satin panniers and cuffs; veil and flounce of Brussels lace; beaded petticoat trimmed with puffs of net on one side only, net ruffle. Quite a magnificent dress.

Illustration 17. Fashion plate from the *Journal des Dames et des Modes*. 1913. Simple dress with long sleeves and concentrated decoration at the hem. Elaborately beaded and embroidered veil with large tassels. The only touches of color are the green leaves decorating the hem and the headdress.

Illustration 16. From a paper doll dated 1911. The wide ruffled sleeves, open-fronted overdress and pointed belt suggest that the model was created around 1905. A heavy lace applique trims the borders of the overdress, the underdress is tucked and long gloves complete the costume.

Illustration 18. Fashion plate, circa 1922. Wrapped dress closed with flowers on the left hip, fringed drapery and train. The underdress and veil are of the same lace.

Beautiful Brides, 1892 to 1908

by **Lyn Alexander & Janice Miller**

Illustration 1. Spring bridal gown, *Harper's Bazar*, 1894. *Reprinted courtesy of Harper's Bazaar.*

Editor's Note: The magazine *Harper's Bazaar* was spelled *Harper's Bazar* before 1929 and after 1929 it became *Harper's Bazaar*.

Wedding gowns of the years 1892 to 1908 ranged from expensive and elaborate to simple and economical, depending on the bride's situation. No longer were gowns quickly packed away after the ceremony, but were used for subsequent occasions by the ecomony-minded bride. The gown could be easily modified at the neck or sleeves for future functions.

The gown shown in **Illustration 1** was exquisite in its simplicity, made of milk white satin with the sole trimming of silk muslin. The veil was of tulle, with a hemmed edge and secured with a spray of orange blossoms.

Daintiness and delicacy were the fashion guidelines for the era. Fabrics used depended on the bride's financial situation and included satin, moire, silk and crepe de chine. Sleeves, draped bodices and trim were made of soft fabrics such as chiffon, lace or silk muslin. For the bride with a strict budget, materials included muslin, swiss, linen, organdy, chevoit, madras and taffeta. These could be very suitably altered for other special occasions. It was important for the fabric to be durable to withstand many launderings.

The gown shown in **Illustration 2** was from *Harper's Bazar* of 1895, and featured a close-fitting waist and leg-of-mutton sleeves.

Many different types of lace were used during this period, in addition to the point lace closely associated with wedding gowns. The bride was encouraged to buy the best lace she could afford, as poor quality lace was never a bargain. Lace could be kept as a valued heirloom for future generations. It held up well over the years, while fine fabrics such as silk or satin could deteriorate with age.

The majority of wedding gowns in the years 1890 to 1899 were made with high necklines and long or elbow-length sleeves. Low necks and short sleeves were considered to be in poor taste in the United States during this time.

Fit was of great importance. The lines of the gown displayed the figure, with proper respect to modesty. Good fit and quality fabric were the mark of a successful gown.

The smartest gowns were those

Illustration 2. Bridal gown, *Harper's Bazar*, 1895. *Reprinted courtesy of Harper's Bazaar.*

Illustration 3. Bridal array, *Ladies' Home Journal*, 1900. *Reprinted courtesy of Ladies' Home Journal.*

made with simplicity. Princess style gowns were popular at this time, with the front of the gown softened by draped folds of material or lace. Another stylish gown included a waist and skirt accented at the waistline with a crushed belt.

Skirts could be slightly draped on each hip, with the material caught up on the left and held there by a garland of orange blossoms. Revealed underneath would be an underskirt of plain satin or lace. Skirts were between nine and eleven yards wide, gored to fit the figure.

Sleeves were of great fullness during the mid 1890s. They were of leg-of-mutton shape, or made with a balloon puff above the elbow.

Illustration 3 shows an organdy gown that could be made by the home seamstress. The skirt was made full with applied trim and the bodice was bloused. In **Illustration 4**, a white liberty satin gown is shown. It featured embroidery of orange blossoms in white with faint touches of pale green. A lace yoke complemented the elegant design.

Trains were an important feature on the gowns of this era. A gown in the late 1800s might have included a train

Illustration 5. Bride's gown for early summer, *Harper's Bazar*, 1901. *Reprinted courtesy of Harper's Bazaar.*

that was several feet in length, while just a few years later, in 1905, 18in (46cm) was the proper length for a train, according to *Ladies' Home Journal*. Just three years later, in 1908, *Harper's Bazar* noted the correct length for a train was 48in (122cm) to 54in (137cm).

Illustration 4. White liberty satin gown, *Harper's Bazar*, 1901. *Reprinted courtesy of Harper's Bazaar.*

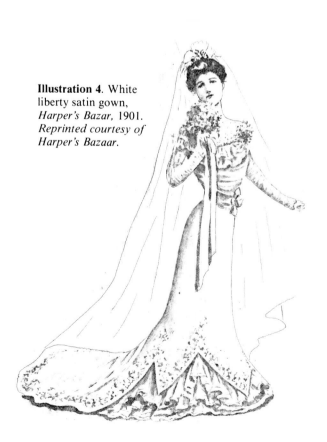

Illustration 6. Bridal gown of white taffeta, *Harper's Bazar*, 1901. *Reprinted courtesy of Harper's Bazaar.*

A tulle veil was considered the most becoming item that a bride wore on her special day. It enhanced the bride's mistique, and was removed immediately following the ceremony. The correct length of a tulle veil was to the edge of the gown in the back and 8in (20cm) to 10in (25cm) below the waist in front, according to *Ladies' Home Journal* in 1903.

Lace veils were also seen; however, special care had to be taken to arrange the hair high on the head. The weight

Illustration 7. Elegant bridal gown, *Harper's Bazar,* 1905. *Reprinted courtesy of Harper's Bazaar.*

of the lace veil had a tendency to flatten the hair unbecomingly.

Shown in **Illustration 5** is a gown with the front of mousseline caught with rows of orange blossoms. Over this fell the gown of white liberty silk. The yoke was made of a delicate white lace.

Illustration 6 shows a bridal gown that could be made of white taffeta or liberty satin with a bolero and a band of lace, combined with a bodice of tucked chiffon.

In 1905, it was becoming more and more fashionable for a bride to be married without gloves, although the taste of the individual was considered. When gloves were worn, those of white glacé kid or suede were to be chosen. It was important that the gloves not

Illustration 8. Simple bridal gown, *Harper's Bazar,* 1905. *Reprinted courtesy of Harper's Bazaar.*

interfere with the overall look of the garment.

An elegant bridal gown is featured in **Illustration 7**. It was developed in soft white satin with a semi-transparent yoke of all-over point de Venise lace. The skirt was trimmed with a deep edging of matching lace.

Illustration 8 shows a simple, yet elegant gown that could be made of various soft fabrics such as chiffon cloth, silk muslin, organdy or batiste; and trimmed with ruffles of lace.

For sleeves of the fashionably short elbow-length, long gloves with 12 or 16 buttons were worn. For gowns with long sleeves, the two button glove was considered proper.

White slippers were worn with white wedding gowns, along with open-work white silk or lisle stockings. White kid slippers were considered permissible by *Harper's Bazar* in 1903, but they were not as smart as those in which the shoe fabric matched the gown.

Harper's Bazar commented that a fad in 1901 was to place a small arrangement of orange blossoms, similar to a rosette, on the slipper. Again, this was left to the individual preference of the bride.

The bridal gown shown in **Illustration 9** was made of duchesse satin

Illustration 9. Bridal gown of duchesse satin, *Harper's Bazar,* 1905. *Reprinted courtesy of Harper's Bazaar.*

accompanied by entre-deux. The dress was decorated with ornaments of Cluny lace and a flounce of point lace.

A bridal coiffure from 1892 is shown in **Illustration 10**. The veil was made of a fine net, and arranged around a tiara of orange blossoms.

The bridal gowns of 1892 to 1908 reflected the traditions of the late Victorian period. They were often elegant and elaborate, and of exquisite design. □

Illustration 10. Bridal coiffure, *Harper's Bazar,* 1892. *Reprinted courtesy of Harper's Bazaar.*

A Fashionable Wardrobe, 1836 to 1853

by **Brenda Paske**

1   2   3a   4   5

This was a very pretty, but restrained and modest period. Hair clung limply to the head in loops or ringlets, sleeves were long and tight and bodices were padded at the chest, giving a pouter pigeon look. Skirts drooped, not yet supported by the cage crinoline. Instead a dozen or so petticoats did the job. Shoulders slumped, no doubt from the strain of bearing all that weight!

Colors were suitably quiet, although sometimes the combinations were not. The color of a dress, its bonnet and mantle need not have any relationship whatsoever!

As a general rule caps were worn with day dress, bonnets outdoors and headdress with ball dress. There are however a few examples of magnificent evening bonnets.

High necks were always worn with day costume and low with evening. Sleeves were not so consistent, and there were short sleeved day dresses and long sleeved evening dresses. Waists were round or pointed, the round waists usually found on day dresses and the pointed on evening gowns.

And, of course, no real lady was to be seen without gloves! □

DAY DRESSES

Illustration 1. Blue and white striped floral silk afternoon dress, trimmed with satin bows and a wide front panel of heavy lace; matching bonnet with lace veil, blue and white tilting sunshade, short blue gloves and painted velvet purse.

Illustration 2. Winter costume of plum-colored velvet, trimmed with matching satin panels, fringe, braid and tassels; "coal-scuttle" bonnet and simple drawstring purse.

Illustration 3a. Indoor dress of brown and yellow silk with deep lace collar; sleeve ruchings of brown taffeta, matching brown taffeta apron — purely decorative of course; early type of cap edged with lace and tied with a yellow ribbon.

Illustration 3b. Matching plaid silk pelerine for outdoor wear. Many skirts had matching pelerines, and separate evening and day bodices to further extend the wardrobe.

Illustration 4. Cross-over dress of plain lilac silk; bishop sleeves date the dress to 1836 to 1837; common type of squared-off morning cap thoroughly trimmed with lace, ruching and ribbons.

Illustration 5. Morning dress of white muslin; underdress trimmed with white embroidery; overdress trimmed with broad bands of pink and yellow embroidered roses with green foliage; late style of lace cap trimmed with pink ribbons, pink ribbon belt; lace edged handkerchief.

Illustration 6. Spring dress of printed muslin with short ruffled sleeves; dotted swiss pelerine trimmed with yellow ribbons; silk shawl with orange and yellow flowers, long yellow silk fringe; plain wide brimmed sun hat.

Illustration 7. Autumn dress of deep red wool trimmed with black velvet scallops; black velvet bonnet with red roses and ostrich feather; red silk fringed parasol; knotted purse.

8   9   10   11

12

13

EVENING DRESSES

Illustration 8. White silk dress with lace overskirt and deep blue velvet bodice; trimmings of ostrich feathers, blue roses and blue velvet ribbons; evening bonnet of white silk with corded edge; medium length gloves with ruched trim.

Illustration 9. Yellow silk dress with lace trimmed draperies, decorated with bunches of crimson and violet flowers, matching bouquet.

Illustration 10. Pink silk dinner dress with unusually long sleeves; deep bertha and overskirt of black lace, rows of pink tulle ruching and pink satin bows; short black mitts and pink ostrich feather in hair.

Illustration 11. Simple white embroidered muslin dress with the popular three flounces; medium length white silk mitts, lace edged handkerchief and diamond slide on black velvet neckband.

Illustration 12. Pale green silk dress with six small flounces (note that the flounces do not extend all the way to the waist); lace trimming on bodice, sleeves and flounces; lace shawl.

Illustration 13. Rich brown silk brocade with gold flowers; long gold shawl with deep fringe; turban type headdress; parure of inlay work; typical large fan with deep gold scroll borders.

14 15 16 17 18

19 21 20 22 23 24 25

SPECIAL DRESSES

Illustration 14. Blue wool riding dress with very long train to totally conceal the legs.

Illustration 15. Mourning dress trimmed with braid; plais collar and cuffs; drawn bonnet.

Illustration 16. Wedding gown cut on day dress pattern but with evening trims; lappets instead of veil.

Illustration 17. Court dress; white satin with triple lace flounces; gold embroidered velvet train of any rich color.

Illustration 18. Simplest style of winter dress in turquoise velvet with deep fur border; fur set of muff, pelerine and cuffs.

OUTER WEAR

Illustration 19. Visite of lace with silk ribbons.

Illustration 20. Gold silk jacket trimmed with ruching, bows and black lace.

Illustration 21. Green silk coat trimmed with darker green velvet.

Illustration 22. Pelerine of dark blue velvet embroidered with red roses.

Illustration 23. Opera mantel of black velvet trimmed with gold quilted satin, braid and tassels.

Illustration 24. Pelisse of cream wool trimmed with crimson velvet and braid.

Illustration 25. Green wool mantle trimmed with braid and lace.

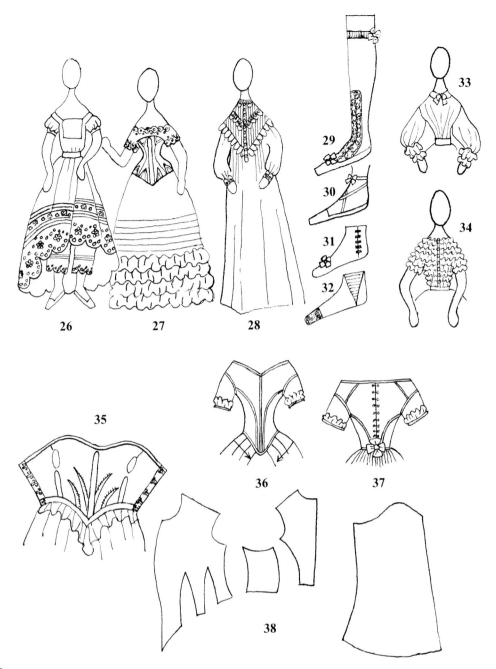

UNDERWEAR

Illustration 26. Chemise with falling front flap to conceal the corset; straight legged drawers trimmed with lace and ruching; matching decorative petticoat (several plain ones would be worn under it).

Illustration 27. Fancy embroidered chemise; white satin corset, heavily boned; horsehair petticoat further stiffened with wadding and cording.

Illustration 28. Nightgown.

Illustration 29. Stockings were generally plain, in white or black; evening stockings might have a band of white embroidery and openwork; elastic garter with rosette; flat slipper trimmed with a bow.

Illustration 30. Another flat ballet-type slipper, tied around the ankle.

Illustration 31. Satin boot with rosette.

Illustration 32. Utilitarian elastic side boot with black toe.

Illustration 33. Plain gathered blouse with wide sleeves.

Illustration 34. Ruched blouse with short sleeves.

Illustration 35. Interior, showing interlining, whipped-over darts bones at sides and center front. Note waistband and turned over top edge of skirt. Hooks and eyes were the most common fastening.

Illustration 36. Front, showing piping on every seam and skirt pleats facing front. The quality of workmanship was very high, although the sewing machine was not yet in general use. Note the very long, curved bust darts.

Illustration 37. Back, showing lacing holes. Note curved back seams and set back shoulder seam. Dresses often had a little rosette at the waist in back.

Illustration 38. Typical bodice pattern shapes. The sleeve is the bell shape of **Illustrations 5 and 7.**

Costume Guide for 1837 Day Dress

by **Kathleen Songal**

INTRODUCTION

The following guide was written to help the doll costume maker design historically accurate 1837 costume styles. The numerous illustrations were deemed essential in order to achieve two goals. First, it was necessary to offer a large variety of costume illustrations to increase the scope of the designer's creativity. All too often, costume books illustrate only one or two dress examples for any given year, limiting the designer's chances of creating an interesting and varied wardrobe. Next, it was considered important to have drawings augment the text; especially, where descriptive terms such as large, tight, long, were open to subjective interpretation. This guide, for one year at least, then, attempts to offer Miss Doll's dressmaker the opportunity to create for the first time a truly haute couture 1837 wardrobe.

Finally a few words regarding the costume terms and their definitions used in this guide. Wherever possible, articles of clothing have been called by the names popularly used in 1837. Do keep in mind that these names were often quite distinct to that particular year. Indeed, the fichu of 1837 was quite a different garment from the fichu of 1860. Bearing these thoughts in mind, the guide will help you acquire a new costume language unique to its day.

I. BODICES

In 1837, most bodices for daytime wear were cut tight fitted with a dropped shoulder effect. Most were cut from the same fabric as the skirt. The seams and darts were usually boned and the bodices lined with a sturdy fabric. Most seams including the armseyes were piped. When the bodices opened and fastened down the front, they were called *pelisse-robes*; when they opened and fastened down the center back, they were called *robes*.

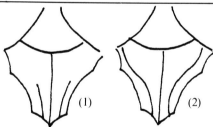

Illustration 2. *Marie Stuart bodices* had waistlines in front that dipped (below the normal waistline) into U shapes. They were cut either (1) with darts or (2) in the stomacher style.

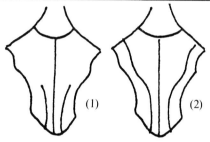

Illustration 3. *Pointed bodices* for daytime wear in 1837, had natural waistlines that dipped just ever so slightly into a point in center front. They were cut either (1) with darts or (2) in the stomacher style.

Illustration 4. *Drawn bodices* were arranged in small tucks or pleats to achieve a smocked effect. The smocking was drawn either in horizontal or vertical rows and was made with either a round waistline or a Marie Stuart waistline.

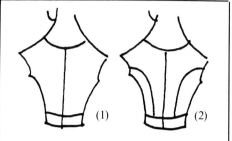

Illustration 5. *Back bodices* were usually cut tight fitted with natural round waistlines. They were cut either (1) *plain* or (2) *lozenge style.*

Illustration 6. Waistlines were often covered with belts of rich fabric called *ceintures*. They could be (1) *buckled* or (2) *plain.*

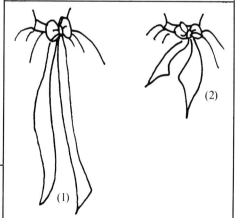

Illustration 7. At other times, *ceintures* could be tied in bows and hang in lappets either (1) *long* or (2) *short.*

II. NECKLINES

Necklines for daytime wear in 1837 took on a variety of shapes and heights.

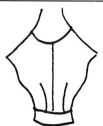

Illustration 1. *Round bodices* had darts, two or more, in the front and were cut with natural round waistlines sewn to wide waistbands.

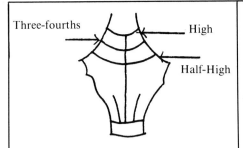

Illustration 8. The amount of neck and shoulder exposed named the *height of the corsage.*

III. BODICE COVERINGS

The real variation in bodice design lay in the decorative collars, pelerines, fichus, drapery and V-shaped trims that covered the bodices. Although these applied decorations varied greatly from one dress to another, one general theme remained constant; that is, most decorations were at first wide at the shoulders then descended to a point at the bosom or waistline creating a V-shaped design.

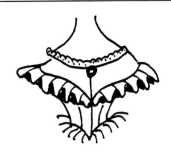

Illustration 15. *Fichu* was another name for pelerine. There was the *heart-shaped fichu.*

Illustration 9. Other necklines had specific names. *Corsage a la Paysanne* was cut high in the back and low on the bosom.

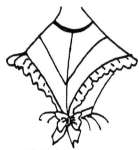

Illustration 12. *Pelerines* were very popular. They were worn over the basic bodice and could be V-shaped in the front and squared or V-shaped in the back. Usually they were made of the same fabric as the bodice. The edges of pelerines were trimmed in a variety of ways, including *self-fabric ruffles.*

Illustration 16. The popular *shawl fichu* was often edged with fringe.

Illustration 10. *Corsage a la Couer* was cut heart shaped in the front and three-fourths high in the back.

Illustration 13. Sometimes the edges of *pelerines* were trimmed with *coques,* strips of fabric or ribbon folded over in loops.

Illustration 17. The *Fichu en Bretelles* was also known as the *Pelerine a la Paysanne.*

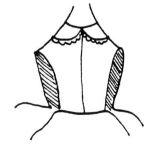

Illustration 11. Sometimes *chemisettes* (also called *tuckers*) were worn under the main bodice to achieve a higher neckline. Tuckers were usually made out of white muslin, with or without collars. They were not sewn together at the sides, but rather, the backs were tied to the fronts at the waistline using drawstrings.

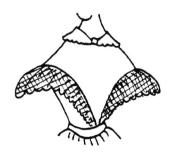

Illustration 14. *Pelerines* were also sometimes edged in *ruffled* lace.

Illustration 18. *Drapery* also played an important feature on 1837 bodices. Usually drapery was made of the same fabric as the bodice. There was *criss-cross drapery.*

Illustration 19. There was *heart-shaped drapery* also called *fan-shaped drapery.*

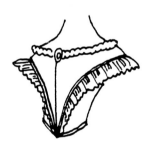

Illustration 20. Some *V-shaped trims* were applied directly on the bodice, such as, *boullions* and *ruffles.*

Illustration 21. At other times, *ruffles* and *piping* were employed to achieve this favorite of designs.

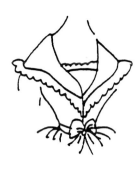

Illustration 22. *Collars* in 1837, were at times, quite large and *cape-like.*

Illustration 23. At other times, collars followed the contour of the neckline creating *lapel collars.*

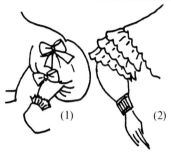

Illustration 24. Or *collars* could be of a *moderate size* as when finishing off the neckline of a chemisette.

IV. SLEEVES

Sleeves for day wear always covered the entire arm. Note that all sleeve styles could be finished at the wrist with just a cord of piping, a frill of lace, or a small white muslin cuff.

Illustration 25. After the demise of the popular exaggerated beret sleeves of the early 1830s, *coat sleeves* made close, and to the exact shape of the arm, were introduced. They were worn plain except for the occasional lace *en manchette,* (lace ruffle at the elbow).

Illustration 26. More commonly worn than coat sleeves were those sleeves deemed *demi-large.* Several different forms of demi-large sleeves were popular. One style, was basically the coat sleeve adorned above the elbow either with (1) *one large bouffant* or (2) *several ruffles.*

Illustration 27. Another *demi-large* sleeve style was the *Orleans.* It was worn perhaps more often than any other style. It consisted of a close fitted upper cap and a bishop sleeve that began just above the elbow terminating at the wrist.

Illustration 28. The upper cap of the *Orleans* sleeve was also sometimes decorated with *ruffles.*

V. SKIRTS

Most often skirts were cut with straight panels of material sewn together; then gauged with cartridge pleats to the bodice or waistband. Length just swept the floor. Skirts either opened in the front or back, depending on the bodice aperture. Plain skirts were always popular, but frequently they were decorated in the same trim that was used on the bodice.

Illustration 31. Skirts were also frequently decorated *en tablier;* they were usually one skirt trimmed to simulate two.

Illustration 29. *Pelisse-robes* had skirts that opened down the center front or left center front and were decorated along that opening.

VI. COLORS, FABRICS, PATTERNS FOR SUMMER

Colors for day wear in the summer months were usually light; such as white, yellow, pale blue, pink and apple green. Those fabrics that were figured or striped, for the most part, had white grounds with simple patterns of primary colors. Small and delicate patterns, both quadrilled and striped were often seen. Striped fabrics with scattered bouquets of flowers were also fashionable. Silk fabrics were often worn, as were muslins of india, jaconet and clear. Cashmeres of the half transparent kind were also found.

Illustration 30. At other times, the *lower third* of the skirt was trimmed; the decoration was never higher than the knee.

VII. COLORS, FABRICS, PATTERNS FOR WINTER

Colors for day wear in the winter months were generally drab; such as gray-blue; dark green, gray-green, brown, gray-violet and pea green. Fabrics that were figured or striped had, for the most part, brown grounds with green, blue or ponceau patterns. There were also some other fabrics that had rose, green or wood-colored grounds with black patterns. Stripes, both narrow and wide were popular. Small delicate patterns were the order of the day. Silk fabrics such as gros de Naples and pou de soi were often worn; as were woolen materials of cashmere, chaly and merino.

VIII. BONNETS

The lady of 1837 never ventured out of doors without a bonnet on her head. The *fashionable* lady had bonnets made to match all the day dresses she owned.

Winter bonnets were made out of velvet, satin and quilted silk. They were decorated with features, ribbons and velvet flowers in a myriad of styles.

Summer bonnets were made out of rice straw, silk and shirred muslin. They were also decorated with flowers, ribbons and laces in countless ways.

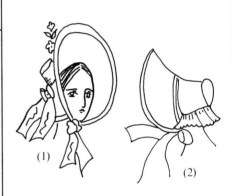

Illustration 32. The basic shape of the 1837 bonnet consisted of a high deep oval or round brim that descended to the chin. Ribbons usually tied under the chin and curtains generally covered the back of the neck. The *crown* could be made either (1) *high* or (2) *low.*

Illustration 33. Many bonnets came with *caps* inside the crowns.

IX. CAPS

Married women during the day in 1837, for the most part, covered their hair indoors with beautiful white caps. They were usually made out of tulle, muslin or lace; arranged in many novel and varied, pleated and shirred, arrangements. Often adorned with colored ribbons and flowers, they sometimes tied under the chin, other times not.

Illustration 37. However, the most popular side hair arrangement was *curls*.

Illustration 34. Note that the *cap* sat several inches away from the forehead, where it encircled the head from ear to ear.

Illustration 35. The back of the cap that covered the head was called the *caul*.

Illustration 36. Women usually parted their hair in the center front. The hair on the sides could then be arranged in a variety of ways; including (1) *braids* or (2) *bands* or (3) *loops*.

Illustration 38. The back hair was then generally fashioned into a *top knot*.

X. OUTDOOR MANTLES

Shawls, mantlettes, canizons and cloaks were all worn for outdoor wear in 1837.

Illustration 39. *Shawls* were a common accessory. In the mild summer months, they were made out of white china crepe embroidered in primary colors. Cashmeres, gauzes, embroidered muslins and laces were also popular. In colder weather, shawls were made out of dark-colored velvet or satin, lined and wadded for extra warmth.

Illustration 40. *Mantlettes* were worn when it was not yet cold enough for an all-emcompassing cloak. Note that in the front, mantlettes hung in lappets nearly as long as the bottom of the dress. In the back, they were squared or rounded at the hip line. In the winter, they were made of black velvet or black taffeta and trimmed with sable or black lace or swansdown. In the summer, mantlettes were made out of costly lace, gauze, muslin or silk trimmed with lace. Some were made of the same material as the dress; or of organdy lined with colored silk. However, the majority were made of black silk or black silk net.

Illustration 41. *Cloaks*, also known as *mantles*, were usually worn only in the coldest weather. Cashmeres, velvets and various kinds of rich silks and satins were all employed for mantles. Some were confined at the waist and made with sleeves.

Illustration 42. Other *cloaks* were loose at the waist and had no sleeves.

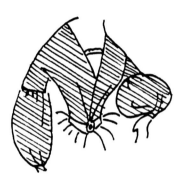

Illustration 43. *Canizons*, also known as *spencers*, were tight fitted jackets worn over the basic dress. They covered the bodice and were made with sleeves. They opened and fastened down the center front. Usually they were made of lace, transparent fabric or fabric contrasting with the basic dress.

XI. ACCESSORIES

Brooches were worn on many bodices at the center of the neckline. In lieu of brooches, *breast knots*, (ribbons tied in bows) ranked next in favor.

Short *gloves* were indispensable.

Boas, muffs, parasols, fans and handkerchiefs were all commonly carried as accessories.

Illustration 44. *Aprons* were worn over dresses for "home wear." They were made of silk or muslin and trimmed with lace and ribbons. They were made either (1) *with bibs* or (2) *without bibs*.

CONCLUSION

It is hoped that this guide will inspire you to design some original, but at the same time, authentic-looking 1837 day costumes. **Illustration 45** is an example of what you, too, might be able to accomplish using your sewing skills and this *1837 Costume Guide* as a compendium for inspiration.

Accompanying the following 1837 costume plates are the original costume descriptions written exactly as found in *The Ladies Pocket Magazine.* □

Illustration 45. 12in (30cm) cloth doll dressed in 1837 Paris Morning Dress. Both doll and costume designed and sewn by author.

Illustration 46.
The Ladies Pocket Magazine
                    August 1837
English   P. 67

LONDON PROMENADE DRESS
White cambric under dress; open pelisse of French gray gros de Naples. The corsage high and tight to the shape, is trimmed round the top with black lace disposed en cour. Tight sleeve, the upper part finished with three black lace flounces. The skirt is trimmed down the front on each side with black lace set on full, and a rouleau of black gros de Naples round the border. A black ceinture and bracelets complete the ornaments of the dress. Rice straw hat, a round and rather deep brim, the interior trimmed with blond lace, and black foliage; black aigrettes and white satin striped gauze ribbons ornament the crown.

Illustration 47.
The Ladies Pocket Magazine
December 1837
English
P. 240
LONDON PUBLIC
PROMENADE DRESS
Pelisse robe of gorge de pigeon satin; the skirt is finished down one side of the front with a full trimming of the same, and a butterfly knot of ribbon to correspond, placed near the bottom. The corsage, high and plain, is partially covered with a pelerine disposed in folds, and finished with full trimming and a breast knot of ribbon. Victoria sleeve, the bouffant at top surmounted by a trimming, and a knot of ribbon en suite. Ceinture arranged en papillon before and terminating in long floating ends. White cashmere shawl, with a richly embroidered border. Velvet bonnet of a bright red currant colour; the brim is close at the sides, but deep and standing out very much from the forehead; the interior is trimmed at the sides with very small white flowers; two superb follettes adorn the crown.

Illustration 48.
The Ladies Pocket Magazine
October 1837
English
P. 140
LONDON MORNING DRESS
Pelisse robe of French grey *gros De Naples*, a tight corsage partially high, and trimmed with a heart pelerine, bordered with black double-grounded lace. The sleeves tight at top and bottom, but very full in the center, with gauntlett cuffs, which are trimmed, as are also the tops of the sleeves, with black lace. The fronts and the round of the skirt are likewise edged with it. The headdress is a fichu of tulle, edged with the same, and disposed on the head in the cape style. The hind hair is gathered in a knot at the back of the head, under a bow of pink ribbon, from which floating ends descend; the border part of the fichu is ornamented in a light style with ends of ribbon, which terminate in brides tied under the chin.

Illustration 49.
The Ladies Pocket Magazine
September 1837
English
P. 103
WALKING DRESS
Pelisse of one of the new summer silks, a white ground striped with blue; it is fastened down the front by rosettes of blue ribbons, and the sides and border trimmed in the tunic style, with a double bias band of the same material. A tight high corsage, partially covered by a fichu a la paysanne. The sleeves made to fit the arm, are trimmed at the upper part with three flounces. Victoria bonnet of pink pou de Soie; the edge of the brim is finished by a tulle ruche, and the interior trimmed in the cap style, with blond lace. Pink ribbons, and a bouquet of roses, with their foliage, adorns the crown.

Fancy Needlework, 1900 to 1930

by **Lyn Alexander**

Filet lace in pointed design effectively trims this dainty frock of fine dotted Swiss. The dress fastens down the front with crochet buttons.

An adorable Dutch frock of sheer linen! — fine tucks and real Valenciennes lace form the yoke and the hand-embroidery is exquisite.

Drawings by Christine Challenger

Illustration 1. *Harper's Bazar*, 1916. Copyright ©1916, The Hearst Corporation. *Courtesy Harper's Bazaar.*

Needlework is a creative and satisfying art form that has been enjoyed for centuries. Though the basic stitches have existed since ancient times, they may be combined in innumerable ways, and worked in a myriad of threads, creating designs that are fashionable at various periods in history.

While doing research for my new book, *Toddlers' Togs 1910-1930,* I discovered a wealth of handwork information in the women's magazines of that time. Since nearly all of the clothes for women and children were decorated with embroidery, tatting, crochet, smocking, drawnwork, binding, piping or ruching, the instructions, patterns and designs were popular subject matter.

During this period between 1910 and 1930 the most delightful dolls were produced. *Kewpies,* googlies, pouties, character dolls, *Dolly Dingle* and the

Campbell Kids were a few that made their appearance. Rose O'Neill, Grace Drayton and Käthe Kruse were some of the artists that successfully captured elfin, impish, positively delightful expressions that captivated everyone. Most of the major doll companies produced realistically child-like dolls, or personable caricatures of toddlers and babies. Nearly all were dressed like contemporary children.

Fancy needlework used tastefully on doll clothes can turn an ordinary garment into one of exquisite beauty. Appropriate trim can date the clothes correctly and enhance their appearance of authenticity. The tasteful combination of garment design, thread and color brings enjoyment to everyone involved.

A few of the most basic forms of handwork that were extremely popular during the first quarter of the 20th century are embroidery, cross-stitch and hemstitch.

EMBROIDERY

RUNNING STITCH. Pass the needle back and forth through the fabric taking even stitches of desired length. This stitch is basic to both sewing and embroidery. To further enhance its decorative effect, the stitches may be threaded by passing a separate thread back and forth under the line of running stitches, but not through the fabric. Or the line may be whipped by passing a separate thread over and over the stitches. This thread may be the same as the running stitches, or contrasting.

BACK STITCH. Working from right to left, take a small stitch. Insert the needle at the beginning of this stitch and bring it out a stitch ahead. Pull the needle and thread through. The stitches on the wrong side will be twice as long as on the front. The stitches form a solid line on the front, and since they do not pull out easily, they can be used in sewing to make a strong seam. Back stitch may be threaded or whipped the same as the running stitch.

SEED STITCH. Make two small back stitches in the same place. They may be arranged at random, close together or spaced. They are often used in the center of embroidered flowers.

STRAIGHT STITCH (not illustrated). Make single stitches of any length in any direction. Variety may be achieved by using different colored threads. Worked close together they can be used as a border on hem, neckline or sleeves.

SATIN STITCH. Work straight

DESIGN IN CROSS-STITCH.

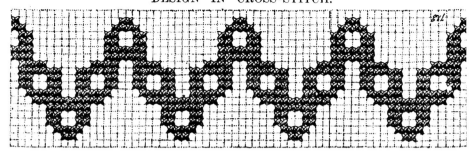

The chain design in cross-stitch is suitable for ends of towels, borders for tea-cloths, or skirts and aprons for children, and many other purposes.

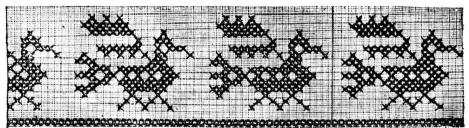

This very pretty border can be used for napkins, carving-cloths, or other table-linen. It is done in cross-stitch, with red embroidery-cotton.

Illustration 2. *Peterson's Magazine,* 1892.

stitches side by side close together so they cover the fabric. The area under the satin stitch may be padded with outline or back stitch. Satin stitch is often used for flowers and leaves.

KENSINGTON STITCH (not illustrated). Work satin stitches alternating long and short lengths. It is used for filling in designs, or for shading colors or values.

COUCHING (not illustrated). Lay a heavy thread, yarn or braid in a design on fabric. With a second thread, secure the first thread with short stitches passed over the top. Couching is used for edges, or for outlining designs.

FRENCH KNOT. Bring the needle out through the fabric, and wind thread around the point two or three times. Insert needle close to where it came out, pulling thread through the loops to form a knot. French knots may be used with embroidered designs, or scattered to decorate an area or a band.

BULLION STITCH (not illustrated). Similar to French knot except longer. Take a short stitch leaving the needle in the fabric. Wrap the thread around the needle five or six times. Pull the needle through. Bullion stitches may be used to form roses, daisies, stems or other designs. It is very pretty when used in the center of smocking.

SNAIL'S TRAIL (not illustrated).

Work from right to left taking short slanting stitches along a line, with the thread lying over then under the needle. Snail's trail is pretty as an outline stitch on collars, sleeves or hems.

OUTLINE STITCH is worked from left to right or away from the worker. Take short stitches with the thread always on the same side of the needle. The stitches will be longer on the right than the wrong side. As the name indicates, it is used for outlining. It is sometimes called stem stitch.

BLANKET STITCH. Work from left to right and take an upright stitch with needle pointed down and thread under the needle. A few of the many variations of this stitch are shown. It can be used instead of overcasting to finish the raw edges of heavy fabrics, as trimming for necklines, sleeves or hems and to outline applique designs. (See **Illustration 4.**)

EMBROIDERY BLANKET STITCH gives a hard even finish for scalloped edges. Mark the scallops by stamping or tracing and pad the design with chain or long and short stitch. Work the stitches very close together so they fill the space like satin stitch. Leave material beyond the edge of the scallop and trim it away when the embroidery is finished. Embroidery scallops were often used on lingerie and children's dresses, suits and underwear. Babies' white wool Barrow-coats were sometimes finished with scallops.

FEATHERSTITCH is a series of blanket stitches in varying numbers at varying angles to the center line. When the stitches are taken in a slanted direction toward the center a delicate vine-like effect is achieved.

A. Single featherstitch.

B. Double featherstitch. (May also be done with three stitches on each side.)

C. Coral stitch is done with the needle

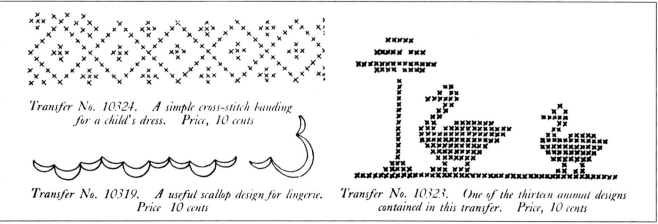

Transfer No. 10324. *A simple cross-stitch banding for a child's dress.* Price, 10 cents

Transfer No. 10319. *A useful scallop design for lingerie.* Price 10 cents

Transfer No. 10323. *One of the thirteen animal designs contained in this transfer.* Price, 10 cents

Illustration 3. *The Delineator,* 1911. Reprinted from *The Delineator* magazine by the permission of Butterick Co., Inc.

Illustration 4. Embroidery stitches.

Running Stitch

Back Stitch

Satin Stitch

Outline or
Stem Stitch

Chain Stitch

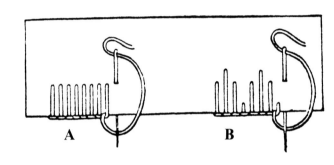

A, Blanket Stitch; B, C, D, E,
Decorative variations of the Blanket Stitch

Lazy Daisy Stitch

Fly Stitch

Seed Stitch

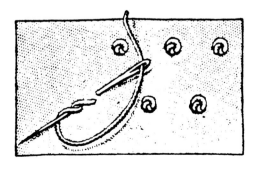

French Knots

106

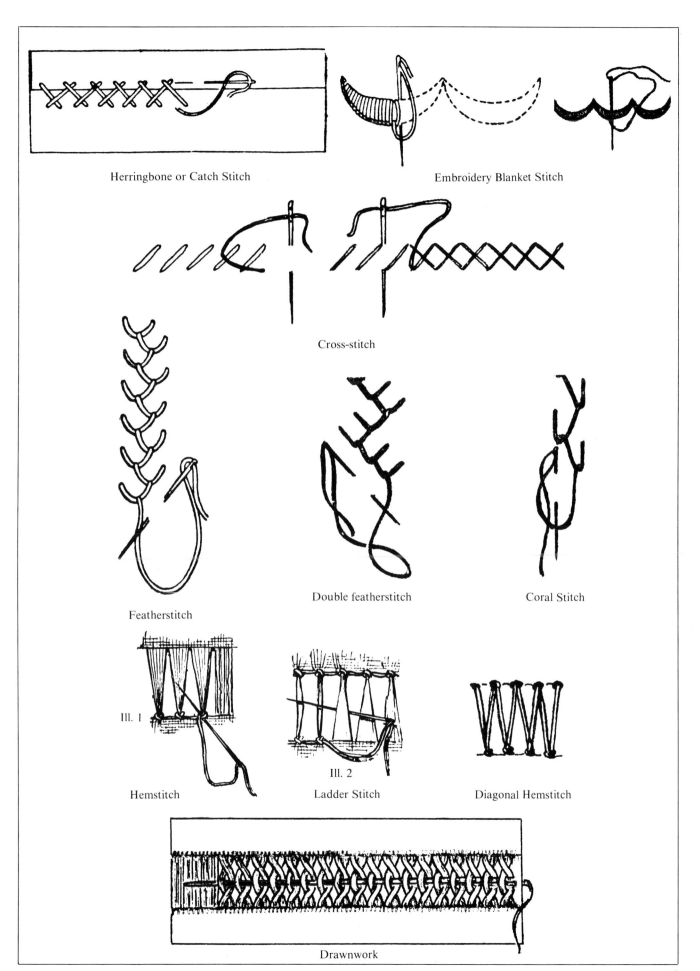

Herringbone or Catch Stitch

Embroidery Blanket Stitch

Cross-stitch

Featherstitch

Double featherstitch

Coral Stitch

Ill. 1

Hemstitch

Ill. 2

Ladder Stitch

Diagonal Hemstitch

Drawnwork

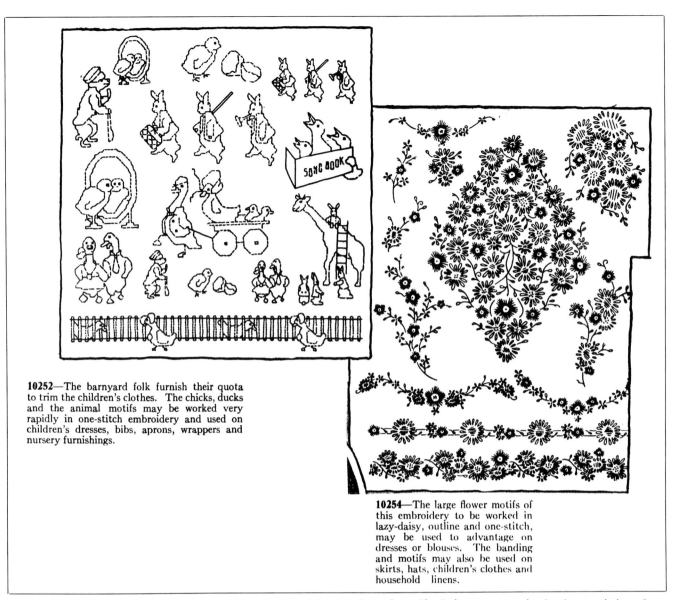

10252—The barnyard folk furnish their quota to trim the children's clothes. The chicks, ducks and the animal motifs may be worked very rapidly in one-stitch embroidery and used on children's dresses, bibs, aprons, wrappers and nursery furnishings.

10254—The large flower motifs of this embroidery to be worked in lazy-daisy, outline and one-stitch, may be used to advantage on dresses or blouses. The banding and motifs may also be used on skirts, hats, children's clothes and household linens.

Illustration 5. Embroidery designs from *The Delineator*, 1924. Reprinted from *The Delineator* magazine by the permission of Butterick Co., Inc.

in a straight position.

Featherstitching was frequently used on dainty garments from baby clothes to lingerie. It was used on neck, sleeve or hem edges as a border, in the space between rows of tucks, in the center of ribbon or covering seams. Featherstitching was often done with embroidery floss in white on white fabrics.

CHAIN STITCH is similar to featherstitch except that the stitches are closed at the top, forming a series of loops. It may be worked with embroidery floss, or, for a coarser effect, in Pearle cotton or wool yarn. Chain stitch is used as a border or outline stitch.

LAZY DAISY is a series of separated chain stitches that can form flower designs. The work is easy and progresses rapidly. (See **Illustration 4.**)

FLY STITCH is similar to Lazy Daisy except that the top is open. It may be worked in a regular pattern or in a random design. For a textured effect stitches of different sizes can be worked close together.

HERRINGBONE or CATCH STITCH is used to finish raw edges of seams, to hold seams open when the fabric is heavy, or as a hemming stitch. It also has many decorative variations. Work from left to right along two imaginary parallel lines. With the needle always pointing left, take a stitch on the lower and then on the upper line alternately. The thread should be under the needle. This stitch was often used on baby clothes, especially those made of flannel. Sometimes it was called cat stitch.

Other variations of this stitch that are not illustrated are closed herringbone and double herringbone. Closed is worked with the stitches touching which gives a more solid effect. Double is widely spaced single herringbone with a second row worked over the first in contrasting color. Place the stitches in the spaces between the first row and interlace the threads as you work. It is very decorative done with coarse threads and makes an interesting border on necklines, sleeves or hems.

Shadow embroidery is closed herringbone stitch worked wrong side out on sheer material so the design shows through in shadow effect. It can be in straight lines or simple curves. It is most effective in contrasting thread. Herringbone stitch is pretty in a single row, or interesting effects are possible when several rows are worked close together using contrasting threads.

CROSS-STITCH

CROSS-STITCH. Starting either at the right or left, make a row of evenly

Illustration 6. *The Delineator*, 1923. Reprinted from *The Delineator* magazine by the permission of Butterick Co., Inc.

Dress 4120
Embroidery
design 10734

HEMSTITCH

HEMSTITCHING is always done on the straight of the cloth. Draw out the threads necessary for the design. This may either be directly above the fold of a basted hem, or cut out in an isolated pattern on the front of a blouse, skirt or pocket. Working from left to right count four or five threads and form a loop around them. Take a tiny stitch through the edge of the hem and fabric and pull up tightly. Continue across the row. The threads between the stitches should be loose, but the knots should be tight. To finish, work another row of hemstitching along the opposite side as in Ill. 2 in **Illustration 4.** This is sometimes called double or ladder hemstitching.

For diagonal hemstitching pick up an even number of threads (either four or six) when you work the first row. For the opposite row, pick up half from each group, making a zigzag line. DRAWN WORK is done in a wider space than hemstitching and may be in a single row or a grouping of rows. Work plain hemstitching on both edges of the row. Bring the needle from right to left under the second group of threads, then turn the needle and pick up the first group. This will cause the groups to cross each other as illustrated. This is one of several basic stitches that may be combined to make many interesting patterns. Drawn work was used to decorate the straight edges of collars, cuffs and hems, or on cut out designs on the front of blouses or lingerie.

From the plethora of fancy needlework designs published between 1900 and 1930 one could easily conclude that every item of clothng or household linen was so decorated. Each issue of the women's magazines usually had pages of instructions for crochet, knitting, tatting, embroidery and smocking. Occasionally peasant embroideries from Russia, Romania, Bulgaria or Italy were featured. The *Ladies' Home Journal* had a regular series of articles compiled under the direction of the Guild of the Needle and Bobbin. Some of these are included in the Fancy Needlework chapter of *Toddlers' Togs*.

Handwork was an integral part of the fashions of the early 1900s and few garments were bereft of embellishment. If you are duplicating these fashions, see to it that they are decorated with at least a small bit of exquisite fancy needlework. □

spaced stitches. Work back over them with the same stitch, slanting in the opposite direction. On the right side the stitches will cross, on the wrong side the stitches are straight.

The designs may be traced or transferred on the fabric, or followed by counting threads in coarse, even-weave cloth. Cross-stitch canvas may be basted to the fabric, and the design worked by counting threads in the canvas. When the work is finished the threads of the canvas are pulled out, leaving the cross-stitched design on the fabric. Cross-stitch canvas may be found in the needlework section of fabric stores.

Cross-stitch designs, were frequently used on women's and children's clothes, and household articles. Two of the designs in **Illustration 2** were from 1892 *Peterson's Magazines*, and the other from a 1911 *The Delineator*.

World War I brought about an interest in the peasant costumes and needlework of the Allied countries. After the war there was great social and political upheaval in Europe and Russia, and many displaced members of the former aristocracy supported themselves by doing fine needlework. Peasant designs and wool embroidery were frequently used on women's and children's clothing. Cross-stitch was one basic stitch used in peasant embroidery.

The next three pages have been reprinted from the 1904 issue of *The Designer.* Submitted by *Lyn Alexander.*

FOR NEW ARRIVALS FROM STORKTOWN

SACK 6973

SACK 7935

SHAWL HOOD 7515

SACK 7724

VERY consequential personages are the immigrants from Storktown. Quite out of proportion is their size to their importance, and a singular thing about the matter is that nobody dares ever question their claim to rule all about them, strangers though they be. From the moment they enter the domain in which they elect to dwell the best of treatment must be theirs or they threaten immediate departure, and, far from rejoicing at the prospect of release from such tyranny, at the mere suggestion of their abdication their subjects bow trembling before their displeasure and humbly hasten to propitiate them.

Royal robes must await the wee immigrants' arrival, for they bring no luggage, and their traveling suits consist at the utmost of skins of rose-leaf texture and a fluff of downy hair for head covering, neither of which is available protection against this rough atmosphere of ours. Hence, months before the Storktown Flyer is scheduled to make a stop at Home-Nest Station nimble and skillful fingers are plying needle and thread on the softest, finest fabrics the shops can furnish, and day by day the daintiest garments of doll-like proportions are laid away in rose-scented baskets and boxes to come forth for the arraying of His or Her Majesty, as the case may be, the instant he or she puts in an appearance.

On this page are shown some exceedingly pretty little cloaks for the first outing, and some little wraps to be donned when the wee one is carried through draughty halls, or from one room to another. The designs explain themselves, and the mother may make her own selection by the numbers put under each illustration. The sacks and the shawl hood—the latter a quaint and most convenient little garment, by the way—may be made of Chinese crêpe, opera flannel, lady's-cloth, cashmere, nun's-veiling or albatross, and may be hand-embroidered or trimmed with narrow ribbon or lace. Sacks of this kind are much to be preferred to the knitted or crocheted worsted ones, in the sleeves of which the baby is certain to entangle his fingers, to his no small irritation and discomfort. Any of the little wrappers which are shown on page 367 may also be made in sack length. The head portion of the shawl hood should be lined with Florentine silk, or the entire garment may be lined with it.

CLOAK 8233   CLOAK 8058   CLOAK 8327 AND CAP 2933   CLOAK 7687

Every layette should contain at least two of the sacks and one shawl hood or large cashmere shawl.

Of cloaks, one will be found sufficient, for the new arrival soon outgrows his first outfit, and it is not as easy a matter to alter a cloak as a dress or slip. Cashmere, merino, China silk, bengaline or piqué is generally used for the first cloak, and it may be trimmed with lace, insertion braid, ribbon or hand-embroidery. The little cap shown at the foot of page 365 is the simplest kind of head covering and may be made of linen lawn or lace over a Florentine silk lining, in which for cold weather a thin interlining of wadding may be inserted.

On this page are shown two sets for infants' wear, the first at left of page comprising a dress, slip, petticoat, barrow and sack, while the second at the upper right of page consists of a dress, wrapper, slip or nightgown, white petticoat and flannel petticoat. Nainsook, India or Persianlawn is generally used for the dresses, while fine cambric is used for the slips and white petticoat. The wrapper may be made of the same material as described for the sacks. Six each of dresses, slips and petticoats will be an ample allowance for any baby, and if it be desired to cut down the supply, four of each will be sufficient if there is good laundering facilities. Two wrappers will be needed.

Slips may be worn as morning dresses, and two pretty ones, also two little yoke dresses are shown at the foot of this page. For trimming the dresses fine narrow Valenciennes lace and insertion or nainsook or swiss embroidery may be employed, while the wee slips will require only narrow edging at the neck and wrists.

The bibs shown on this page may be made of piqué, marseilles or quilted linen, and may be trimmed with narrow edging, or the edge may be worked in scallops.

A set of underwear is pictured on page 367, and consists of a slip or nightgown, wrapper, white petticoat, flannel petticoat and barrow. The wrapper may be made in sack length as pictured in the back view.

The shirt and band pictured at upper left of page 367 may be made of silk flannel, a peculiarly soft fabric particularly well suited to delicate baby skins, or of merino, and may be bordered with buttonhole embroidery in white silk or with a narrow crocheted shell made with Shetland floss or silk. Four shirts and two bands will be needed.

The garments pictured at the foot of page 367 are sold separately. The first petticoat, 6475, requires neither buttons nor pinning, the waist portions tying in such a manner as to give great comfort to the child. The second petticoat, 7856, may be buttoned or tied on the shoulders, and the gabrielle, which may be used as a slip, nightgown or petticoat, fastens down the back. The wee slippers or shoes in the upper right corner may be made of merino,

BIBS 2332

SET 8329

SET 8231

DRESS 8679

SLIP 8260

SLIP 2129

DRESS 8374

piqué, cashmere or silk, and prettily decorated with hand-embroidery. "Points on Dressmaking" in this issue gives some valuable suggestions and advice regarding making baby clothes, and indeed all the directions the average needlewoman will require can be found on the labels which accompany each little pattern. Even if the greater part of the layette is given into other hands to prepare the mother always wants to make some of the pretty

SHIRT AND BAND 6564

WRAPPER 8572

8572

8512

·8454

872

WRAPPER 8414

things with her own fingers, and as fine needlework is once again regarded as an accomplishment, she can lavish the daintiest stitchery on the wee garments if she does not have to make the entire outfit herself. If, however, she is to construct the whole of the miniature wardrobe, it is advised that she forego the pleasure of laying a multiplicity of tucks, and so not tax her eyesight with elaborate embroidery, for the first garments are so soon outgrown that it is far better to keep them as daintily simple as possible. Of the finest, softest material they should certainly be made, and the seams and hems should be finished with all the skill possible to the accomplished needlewoman, but a frill of fine Valenciennes lace of narrow width will finish the neck and sleeves of even the "best" frock quite as pleasingly as would one of hand-embroidery, and the tiny round or square yokes may be made from the exquisitely fine all-over yoking which, although it is made by machinery, will present a far better effect than would hand-made decoration wrought, perhaps, at the expense of the prospective mother's health and nerves.

There are, however, many trimmings which can be quickly made by hand, such as fine fagoting, her-

WRAPPER 8512

UNDERWEAR SET 8403

ring-boning and simple hemstitching, all of which when made with rather coarse soft cotton on fine material, such as nainsook, linen lawn or Persian or India linen are lovely in the extreme. French knots, too, made with the cotton, may be placed between wide hems or rows of very narrow tucks. Bias bands of the material may be feather-stitched or decorated with rows of the knots and used to finish the edges of yokes or the neck and wrists of the little gowns, or such bands may be joined by fagoting made with wash silk and used for the yokes themselves.

PETTICOAT 6475   PETTICOAT 7856   NIGHTGOWN 6220   GABRIELLE 5555

On Dressing the Schoenhut Doll

by **Ruth H. Zimmerman**

Photographs by **Robert W. Zimmerman**

Illustration 1. 11in (28cm) seated infant doll with natural arms and legs. This baby doll has been correctly redressed in a gray and white striped romper suit made of old gingham with a contrasting collar. The self-belt fastens at the natural waistline with a mother of pearl buckle. This doll is an excellent example of the proper use of old material to recostume a doll. He wears an original Schoenhut pin, 7/8in (2.2cm) diameter, which reads: "MADE IN USA STRONG DURABLE and UNBREAKABLE//SCHOENHUT//ALL WOOD// PERFECTION//ART DOLL."

We all have seen it happen! The appearance of an otherwise attractive doll is spoiled because of inappropriate dress. A doll dressed in the wrong style or costumed in a manner that does not correctly mirror its period in history grates on the sensibilities of a collector like the sound of fingernails on a blackboard. The total picture presented by a doll can be completely destroyed when its clothes do not reflect the doll's historical age or social position. Disregard either of these considerations, and the appearance of the doll will suffer. The *All Wood Perfection Art Doll* produced by The A. Schoenhut Company illustrates this point.

Schoenhut dolls were among the best dressed dolls of the time. Each doll came from the factory with a union suit, stockings and shoes. The dolls could also be bought dressed and extra clothing was available for separate purchase. In 1915, 18 styles of girls' dresses and six styles of suits for boy dolls were available from the factory.

There were also baby dresses for the infant dolls, both natural limb and toddler. The A. Schoenhut Company repeatedly advertised that its dolls "...are dressed in the latest style of childrens' clothes." The clothing was sturdy and easy to care for and followed the pattern of dress favored by the emerging middle class. American children of this period (1911 to 1921) wore simple clothing trimmed with tucks, embroidery, smocking or topstitching. A Schoenhut doll dressed as a French Bébé, in lace and satin, or in the ethereal daintiness of the Kate Greenaway period appears overdressed and uncomfortable.

Dresses and suits for many Schoenhut dolls were also made at home by loving mothers, grandmothers and aunts. Since sewing for a doll was encouraged as a way "to teach the growing girl the satisfying art of fine needlework" (*Ladies' Home Journal*, December 1913), clothes were often made by the child herself. Women's magazines carried, in their Christmas issues, patterns and directions for making a wide range of dolls' clothes. Though these patterns were not specifically designed for the Schoenhut doll, they were suitable for most dolls of the period.

During the time when Schoenhut dolls were popular, babies of both sexes wore dresses of white lawn or fine cotton. Small infants were clothed in long dresses with skirts that extended well below the feet. Toddlers wore short (ankle length) walking dresses. Whatever the length the dresses usually had several rows of horizontal tucks at the hemline, so that the dress could be lengthened as the child grew. The dress might fall in gathers or fine pleats from the neckline or the skirt might be gathered to fit a lace-trimmed yoke. The sleeves were almost always long. Under the dress, a full-length slip and a

113

ABOVE LEFT: Illustration 2. 17in (43cm) doll with sleep eyes and a wig. The blue paisley material for this was found in an old box of remnants. The pattern was taken from Anna McQuilken's book, *Sew for Schoenhuts*. The doll has her original underwear and shoes. An otherwise perfect costume is marred by the use of synthetic material for the dickey.

ABOVE RIGHT: Illustration 3. 16in (41cm) Schoenhut all-wood character doll. This carved hair girl with a blue bow has been redressed in a blue and white dotted swiss dress. The bodice has vertical tucks and is trimmed in lace. The self-belt is worn just below the natural waistline; a belt of wide blue ribbon would also be correct. The dress is similar in style to one shown in the 1915 Schoenhut catalog. The stockings are not original.

flannel petticoat were worn for added warmth and a rubber diaper cover was worn for dryness. Toddlers wore high shoes, either laced or buttoned, to give extra support to the ankles. In an early Schoenhut ad, *Tootsie Wootsie* and *Schnickel Fritz* are both shown wearing walking dresses with lace-trimmed slips and high button shoes. Other advertisements show the infant dolls wearing machine embroidered dresses in two lengths.

"The Little Mother's Doll" in the December 1913 *Ladies' Home Journal* illustrates "every necessary garment for the baby." Included in the listing are: a long dress with matching slip, a flannel petticoat and shirt, a nightgown, a long robe and a short sacque. All tie in the front. The coat that is pictured is long with a shawl collar and a peaked

cap. The article concludes, "The clothes have been designed and made along the same lines as the most approved of hygenic clothes for the real infant." Patterns for the clothes pictured in this article on dolls' wear were available from *Ladies' Home Journal* and would have been readily adaptable to the bent-limb baby.

Pre-school boys wore rompers. These were generally knee length but some styles extended to the ankle. The 1915 Schoenhut catalog shows a gingham romper with long sleeves and a rounded collar. It has a square yoke and a self-belt worn at the natural waistline. A romper suit with a sailor collar in white or gray with blue trim was a popular outfit for young boys. Another type of suit was the "blouse suit" which consisted of pants that

ended just above the knee with a long overblouse or tunic. The blouse was usually trimmed with braid or binding and had a belt of matching material which fastened just above the hip. The blouse usually fastened at the center front and was worn over a dickey. Materials used were linen, chambray and rep, a ribbed fabric. Brown and blue were favored colors, but in 1914 rose became a popular color for small boys.

For school age boys knee-length pants with a white shirt was the most common outfit. This was called an "Oliver Twist" suit. Often the pant legs fastened at the knee with three buttons. Suspenders, more commonly called braces, were used to hold up the pants. The use of leather belts to hold up trousers did not become general until after World War I. The crew neck sweater had become popular before the turn of the century and continued to be a favorite for sportswear. Overalls and sports uniforms were worn by boys, although the Schoenhut catalogs have these items worn by the manikins not the boy dolls.

Sailor suits had been made popular in the late 19th century by the sons of Queen Victoria and their popularity continued well into the 20th century. Boys of all ages wore sailor suits. Boys wore dark stockings with either oxfords or high shoes. Sailor hats, large straw hats and golf caps were the favored headgear.

Girls of the period between 1811 and 1921 wore their dresses at knee length. Big hair bows were worn, either at the crown or at the side part. Shoes could be high —either buttoned or laced, oxfords or sandals. Long stockings were worn. Ankle socks became popular only after 1918. Dresses of wool or gingham were worn over a guimpe or blouse. The dress was usually low-necked and short-sleeved so that the high neck and fine tucks of the guimpe could be seen. The dress itself might have been plaid with a solid color belt or plain with a contrasting trim. This type of dress seems to have been very popular as there are several variations shown in the Schoenhut catalogs.

The middy or sailor dress had first gained popularity in the 1880s and continued to be worn into the 1920s. The middy was made of linen or chambray. Favorite colors were red, blue and tan with white trim and a white piqué dickey. The dress might be a two-piece outfit consisting of a pleated skirt with overblouse or a one-piece dress with pleats falling from the shoulder. The one-piece version had a belt contrasting material. Both styles of middy dress are shown in the Schoenhut catalogs.

A simple dress with a pleated skirt and finely tucked bodice was an all-around garment, suitable for many occasions. In white lawn or fine cotton it could be worn for "Sunday best." Made of brown or other dark checked material it was suitable for school or play. It was often covered by an allover apron that protected the dress completely. The apron could be worn alone as a play dress in summer.

The A. Schoenhut Company did not make coats for its dolls, but the magazines of the day show several popular style coats. Infants wore long coats in white or cream wool or silk, trimmed in ribbon and lace. Often the coat had an attached cape, and the lining was usually silk. Babies, more often than not, wore matching lace-trimmed caps.

Both boys and girls wore reefers, a double breasted short coat with either a square or sailor type collar. Dressy coats for girls were skirt length and often trimmed with fur collar and cuffs. A muff was an important acces-sory. Boys' coats might have flannel or velvet trimmed collars and cuffs. In cold weather both boys and girls wore leggings which buttoned up the side of the leg and were held in place by an elastic strap under the instep. The leggings could match the coat or be of white wool.

Collectors who wish to recostume their Schoenhut dolls have many sources for finding correctly styled clothing. There are reprints of the Schoenhut catalogs. *Ladies' Home Journal, Woman's Home Companion* and other magazines of the period are well illustrated with both dolls' and children's clothing. Once a desired costume has been found there are several sources for patterns. Anna McQuilken's book, *Sewing for Twentieth Century Dolls* by Johanna Gast Anderton has a section devoted to Schoenhut patterns. The chapter on the period 1910 to 1920 has some valuable tips on material and colors. Doll patterns for the period 1911 to 1921 are usually suitable to use in dressing Schoenhut dolls. The time and effort that go into research before starting to sew are well worth it when the result is a well-dressed doll that correctly reflects its historical background. □

Illustration 4. 16in (41cm) Schoenhut all-wood character doll. "Ted" wears a contemporary sailor suit of white linen with -light blue soutache trim. The trousers are buttoned to the shirt with six handmade buttonholes. The light blue dickey matches the trim on the collar and cuffs and is embroidered with a red star and chevron. Not only is the entire suit hand-stitched but the stockings are knit from white crochet cotton. Only the shoes are not original. He wears a Schoenhut pin identical to the pin shown in **Illustration 1**. His companion is an 8½in (22cm) (without his hat) *Danny Daddles*, also made by The A. Schoenhut Company.

Illustration 6. A page from the 1915 Schoenhut doll catalog showing six of the over 20 costumes available from the company.

Illustration 5. 14in (36cm) walkable doll. The commercially made suit is not original to the doll; note that the sleeves are too short. However, this two-piece blouse suit is correct for the period. It is made of white cotton with dark blue trim and tie. The pressed metal anchor is sewn to the bodice of the suit. Anchors also trim the ends of the tie. The matching hat adds to the charm of this costume. His shoes are not original and he would look better with long stockings.

Miniature Sewing Techniques

by Lauren Welker

There is a fascination with the tiny. Small things seem to capture our fancy and draw us into their world. Creating the minute can become an obsession, but working in small scale creates demands of its own.

Most miniature sewing techniques focus on eliminating bulk and creating a natural effect. Standard sewing methods would produce an unnatural garment. The following are some of the methods I use when sewing for the miniature dolls in my own collection and for my original line of dolls' house people.

Necklines can be tricky. A real facing would be too bulky, so for a neat finish on a simple untrimmed neckline I make a facing from lightweight iron-on interfacing. First cut a square of interfacing larger than needed. Pin it to the bodice right sides together (the "sticky" side of the interfacing faces away from the garment). Carefully, by hand or by machine, sew around the

neckline making an even circle. Cut your interfacing away so it looks like a real facing. (See diagram.) Turn and press in place.

The high collar is a popular feature on many turn-of-the-century styles. It is a very simple finish. Run a light touch of glue around the neck opening and let dry to prevent raveling. Hand sew 1/8in (.31cm) ribbon along the right side of the neck opening to form the collar. Silk ribbon works best.

If you do not have ribbon to coordinate with your outfit you may make an 1/8in (.31cm) strip by applying some iron-on interfacing along the selvage on the wrong side of your material. Cut to size. Apply as you would the ribbon.

Sometimes a low cut bodice is glued in place. The raw edge must then be trimmed. A lace ruffle may be glued over the raw edge. Cotton laces glue better than synthetics, but are harder to find. If you must use a synthetic lace

Illustration 1. These all-bisque dolls have been dressed in cotton outfits with felt collars. *Buster Brown* has a felt belt and cuffs, too. Silk ribbon makes soft and natural looking bows. Muted colors look best on most older dolls.

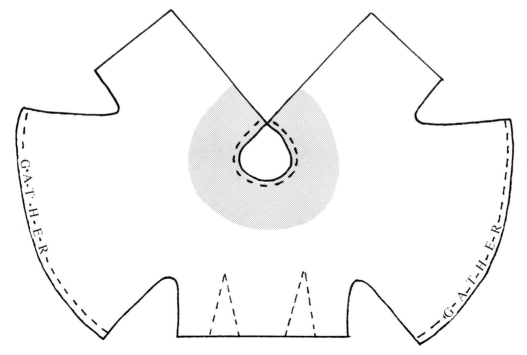

This is a pattern for a basic bodice for a dolls' house lady. The shaded area shows how your facing will look before you turn it to the wrong side and press in place. The sleeves are gathered at the wrist after the garment is finished and in place on the doll.

ABOVE LEFT: Illustration 2. An outfit depicting the mid 1800s had Bunka trim on the bodice front and the sleeves. A tiny felt hat trimmed in feathers and silk ribbon completes her outfit.

ABOVE RIGHT: Illustration 3. These dolls have high collars made of self-fabric. The lace trims are glued in place. Tiny prints are often found among the calicos in any fabric store.

BELOW RIGHT: Illustration 4. A low-necked bodice that has been faced with iron-on interfacing. Bunka, lace and ribbon decorate this Colonial lady's dress.

try a glue like Bond 527 instead of white glue.

Chainette (also called bunka) is often used as a finish or a trim. It is first unraveled. A line of glue is applied where the trim will go. Then the chainette is pressed in place.

Trims on bodices and skirts are often glued in place on little garments. Rows of lace, ribbon or chainette are commonly used. Bows and "buttons" (usually tiny beads) are also glued on.

Hems may be handled in several ways. They may be turned up and sewn or glued, or they may be faced with a strip of tulle if they threaten to unravel. A tulle facing also makes a neat finish for a circular hem.

On many antique dolls felt was used for both garments and trims as it does not require hemming or facing. I find felt useful for making hats, collars, cuffs and belts.

As always, I work "on the flat" as much as possible applying neck treatments, sleeves and trims before sewing the side seams.

I hope you find some useful ideas here and perhaps as you work along you will invent new methods of your own.

The older dolls shown here are from my private collection. The ladies and children in dolls' house scale are from my line of original dolls. □

LEFT: Illustration 5. Occasionally a wider piece of lace may suggest some special use. The lace panel going down the front of this dress was glued first to the bodice before assembly, then to the skirt at the center front. The pieces were carefully matched when the doll was dressed. Tiny pearl "buttons" were glued down the center front of the bodice.

RIGHT: Illustration 6. This tiny *Princess Di* is only 5¼in (13.4cm) tall. The neckline of her silk gown is trimmed in a row of gathered lace. Silk fabric can be marred by glue so hand-sewing is often best for hems and trims.

BELOW: Illustration 7. This group of dolls' house dolls gives but a tiny idea of the many styles that you can create using these sewing techniques.

DOLL DRESSING:

BONNETS AND HAT:

Let's Make an 1898 Poke Bonnet
by Dorothy Noell de Campus [Kern]
Doll Hat for a 12in (30cm) Head Size
by Ruth Dougherty

ACCESSORIES:

The Subject of Sleeves and Collars
by Albina Bailey
Miniature Ribbon Roses
by Doris Rockwell Gottilly
Dolls' Shoes and Socks
by Jeannie Sieg
Parasols For All
by Barbara Guyette
Doll Stockings
by Pat Nelson

Let's Make an 1898 Poke Bonnet

by **Dorothy Noell de Campus [Kern]**
11½in (29cm) to 13½in (34cm) head circumference

This poke bonnet is not a project to undertake and complete all in one sitting. It is an elaborate and time-consuming affair, which, if completed exactly according to the instructions, will produce a beautiful and top-notch quality bonnet for your treasured doll.

The directions are very concise, so even if you are a beginning doll milliner, have no fear — you should be able to accomplish the bonnet with no pain —just patience!

The style and illustration are from the *Butterick Catalog of Fashions, Winter 1898-1899.* This gives the period from which the doll of your choice should date. A few years more or less will make no difference, as the poke bonnet was truly a classic in head wear for many years.

Suggested fabrics are satin, taffeta, velveteen or very fine wool. The lining should be of soft silk; thin satin, china silk or a sheer silk broadcloth would be good. The interlining should be a firm muslin. The foundation should preferably be buckram, although this is somewhat painful to work with. Substitute crinoline if you cannot tolerate the buckram. Other supplies needed are: 1/2in (1.3cm) delicate lace, millinery wire, ribbon wire, bead wire, thread, beeswax, millinery needles and ribbons and flowers with which to trim the bonnet. A source for millinery supplies is: Manny's Millinery Supply Co., 63 West 38th St., New York City, New York, 10018. They have a free catalog.

DIRECTIONS

Explanation of Terms and Functions of Supplies
— The *foundation* is the material upon which the bonnet is "built." It gives the needed stiffness, and when wired, can be made to assume the desired shape.
— The *interlining* is placed upon both sides of the foundation. Its purpose is to provide a covering before the bonnet

fabric and lining are sewn in place.
— The *lining* neatly finishes the interior of the bonnet. Inside the brim (in this particular pattern) it is softly shirred.
— The bonnet *fabric* covers the exterior of the buckram frame.
— Millinery wire is used to stiffen and make bendable all the edges of the bonnet. It is whipstitched to the buckram.
— Ribbon wire is a double thickness stiffened cotton ribbon within which is encased thin wire. This is used to support and make bendable the brim of the bonnet.
— Beeswax can be bought at any sewing store. Always run your thread through several times before sewing, as this will strengthen it greatly.

Illustration 1.

— Millinery needles are extra long and are necessary when sewing the various parts of the bonnet together.
Making the Bonnet
    Cut out all of your pattern pieces in buckram, interlining, lining and fabric. We will first be concerned with the buckram pieces.
A. The frame
1. Taking a waxed thread, whipstitch millinery wire around all edges of the buckram which are designated on the pattern pieces. When you join it on the crown, do so at "A." Overlap the wire 1in (2cm) and bind it tightly together with fine bead wire, wrapping it round and round very smoothly.
2. Stitch ribbon wire in place on the brim, as shown by the guidelines in the pattern.
3. Slash the slash lines indicated on the brim and band pieces.

4. Bend the slashed part of the brim outward, and place the wired edge of the band on top of it; stitch from A to B with a firm backstitch, drawing the thread securely each stitch.
5. The bonnet should now look like **Illustration 2.**

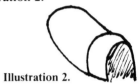

Illustration 2.

6. Bend the slashed edges of the band downward, place the crown up against them, and stitch C to D as in step 4 above.
7. Cut 1/2in (1.3cm) strips of the interlining fabric on the bias. Bind all the wired edges, stretching it as you go. Stitch with a running stitch. The fabric strips covering the A to B and C to D joinings should rest on both pieces of the bonnet.
    (For example, when covering the A to B joining let half be sewn through the brim piece, and half through the band piece.) The purpose of these strips is to prevent the wire from showing through to the bonnet fabric, when the bonnet is completed.
B. Interlining the Frame
8. Clip the brim interlining where marked on the pattern. Do the interior first, turning the edge up over the edge wire of the frame, and basting down. Clip out extra fullness as necessary. Stitch A to B in place. Sew the other interlining piece to the top of the brim, turning the edge under and basting it to the interior. Sew A to B.
9. Clip the crown interlining as shown on the pattern. Baste this in place first on the interior, then do the exterior, turning the C to D straight edge up over the edge wire in each case.
10. Next baste the interlining for the hat band on the interior, turning raw edges under to provide a neat finish.

Now cover the exterior of the band with its interlining piece, turning raw edges under on A to B and C to D, but turning A to C and B to D to the interior.

C. Covering the Bonnet

11. First comes the brim covering. Put this in place, having first clipped A to B as shown on the pattern. Turn the outer edge to the interior, clipping out extra fullness, and slip stitch to the interlining. The clipped edge of A to B should lap against the band. See **Illustration 3.**

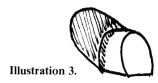

Illustration 3.

12. Next comes the crown covering. Clip the *rounded* C to D edge as shown on the pattern. Put the crown piece in place on the frame, with the clipped edge resting on top of the hat band. See **Illustration 4.** Turn the lower edge to the inside, slip stitch in place to the interlining. Stitch the clipped edge down.

Illustration 4.

13. Finally comes the covering for the band! Place this in position, and tuck raw edges of A to B and C to D under, hiding the raw clipped edges of the brim and crown. It is not necessary to stitch A to B and C to D. With the proper tension, all that is needed is to turn A to C and B to D over the edge wire to the inside and slip stitch firmly in place.

D. Lining the Bonnet

14. Before the actual lining is sewn into place, one needs to attach the neck ruffle. Roll-hem the side and lower edges. Gather or narrowly pleat upper edge. Slip stitch in place on the *interior* of the bonnet, from A to C to D to B. If desired, the ruffle can be lined with silk. In this case, pin lining and fabric right side to right side. Stitch side and lower edges, invert and press. Gather or pleat upper edge and slip stitch to the interior.

15. Clip the rounded edge of the crown piece. Iron under 1/2in (1.3cm) of the straight edge. Place inside the bonnet, and turning the clipped edge out, to lap against the band, slip stitch all edges neatly in place.

16. Narrowly roll-hem by hand the outer edge of the brim lining. Whip fine lace along this edge. Run a gathering thread along the laced edge, and another thread along the raw edge of A to B (two threads). Pin lining in

place inside hat, pull up and adjust gathers and end gathering threads firmly. Carefully tack the laced edge in place every 1/2in (1.3cm), being cautious not to go through to the exterior of the bonnet. Slip stitch A to B in place.

17. Iron all raw edges of the band under, and slip stitch in place on the interior, neatly covering the raw edges of the brim and crown lining pieces, and also the raw edges on A to C and B to D.

E. The Fun Part — Trimming the Bonnet!!

18. Tack artificial flowers on the interior, along A to B, to frame the face.

19. Tack 1/4in (.65cm) ribbon along A to C to D to B on the exterior.

20. Tack 1/2in (1.3cm) or 3/4in (2cm) ribbon along A to B where the brim and band join.

21. Attach 1½in (4cm) ribbon in place on the *exterior* for chin ties, and cover the place of tacking with a small ribbon bow.

22. Now for the gorgeous ribbon cluster atop the bonnet. Take six pieces of 3/4in (2cm) ribbon, each 10in (25cm) long. Turn the ends into the middle and tack. See **Illustration 5.** Run a

Illustration 5.

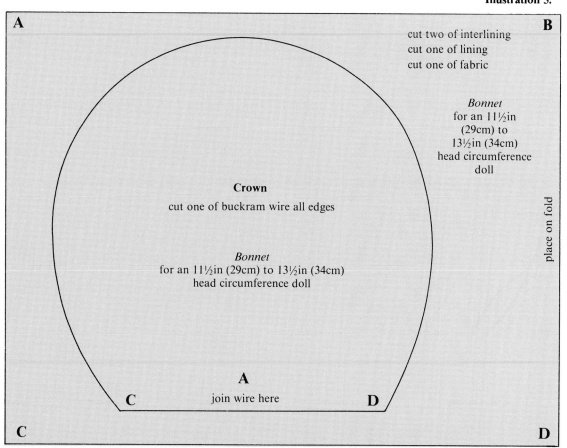

A

B

cut two of interlining
cut one of lining
cut one of fabric

Bonnet
for an 11½in
(29cm) to
13½in (34cm)
head circumference
doll

Crown
cut one of buckram wire all edges

Bonnet
for an 11½in (29cm) to 13½in (34cm)
head circumference doll

place on fold

A

join wire here

C

D

C

D

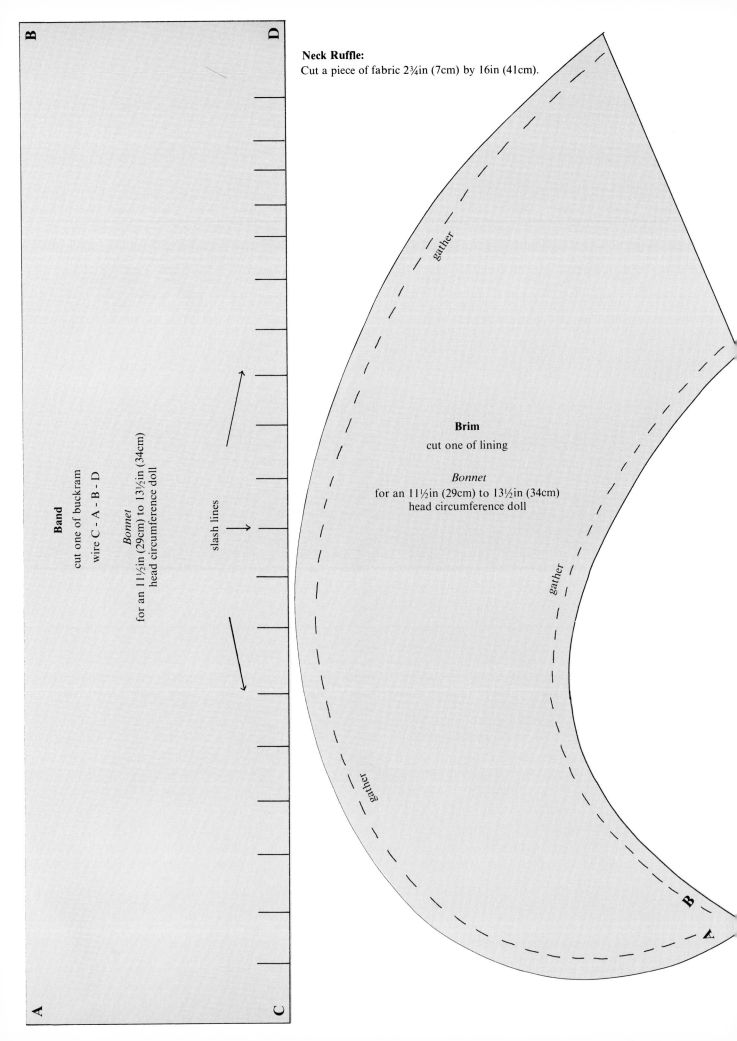

Neck Ruffle:
Cut a piece of fabric 2¾in (7cm) by 16in (41cm).

B **D**

Band

cut one of buckram

wire C - A - B - D

Bonnet
for an 11½in (29cm) to 13½in (34cm)
head circumference doll

slash lines

A **C**

Brim

cut one of lining

Bonnet
for an 11½in (29cm) to 13½in (34cm)
head circumference doll

gather

gather

gather

B

A

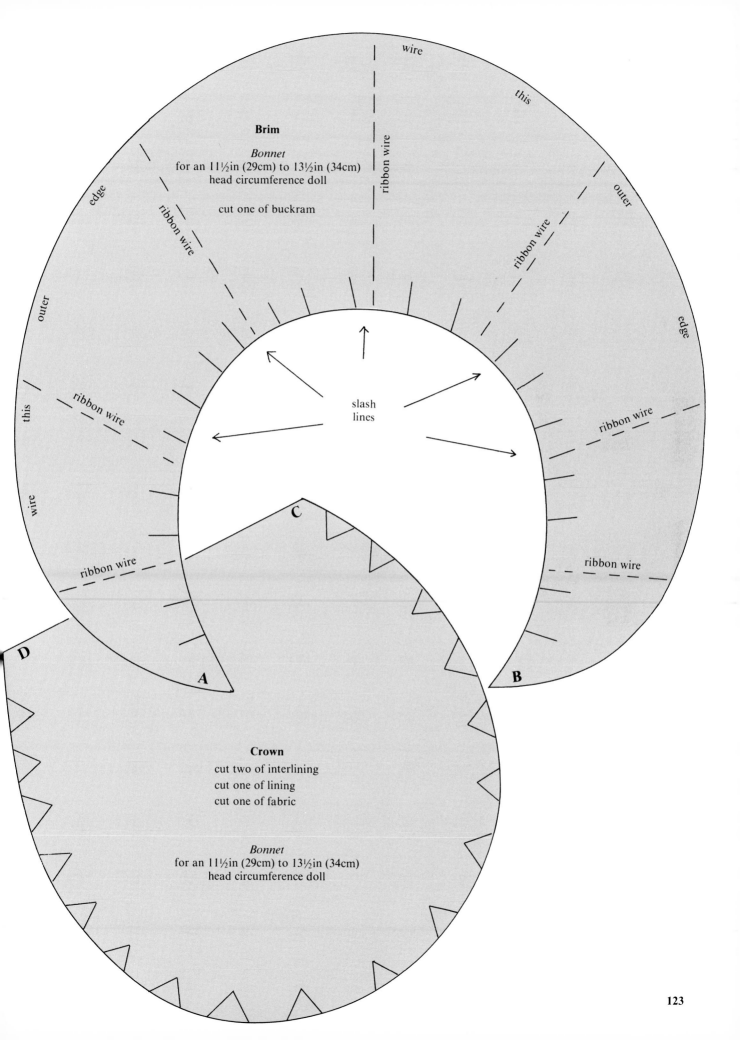

Brim

Bonnet
for an 11½in (29cm) to 13½in (34cm)
head circumference doll

cut one of buckram

wire

this

ribbon wire

outer

edge

ribbon wire

outer

this

edge

ribbon wire

wire

ribbon wire

ribbon wire

ribbon wire

slash
lines

C

D

A

B

Crown
cut two of interlining
cut one of lining
cut one of fabric

Bonnet
for an 11½in (29cm) to 13½in (34cm)
head circumference doll

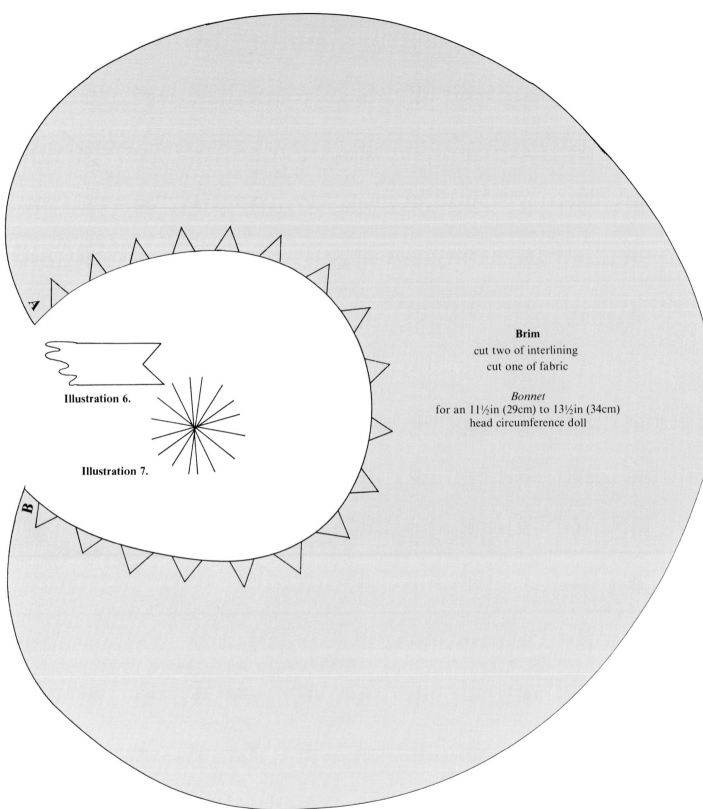

Illustration 6.

Illustration 7.

A

B

Brim
cut two of interlining
cut one of fabric

Bonnet
for an 11½in (29cm) to 13½in (34cm)
head circumference doll

gathering thread through the middle (where you just tacked) and draw up each one individually. You now have six gathered bows. Take two 6in (15cm) pieces of ribbon, clip the ends into double points (see **Illustration 6**), and gather the middle of these also. Lay these eight gathered pieces on top of each other, as in **Illustration 7.** Fasten them securely through the middle. End your thread. Now run a gathering

thread, piercing through completely on each stitch, around a 1½in (4cm) diameter at the center of the cluster, and draw up slightly. Fiddle around with the bows until the cluster is arranged to your satisfaction, then end the thread. Tack firmly in place.

Once the doll milliner has made and completed this bonnet successfully, she need have no fear of any bonnet or

hat pattern in the future. The methods and instructions given here are the most basic and necessary in millinery. Hobby House Press, Inc. publishes a book, *Hat Making for Dolls, 1855-1916,* which has many patterns for some lovely bonnets and hats. The patterns in this book are now the next step. *All* of your dolls deserve a lovely piece of head wear! □

Doll Hat for a 12in (30cm) Head Size

by **Ruth Dougherty**

Photographs by **Charlotte Pack**

Illustration 1. "Holly" wearing white silk brocade bonnet type trimmed with white and pink silk roses. White silk ribbon in loops hangs down on each side.

Illustrations 2 and **3.** "Holly" a Gebrüder Heubach Pouty. Front and back view of bonnet made from old satin bodice of dress. 3in (8cm) old wide lace falls over the back on the shoulder. Trimmed with old French violets.

Front (3)

gather this edge

(2)

cording pull up to fit

This pattern can be made with stiff heavy silk or taffeta. Cut one outside piece for the hat and one inside piece for the lining. Sew right sides together on three sides and leave 3in (8cm) on third side open. Turn and slip stitch the other 3in (8cm). Fold over one length 1/2in (1.3cm) for cording insert: (1) Sew in the cording leaving about 2in (5cm) of cording on each side to pull up for the back crown.

Sew another row of cording 2in (5cm) from the front edge (2).

Pull up the cording on edge (1) and it will look like a circle. Tie cording pieces in a knot and cut off all but 1in (2cm) of each piece. Fasten into lining neatly.

Pull up the cordings on (2) and adjust to head size. A little practice makes perfect here. Cut cording to 1in (2cm) on each side and sew in the lining. The distance between the two cordings makes a lovely pouf — without wiring.

The front edge now becomes a ruffle because of pulling up cording (2). Or you can hand-gather the front edge to fit the face closely. You can also put in cording (3) along front edge and pull up. The effect is much the same as gathering by hand.

To make a smaller hat cut a smaller piece. For example 11in (28cm) by 5in (13cm) makes a much smaller hat. A wide piece of ribbon can be made this way and left unlined.

The hat can be trimmed with flowers, ribbons, bows feathers or any combination of these.

A baby's bonnet can be made by leaving the front edge as a ruffle. A bonnet look is effective by making a small pleat on each side of the front edge folded to the back.

This is a versatile pattern and every hat will look different depending on the size and material. Materials with body look the best. □

Back (1)

one-half pattern — place on fold

cording pull up to fit

one half 15in (38cm) length

Illustration 4. French fashion marked: "B. 12 S." Green silk faille; large self-trim bow in back; front edge bound in lace with red currants and leaf trim.

Illustration 5. "Katie," a Kestner, modeling white lace hat with pointed lace edging.

Illustration 6. "Katie," Kestner, modeling white and green pure silk taffeta hat made from scarf made in France; trimmed with miniature fruit and green velvet leaves.

Illustration 7. "Holly" modeling red satin brocade hat with lace edgings and pink silk French lilacs.

The Subject of Sleeves and Collars

by **Albina Bailey**

During the 19th century ladies looked forward to receiving their *Godey* and *Peterson* books each month because the fashions changed so frequently. They found reading "The General Remarks" most important in describing the new changes of every part of the costume, including sleeves, collars, trimmings, color, fabrics and so on, in making up their costumes.

During the 1850s and 1860s, sleeves and undersleeves of every variety and form were fashionable: hanging sleeves, sleeves with bands at the wrists, finished by narrow insertions or a border of lace falling over the hands; and puffs, separated by rows of insertion, some richly embroidered. Open sleeves were very popular for summer wear.

A convenient style of sleeve introduced in 1869 was the Coat Shape sleeve. This novelty sleeve allowed for the cuffs to be buttoned on, which enabled one pair of sleeves to answer for several pairs of cuffs. These deep cuffs were trimmed in several different ways; of black silk or satin, embroidered in jet, and some were ornamented with an application of colored velvet or silk. Others were plain with topstitched edge. The choices were numerous.

Undersleeves were worn under the wide sleeves, such as the Pagoda sleeve and others. They were extremely popular for winter wear to keep the arms warm in addition to being fashionable.

Collars changed as frequently as sleeves and undersleeves. Often, cuffs

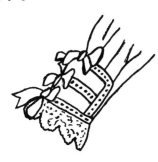

Illustration 1. La Comptess sleeve of very thin muslin, finished on the back with bands of insertion and bows of ribbon, and a deep frill over the hand. This sleeve is exceedingly dressy, especially if made of illusion or thin lace. *Godey*, April 1855.

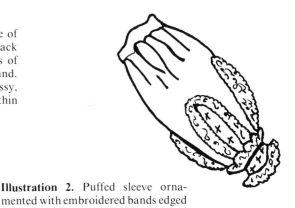

Illustration 2. Puffed sleeve ornamented with embroidered bands edged with lace. *Godey*, April 1855.

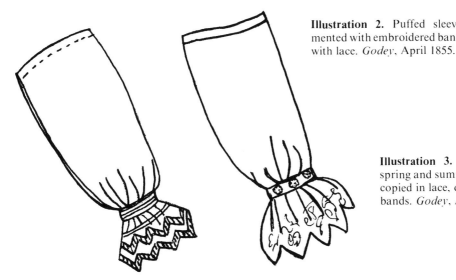

Illustration 3. Duchess sleeves for spring and summer wear; they may be copied in lace, or with worked muslin bands. *Godey*, April 1855.

were made to match the collars and many times the collar was used as a pattern for making the cuffs. They were worn in all shapes from the large Shakespearean to the very small dainty collars. The Elizabethan collars were fashionable in the late 1860s; in Paris they were called a la Medicis and trimmed with lace. Linen collar sets were sometimes ornamented with English openwork embroidery. Standing collars with wide lapped ends were another style worn by the ladies for day wear.

The variety of sleeves, collars and cuffs, of the 19th century is so vast that it is impossible to give them all.

Any of the sleeves and collars given in this article may be authenticated when making up a wardrobe for your dolls. □

Illustration 4. Medici undersleeve. The wristband is just large enough to let the hand through. *Peterson*, May 1857.

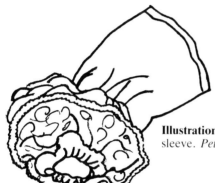

Illustration 5. Mousquetaire Under-sleeve. *Peterson, May 1857.*

Illustration 6. Muslin sleeve with slashes, separated by wide embroidered insertions: the sleeve is terminated by a deep band of embroidered muslin. *Peterson*, May 1857.

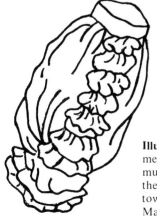

Illustration 7. Muslin sleeve ornamented with slashes forming puffs of muslin, running all along the seam; these puffs should gradually diminish toward the top of the arm. *Peterson*, May 1857.

Illustration 8. Narrow collar, with ends to cross in front. This is to be worked in satin stitch and raised dots on very fine cambric or muslin and the edge in buttonhole stitch with embroidery cotton No. 30. A large stud or button should be worn with it which should be placed in the buttonholes, as shown in the illustration.

A stud or button, to correspond with that worn with the collar, should also fasten the cuffs. *Godey*, April 1862.

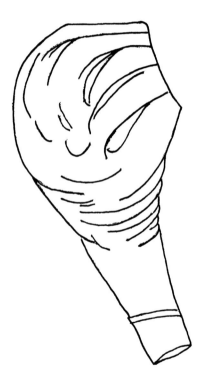

Illustration 9. The gigot, or "leg of mutton," sleeve which used to be such a favorite with our grandmothers, has now come into fashion again, and it is a style which is more used for morning wear than any other. It is very simple in its construction, being cut in one piece, with a very decided slope at the top, and, when pleated into the armhole, very much resembling the shape of a leg of mutton. It is made to fit tightly to the wrist, being fastened by means of buttons and loops, or hooks and eyes, over which a pointed white linen cuff should be worn. A plain gigot sleeve is illustrated as being the easiest to make, but these sleeves are also worn trimmed in a variety of ways, and are much more elaborate in their making. *Godey*, July 1862.

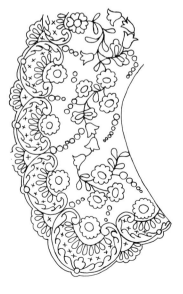

Illustration 10. New style collar. *Peterson*, February 1858.

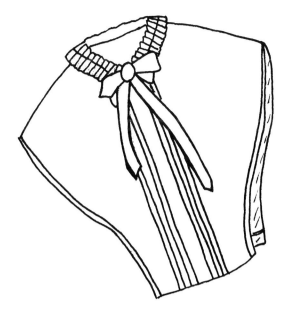

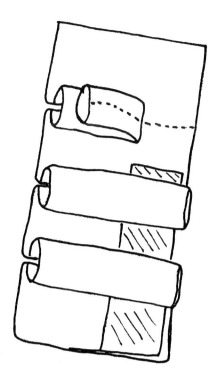

Illustration 11. A new style for collars and cuffs. The collar and cuffs can be made by following these diagrams. *Godey*, January 1863.

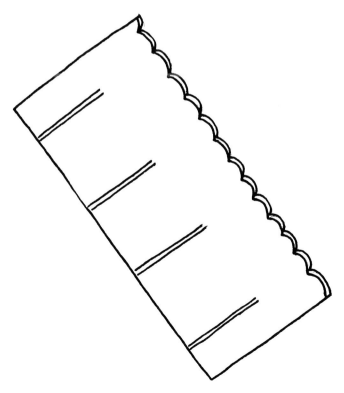

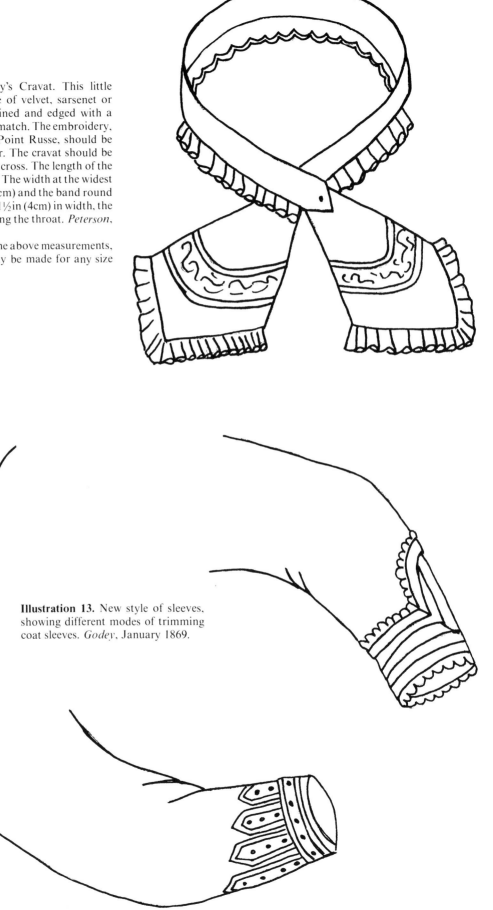

Illustration 12. Lady's Cravat. This little cravat may be made of velvet, sarsenet or satin. It should be lined and edged with a quilling of ribbon to match. The embroidery, which is worked in Point Russe, should be very brilliant in color. The cravat should be cut absolutely on the cross. The length of the lappets is 5in (13cm). The width at the widest part should be 3in (8cm) and the band round the throat should be 1½in (4cm) in width, the length of course, fitting the throat. *Peterson*, July 1865.

NOTE: In reducing the above measurements, this cravat may easily be made for any size doll.

Illustration 13. New style of sleeves, showing different modes of trimming coat sleeves. *Godey*, January 1869.

Miniature Ribbon Roses

by **Doris Rockwell Gottilly**

I first learned to make the lovely miniature ribbon roses in 1978. I was teaching some friends from Japan how to make dolls of papier-mâché. While teaching them how to make the dolls, they taught be how to make the lovely roses of ribbon. I have used the rose many times since then to decorate the original dolls I design and make. Recently while reading Kate Green-away's *The Language of Flowers,* I looked up her meaning for the rose. She has given the rose many meanings; the first meaning is "love." Here are a few of the other meanings that are favorites of mine. Keep them in mind when you make your roses for your dolls.

Rose, multiflora . . . . . Grace
Rose, single . . . . . . Simplicity
Rose, white and red
   together . . . . Unity
Roses, crown of . . . . Reward
   of Virtue
Rosebud, red . . . . . . Pure and
   lovely
Rosebud, white . . . . Girlhood

Gather the materials needed to make the basic rose, find a quiet corner and begin to make your first miniature ribbon rose.

MATERIALS needed for making the Basic Practice Rose:

Acetate ribbon, fused edge 1in (2cm) wide about 5yd (4.55m), your color choice
Green floral tape
Florist wire 32 gauge
Scissors
Green velvet ribbon, acetate backing (leaves)
Brown fine-tip magic marker (to make leaf pattern)
Thread to match the color of the ribbon

When you first practice making the rose all you will need is the ribbon, your hands and the thread to tie around the base. We will use the 1in (2cm) wide ribbon because it is easier to learn the folding steps and turning procedure on the larger size ribbon. When your fingers know how to **hold with the left** hand and **fold with the right** hand (the opposite if your are left-handed) **at the same time** you will be able to use the smaller width ribbons. You will be able to make approximately 20 roses from your 5yd (4.55m) of ribbon (9in [23cm] per rose, four to the yard, 20 from the 5yd [4.55m]). Use the practice roses to fill a miniature wicker basket. Attached to the florist wire, wrapped with the floral tape you will have lovely long-stemmed roses.

Now to begin. This is the basic procedure, read it carefully. Cut your ribbon to measure 9in (23cm) (the length of ribbon determines the number of petals your rose will have).

Hold ribbon in left hand (1in [2cm] wide, 9in [23cm] long).

Fold ribbon forward and down with right hand; note the angle of the fold. There will be about 1in (2.5cm) hanging down.

Twist and roll the ribbon (hold in right hand the ribbon hanging down from the bottom). Twist to the right three times, to form the center "core" of the rose.

Now **hold the core of the rose in the left hand,** fold ribbon back, note the angle, with the right hand, for the **first petal.**

Wrap the petal to the left with the right hand while you turn the core with the left.

Fold ribbon back for second petal.

Wrap around to the front, hold with left hand, wrap with right hand.

Fold back, form point of third petal, wrap around to left. Note all the time you hold with the left hand while folding and wrapping with right.

Note petal point in the illustration, as you fold back and wrap to the left (fourth petal).

Fold back and wrap around again. Note the point the petal makes, (fifth petal).

To make the last petal, fold ribbon back with right and wrap around the core, to the left (sixth petal).

Take thread about 6in (15cm) long and tie tightly around base of the rose. Tie all the petals real tight. Wrap thread tightly. Next take a piece of florist wire about 2in (5cm) long and tie around base of rose. Take your floral tape, (made from a waxy crepe type of paper about 1/2in [1.3cm] wide).

Start at the base of the rose and wrap with floral tape, pulling gently downward as you wrap. Wrap the waxy floral tape around and around to the bottom of the wire.

Using the leaf pattern, cut three leaves, using the green velvet ribbon, draw the leaf markings with the magic marker. Cut 1in (2cm) of wire and tie to base of leaf. Wrap wire with floral tape. Attach the leaves to the rose with a piece of floral tape. The tape is waxed and sticks very easily when pinched with your fingers. Now you have completed your first *basic* rose. As you make your other practice roses, just tie them with the thread and place them in a small basket until you have completed

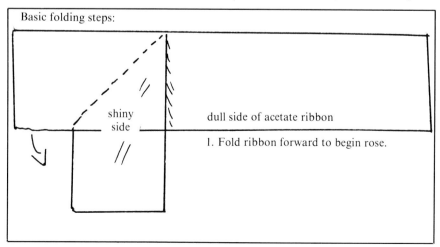

Basic folding steps:

shiny side

dull side of acetate ribbon

1. Fold ribbon forward to begin rose.

all the roses. It is more convenient to make all the roses first, then all the leaves, then assemble the complete rose as you make the stem.

After you have mastered the art of folding and turning and know how to make the rose, you can vary the size of the ribbon length and width. For example:

3in (8cm) creates a lovely rosebud, try it.

6in (15cm) creates a rose just beginning to bloom.

Continued on page 136.

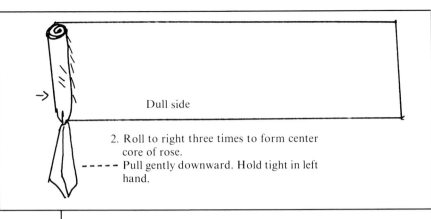

2. Roll to right three times to form center core of rose.

- - - - - Pull gently downward. Hold tight in left hand.

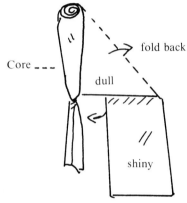

3. Turn as you make point of rose petal. Do not gather, just wrap gently around to the left.

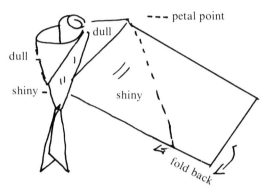

4. Fold back and wrap to left to form petal. Hold core with left hand, wrap with right hand.

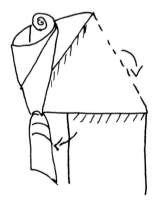

5. Fold ribbon back; note angle of fold, and wrap to left.

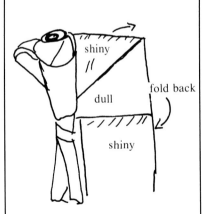

6. Fold back and wrap to left.

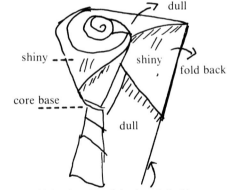

7. Fold back with right hand, hold core base in left hand and wrap to left with right hand.

Repeat the fold back with right hand and wrap to the left. Hold core base in the left hand and continue until all the ribbon is used. Then tie firmly at the base, wrapping thread around and around and pulling tight to keep all the petals secure.

Patterns for rose leaf:

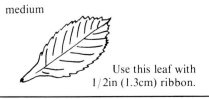

small
Use this leaf with 1/4in (.65cm) ribbon.

medium
Use this leaf with 1/2in (1.3cm) ribbon.

large
Use this leaf with 1in (2cm) ribbon.

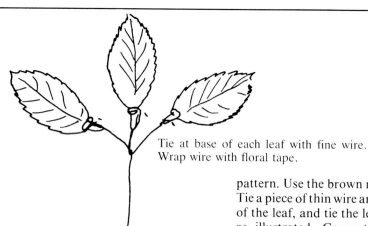

Tie at base of each leaf with fine wire.
Wrap wire with floral tape.

First trace the outline of the leaf pattern you need. Cut out the leaf pattern and place it on the back of the velvet or satin ribbon. Draw the leaf shape with the magic marker. Turn over to the right side of the leaf and draw the markings as shown on the leaf pattern. Use the brown magic marker. Tie a piece of thin wire around the base of the leaf, and tie the leaves together as illustrated. Cover the wire with floral tape. The floral tape is waxy and sticky. When the leaves are to be attached to the main stem, twist the wire around the stem three times. Always cover the wire and base of rose with floral tape for neatness and contrast.

Use floral tape to unite leaf to stem. Twirl the stem in right hand and stretch tape in left hand. Guide tape down the stem on the bias.

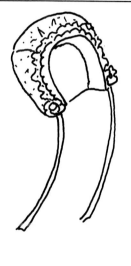

White satin ribbon roses add a special touch to a doll's christening outfit: Use 1/4in (.65cm) satin ribbon. Sew the rose to the ribbon tie on the hat. Add tiny rosebuds to the dress.

White satin roses for doll's bridal veil and bouquet:

Use 1/2in (1.3cm) white satin ribbon. Make six medium roses and sew them to white satin ribbon. Attach the roses to a piece of white netting for a veil. Again adjust the size of roses to the size of the doll. For the bouquet make three medium white roses and three rosebuds, attach to floral wire and wrap with floral tape. Add some dried baby's breath and a white satin ribbon.

9in (23cm) creates the basic rose you have just completed, a full rose.

The stems for the rose are not always necessary to make. They are not needed when you decorate the dolls' hats, dresses or undergarments. When the miniature roses are attached to a dress or a petticoat or soft bonnet, a needle and thread is inserted through the leaves and then through the base of the rose, making sure to catch all the petals. The rose and leaves are sewn directly to the garment; in some cases the floral tape or the leaves will not be necessary. There are a great variety of ribbons available for the miniature ribbon roses. Silk and satin ribbons make beautiful roses. The acetate ribbon roses are perfect to glue to hats and for floral arrangements in baskets or in small vases.

The miniature ribbon rose can also be used to decorate your doll house: Make tiny roses from 1/4in (.65cm) ribbon and fill tiny vases or planter boxes. They can be used in tiny pictures to hang on the walls. In the bedrooms they make lovely tiebacks for curtains and add a decorative touch to dust ruffles, or to add a feminine touch to a bedroom chair. Use 1/2in (1.3cm) acetate ribbon cut to measure 6in (15cm) and make medium-size roses for tiebacks and to trim chair and table. □

Dolls' Shoes and Socks

by **Jeannie Sieg**

Photographs by **Annie McLane**

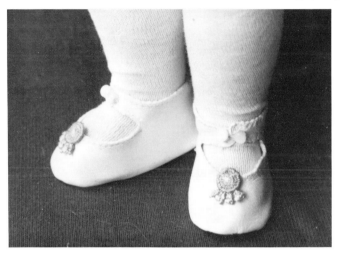

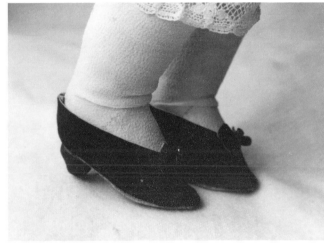

Illustration 1. These shoes are made out of old kid gloves using Pattern A.

Illustration 2. These shoes are made from Pattern E out of black suede gloves.

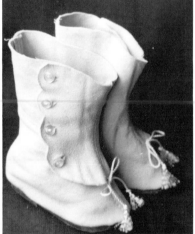

Illustration 3. These shoes are made from Pattern B but with a center back seam to fit a composition doll.

Illustration 4. These shoes are also Pattern A but without the strap.

Illustration 5. Satin shoes from Pattern A.

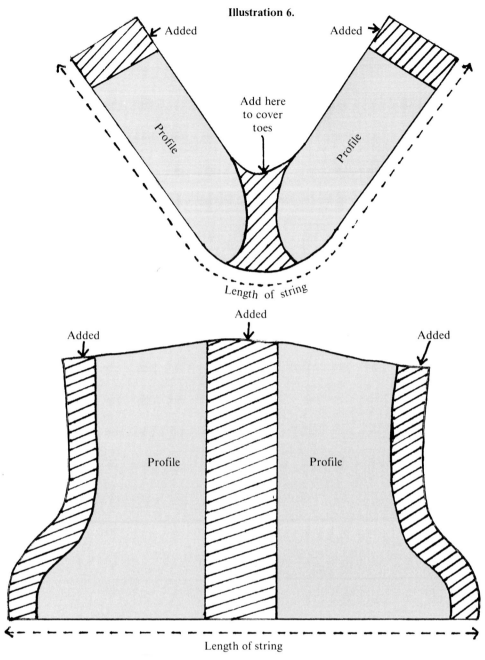

Illustration 6.

Added

Added

Profile

Profile

Add here
to cover
toes

Length of string

Added

Added

Added

Profile

Profile

Length of string

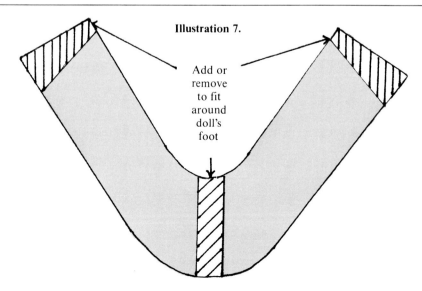

Illustration 7.

Add or
remove
to fit
around
doll's
foot

I used to search the doll shows for shoes that fit and looked appropriate on my antique dolls. Now I find it is easier to make them myself. If you decide to make shoes for your dolls you can have good reproductions of Jumeau and Bru shoes in satin or leather and high button boots that fit perfectly on your French fashion or little girl dolls. The cost is very small. You do not need any elaborate expensive materials, supplies or equipment. Dolls' shoes can be made out of old kid gloves from yard sales or thrift shops or from material that matches the dolls outfit. Inner soles are made from thin cardboard boxes. Soles and heels are leather from old pocketbooks also from thrift shops. Equipment and supplies include a sewing machine, a number 18 sewing machine needle for heavy leather, white glue, transparent tape and scissors strong enough to cut the heaviest leather you will use. To cut high heels from wood it is helpful to have a Dremel moto-tool. High heels could also be molded from Sculpey.

Before fitting her shoes, your doll should have on her socks. I make socks using the doll stocking patterns. Since they are made from knit material, they stretch to fit the doll and size is not much of a problem. I use a man's old cotton undershirt as material. For a dainty French fashion you could try using lace netting or an old silk chiffon scarf.

Finish the top of the sock by turning it to the inside and stitching it down. Next, with the wrong side out, fold the sock in half lengthwise and stitch the curved edge and the back of the sock leaving only the finished top unstitched. Turn right side out and the sock is finished.

Now that your young lady has her socks on, it is time to make her shoes. The most difficult part of shoe making is fitting the doll's feet. Included here are some basic patterns I have used for my dolls. The easiest to use is the U-shaped slipper pattern. Keep in mind that these patterns can only be guides as you will have to make shoes that fit your doll. You can find more patterns for shoes in *The Collector's Book of Dolls' Clothes* by Dorothy S., Elizabeth A. and Evelyn J. Coleman, pages 758 to 759 or in *Antique Children's Fashions 1880-1900* by Hazel Ulseth and Helen Shannon.

Start by making a pattern from tissue paper. I use tissue paper because it is inexpensive, fairly transparent and drapes pretty well around curves, but any paper will do. First put the bottom of your doll's foot on the tissue and draw around it. This tracing will be the pattern for the sole of the shoes; if you do not like its shape, change it now. Of course you cannot make it smaller, but if your doll has undersized feet you can enlarge them by making longer shoes. You can also add a pointed toe or a square toe or develop a more foot-like shape. I never add seam allowances at this time because it is easier to fit the pattern to the doll without them.

Now use a string to measure the circumference of the sole pattern. Lay your doll on her side and draw a profile of her foot, or, in the case of boots, her foot and leg cut out two profile pieces. Pick the upper pattern you will use and put your profile pieces together or cut them apart and place them to conform to the shape of the pattern. Add enough room between the profiles to make the bottom of the upper equal to the length of the string. (See **Illustration 6.**) When you are satisfied with the size and shape, cut it out.

Having made your pattern and cut it out, fit it on the doll. You can use transparent tape to hold it together. Ask yourself:

Do the edges meet in back and/or in front? If not add to these areas on your next pattern. (See **Illustration 7**.) If the edges overlap, remove room on the next pattern.

Will the upper meet the sole in the front over the doll's toes? If not enlarge the toe area. (See **Illustration 8.**) (If the bottom edge of the upper thus becomes too large, it can be gathered into the sole when the shoe is made.)

Does the angle of the curve over the front of the foot fit the doll's foot? If not change the angle at which you put together the two profiles at the front of the shoe. (See **Illustration 9.**)

Will the top of the boot go around the doll's leg? If not you will need to enlarge to the top of the boot. The top can be shaped to fit the large calf by curving it out in back. You will have to make the boot upper in two separate pieces seamed in back as well as open in front. (See **Illustration 10.**)

Will the straps of slippers meet in the front of the doll's foot? If not, lengthen them; if they are too long, shorten them.

You may have to make several patterns before the shoes look the way you want them.

When the shoe pattern fits, draw

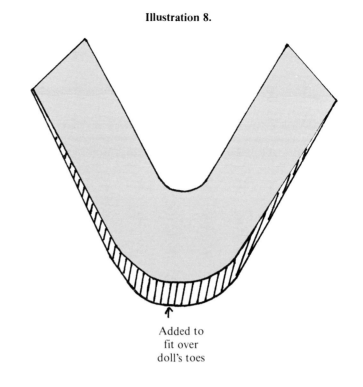

Illustration 8.

Added to
fit over
doll's toes

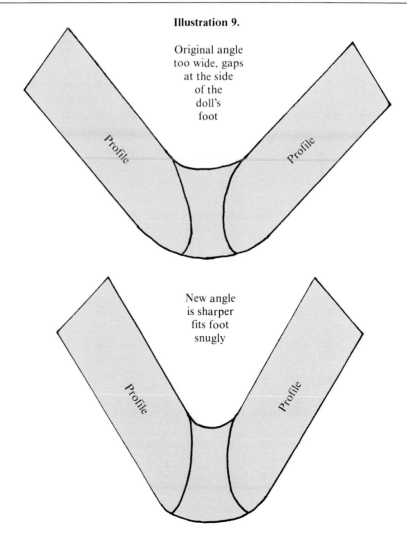

Illustration 9.

Original angle
too wide, gaps
at the side
of the
doll's
foot

Profile

Profile

New angle
is sharper
fits foot
snugly

Profile

Profile

Illustration 10.

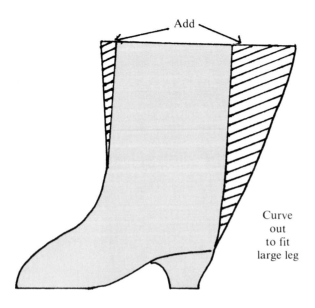

Add

Curve
out
to fit
large leg

Illustration 11.

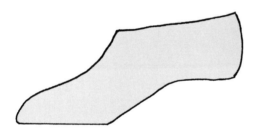

around the sole pattern on a piece of cardboard. Cut this out for the inner sole. Fabric may be placed over the cardboard and glued to its underside for a finished appearance. You may now want to add seam allowances to your pattern at the edge of the sole, the bottom edge of the upper and on any seams in the upper.

Now transfer your pattern to the fabric and/or leather. You may want to line the shoes, especially if you are using a soft woven material. You can use an iron-on interfacing, but this will not be quite as authentic as an old-fashioned material.

After cutting, do all the work you can on the shoe while it is still flat before you sew the final front or back seam and put on the sole. You may want to put the lining and the upper together and finish the top first. Zig-zagging over the edge to make a decorative or satin stitch is the method I often use. Although you may think that zigzag sewing machines were not used until the 1950s, commerical machines that did decorative edge stitches were used to make doll shoes much earlier. In *The Collector's Book of Dolls' Clothes,* on page 364, is a doll shoe from the 1890s with a commercial edge finish you may be able to simulate. Alternately, you could finish the top with narrow braid or trim, or blanket-stitch around the top for a handmade look.

Sew the seams in the upper, then sew the upper to the sole. Be sure to put right sides together and sew the seam on the wrong side. I tape the upper in place on the sole before sewing it when I am working with leather. If you are using a heavier leather for the sole you may need a number 18 sewing machine needle for this seam. After you sew the seam, clip the seam allowance as close as possible. Turn the shoe right side out and insert cardboard inner sole. You may want to glue a heavier leather sole or a heel on the bottom of the shoe, especially if your doll is quite large.

You will probably want a decoration on the front of the shoe. A design cut from lace, a ribbon rosette, a bow, a buckle or beads can make your shoes look more realistic, and they can mask goofs, too. Straps on slippers can be held together with buttons, laces or buckles. Two buttons with an elastic thread loop is a favorite closing for woven materials because I do not have to make any holes in the strap for this closure.

I wanted to dress a Verlingue lady doll from the 1920s in an Alsatian peasant costume. Photographs show these costumes with shoes, not boots. So I set out to make shoes with heels, 1920s style for this doll's imitation leather feet. I could not make the heels very high because the doll's feet are flat. I started by making the pattern as described earlier. The doll's feet are short, the toes square and the legs fat. I lengthened the toes of the shoe and made the sole more "shoe" shaped. See Pattern E. I sewed the upper onto a thin leather sole; then glued on a thicker leather outer sole and a cardboard inner sole. While the glue was still wet, I bent the heel of the shoe up and the toe down forming an arch of the type you would expect on heeled shoes of this height. (See **Illustration 11.**) To make the heel I asked my husband to cut from his wood scraps a 5/8in (1.6cm) square stick of pine which I whittled into the heel shape. Then, using his Dremel moto-tool, he cut off the heel at the correct angle to fit on the bottom of the shoe. The worst problem was getting the two heels exactly alike. Heels could also be molded from oven-hardening clay or built up of thin pieces of leather for stacked heels. To complete my shoes I initialed and dated them on the bottom.

These directions may look long and complicated, but making doll shoes is certainly easier done than said. Care and patience in fitting and sewing will pay off in good results. In fact, yours may look better than the originals. □

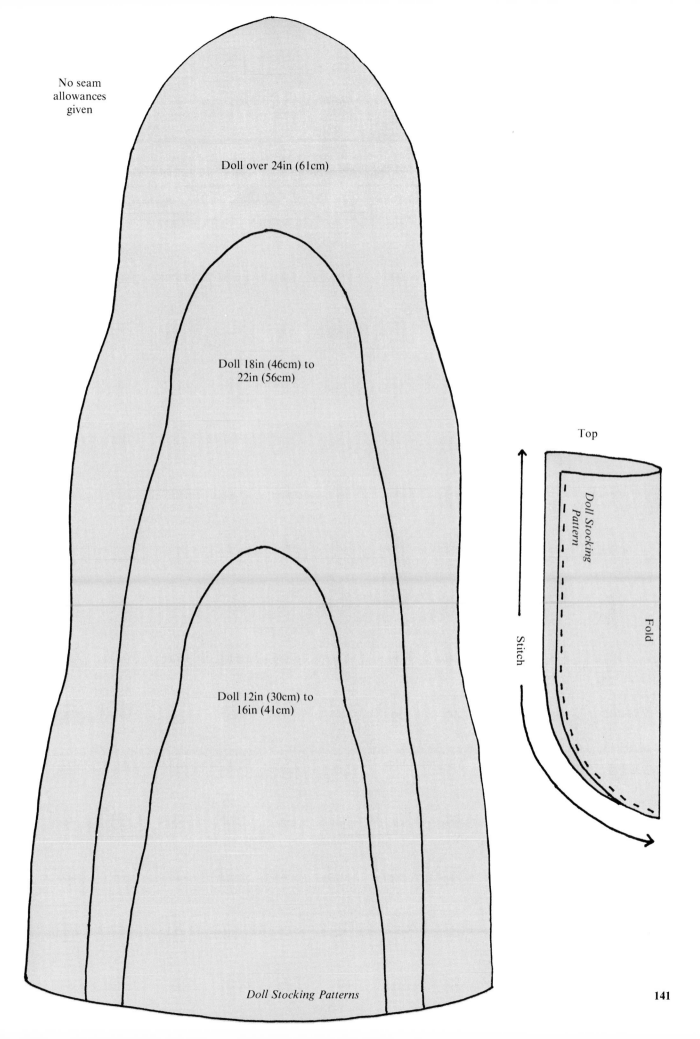

No seam
allowances
given

Doll over 24in (61cm)

Doll 18in (46cm) to
22in (56cm)

Doll 12in (30cm) to
16in (41cm)

Doll Stocking Patterns

Top

*Doll Stocking
Pattern*

Stitch

Fold

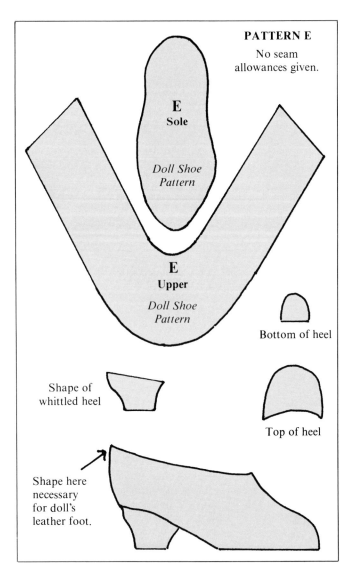

PATTERN E

No seam allowances given.

E
Sole

Doll Shoe Pattern

E
Upper

Doll Shoe Pattern

Bottom of heel

Shape of whittled heel

Top of heel

Shape here necessary for doll's leather foot.

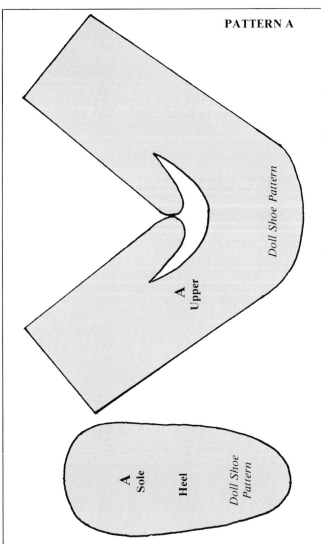

PATTERN A

Doll Shoe Pattern

A
Upper

A
Sole

Heel

Doll Shoe Pattern

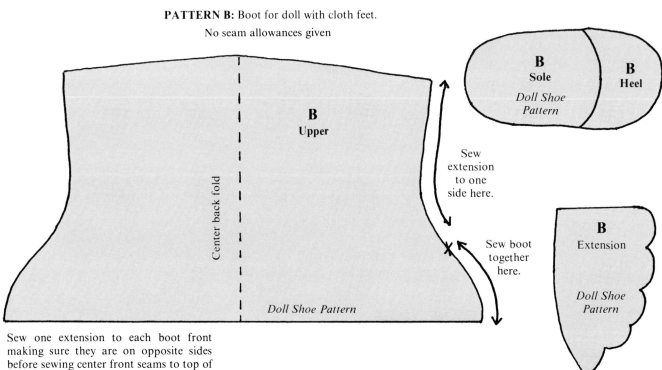

PATTERN B: Boot for doll with cloth feet.

No seam allowances given

B
Upper

Center back fold

Doll Shoe Pattern

B
Sole

Doll Shoe Pattern

B
Heel

Sew extension to one side here.

Sew boot together here.

B
Extension

Doll Shoe Pattern

Sew one extension to each boot front making sure they are on opposite sides before sewing center front seams to top of foot.

142

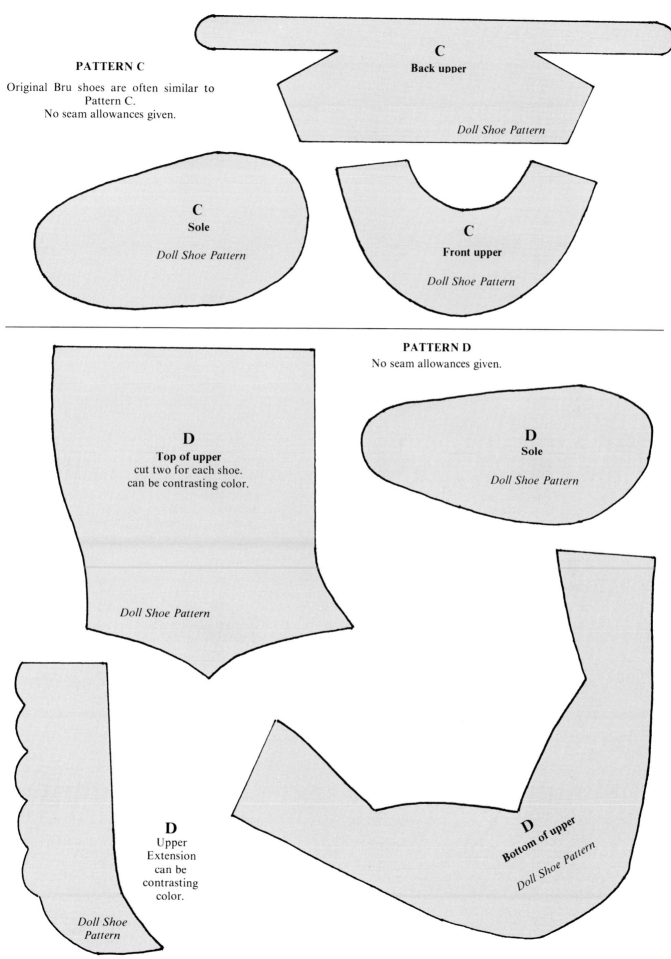

PATTERN C

Original Bru shoes are often similar to
Pattern C.
No seam allowances given.

C
Back upper

Doll Shoe Pattern

C
Sole

Doll Shoe Pattern

C
Front upper

Doll Shoe Pattern

PATTERN D
No seam allowances given.

D
Top of upper
cut two for each shoe.
can be contrasting color.

Doll Shoe Pattern

D
Sole

Doll Shoe Pattern

D
Upper
Extension
can be
contrasting
color.

*Doll Shoe
Pattern*

D
Bottom of upper
Doll Shoe Pattern

143

Parasols For All

by **Barbara Guyette**

In the 19th century, no "proper" lady's fashion ensemble was complete without a parasol. On a sunny summer day parks were filled with a gay profusion of this lovely and elegant fashion accessory. Freckles and tanned skin were considered unfeminine and a curse of the working class! Parasols, to coordinate with every outfit, were carried faithfully, to protect against the sun's damaging rays.

Parasols serve a variety of purposes today. They are decorative reminders of yesteryear, still carried by generations of dolls, or, they act as attractive symbols for wedding and baby showers, as centerpieces or party favors.

Whatever your need, why not try your hand at creating a parasol just for its special beauty? The instructions that follow, show you how to create three sizes of parasols. There is sure to be one sized for that special doll to carry. The large size is 12in (30cm) in diameter, medium size is 6in (15cm) in diameter, and there is even one for a dolls' house-sized doll! What doll's wardrobe would not benefit from such a beautiful accessory? It is sure to make that treasured doll a real eye catcher!

MATERIALS REQUIRED:

For the large parasol:

One 11in (28cm) diameter parasol frame

1yd (.91m) of 2in (5cm) wide pre-ruffled lace trim, white

1⅜yd (1.24m) of 1in (2cm) wide pre-ruffled lace trim, white

Six small embroidered rosettes, pink

1½yd (1.36m) of 5/8in (1.6cm) wide satin ribbon, turquoise

12in (30cm) square of lace fabric, white

Several small pink silk blossoms (may be cut from a large spray)

For the medium parasol:

One 8in (20cm) diameter parasol frame

9in (24cm) square of yellow taffeta

2yd (1.82m) of 2in (5cm) wide taffeta ribbon, yellow

1yd (.91m) of 1/2in (1.3cm) wide double-scalloped edge white craft ribbon

Illustration 1. This 14in (36cm) doll displays her lovely white lace parasol. See the instructions for creating the large-sized parasol.

Several clusters of small yellow flowers, with buds

For the miniature parasol:

One miniature Oriental paper-style parasol (the kind sold for party favors or drink decorations)

1/4yd (.23m) of 1/8in (.31cm) wide velvet ribbon, pink

1/2yd (.46m) or 1/2in (1.3cm) wide pre-ruffled lace trim, white

5in (13cm) square of crisp fine dotted swiss fabric, pink

One small white embroidered flower applique

For all the parasols:

Tacky glue or an electric glue gun and glue sticks

Straight pins, needle and thread, stylus, scissors, small sharp scissors, pencil, ruler, paper for making patterns

INSTRUCTIONS:

For each parasol: Using a stylus and paper, draw a circle of the correct size for the parasol fabric pattern.

Large parasol:

10¼in (26cm) diameter

Illustration 2. A lady of fashion would never be caught promenading through the park without her parasol! The doll shown here is a reproduction of a French fashion doll. She elegantly displays a yellow moire taffeta parasol. See the instructions for creating the medium-sized one.

Medium parasol:
7in (18cm) diameter
Mini parasol:
3½in (9cm) diameter

Using the appropriate circle as a pattern, cut one from the chosen parasol fabric square. Fold the fabric circle into four even pieces, and snip off a tiny amount of fabric at the point for the center hole on the top of the parasol. Place the center point of the parasol frame through the fabric center hole and glue. Let dry before proceeding.

For large parasol: Pull the lace circle taut over the parasol frame, stretching the fabric over the outside points of the frame. Points should poke through the lace and hold the fabric neatly in place. In between the points, along the outside edge on the parasol underside, place a fine line of glue on the frame. Draw the lace fabric tightly over the section of the frame, gluing it in place by doing so. Pin together until thoroughly dry, if necessary. When dry, trim off the excess fabric. Repeat procedure for all sections of the frame.

Following the outside, lower rim of the parasol, glue a flounce of 2in (5cm) wide pre-ruffled lace trim. The lace may be held in place with pins until the glue has dried. When dry, along the top of the first flounce glue a second flounce of 1in (2cm) wide pre-ruffled lace trim in the same manner.

At each of the six parasol frame points, glue a pink embroidered rosette.

Around the top center point 1in (2cm) out, glue a circle of 1in (2cm) wide pre-ruffled lace trim.

Cover the handle of the parasol with 5/8in (1.6cm) wide satin ribbon. Glue one end of the ribbon to the inside top; when dry, tightly twist the ribbon around the handle to the opposite end. Tuck in the ribbon raw end and glue in place. Hold with pins until dry.

Make two bows, approximately 2in (5cm) to 3in (8cm) wide. Each bow should have four loops and two streamers. Glue one to the top center point of the parasol, filling in the center of the lace ruffle circle. Glue the second bow to the parasol handle, just above the lower end. Intersperse and glue several small pink silk blossoms in and around each bow.

For the medium parasol: Attach the circle of taffeta fabric to the parasol frame in the same manner as for the large parasol. The taffeta will not

Illustration 3. The parasol, a miniature version, held by an antique French dolls' house doll.

stretch and poke through as easily and as tautly as the lace fabric so at each point of the frame pull the fabric taut and tack with a needle and thread. Continue gluing the fabric to the frame in the same manner as the large parasol.

Gather the 2in (5cm) wide taffeta ribbon into a ruffle by sewing a gathering thread along one edge. Glue the ruffle around the parasol frame at the outside edge. Overlapping ruffles by 1/2in (1.3cm), place and glue a second ruffle around the top of the parasol.

Make a 2in (5cm) wide bow of the 1/2in (1.3cm) wide craft ribbon with four loops and two streamers. Glue to the center top of the parasol. In and around the bow, glue several clusters of small yellow flowers with buds. Make a second simple bow and glue to the lower end of the parasol handle with a spray of the flowers.

For the miniature parasols: With small sharp scissors, snip and peel all the paper of the parasol off the wooden frame. *Note:* Before choosing a miniature parasol for your project, examine the frame carefully. Choose a sturdy, evenly made frame.

Glue the parasol fabric circle to the parasol frame at the center top. When dry, proceed to glue, evenly spaced, the parasol spokes by spreading a thin layer of glue on the top of each spoke and pressing it lightly to the fabric. Let dry. With a needle and thread, stitch a ruffle of 1/2in (1.3cm) wide pre-ruffled lace trim around the outside edge of the parasol fabric.

Make two small bows of 1/8in (.31m) wide velvet ribbon. Glue one to the center top of the parasol and the other to the lower end of the parasol handle. Glue a small white embroidered flower to the center of the top bow.

Use your imagination and experiment. Parasols may be trimmed in a variety of ways and made in a wide range of fabrics!

SOURCES OF PARASOL FRAMES:

Craft, art, doll and party stores and mail order catalogs.

IMSCO, Doll supplies, 950 North Main Street, Orange, California 97117. Write for their catalog, and request the name of the store nearest you that carries their line of doll accessories. Frames used for this article are the 8in (20cm) and 5in (13cm) pin and sew parasol frames.

Miniature parasols of the type used here may be found in the party supply sections of most supermarkets or at party supply stores. □

Doll Stockings

by **Pat Nelson**

Dressing an antique or a reproduction doll is a rewarding venture, and many of us find old dolls without clothes, so we research and do our utmost to dress the dolls as they were when new. In dressing the doll, we would like a pattern to make stockings, but none are available. We either order from a catalog, or buy some at the doll show — but why? Stockings can be plain or fancy, so after I had dressed a doll in a costume I had made, I wanted some fancy stockings for my French fashion doll. It was then I decided to create and design my own patterns.

I experimented with various materials and found T-shirt material was ideal, as it had stretch and soft weave and shaped the foot well; also, it was cotton.

I measured my doll's foot and tried making a pair. The size and shape was good, but the tops of each stocking needed a finished look. I decided to try a crocheted plain edge around and it worked beautifully. I also did a pair with a buttonhole stitch and that, too, was satisfactory. It was then I decided to do some fancy embroidery in colors to match the doll's dress. The doll was dressed and fitted with her stockings and when our doll group met and I showed my doll, everyone wanted to know where I bought the stockings. Bought — no indeed, I made them, and then told them of my experiment. I dyed a few sets in ecru, brown and red, fitted them to a cardboard form and they looked professional. I measured my dolls, and made various patterns for different sizes of dolls and sketched designs for embroidery. Three patterns are illustrated with designs I used along with my sketches of high and low shoes and how fancy embroidery complemented them.

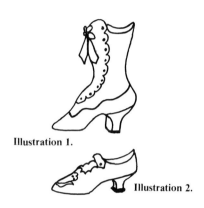

Illustration 1.

Illustration 2.

PATTERNS: (cut two on fold)
FOR DOLL
12in (30cm) to 14in (36cm)

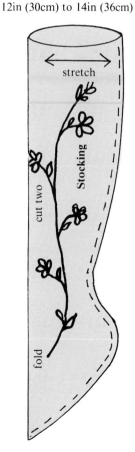

stretch

Stocking

cut two

fold

16in (41cm) to 20in (51cm)

stretch

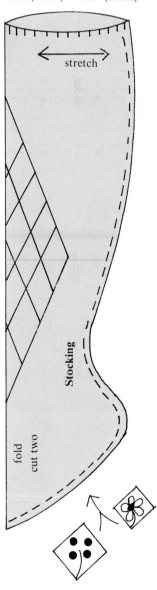

Stocking

fold

cut two

Stockings can be made in any length or width, plain white or dyed colors, also in plaids or stripes as illustrated in old fashion magazines. Color combinations of embroidery can be on the middle ankle section of the stocking or on the side. Low cut shoes can take most designs, but a high cut shoe must have fancy work to show above the shoe.

French dolls lend themselves to elaborate costumes, accessories, hair styles and hats — and yes — fancy stockings. Small mesh materials can have gold or silver thread needlework and tatting can be stitched for flower designs. Keep designs simple and in scale, not to overpower but complement the costume. My dolls have taken on a special quality now that I make all my stockings. Next time you go to a doll show, observe a doll's stockings. Are they the run-of-the-mill purchase? Everyone loves a handsome well-dressed doll, and you will too. Like shoes, stockings make the difference, so make a pair and have your doll stand tall. You will love it!

STOCKINGS FOR ANTIQUE AND REPRODUCTION DOLLS
MATERIALS:
Stretch woven material (solid, plaid or stripe)
Sewing thread, color to match material
Pins and sewing needles
Scissors and pattern for stockings
Thin but firm gray cardboard

DIRECTIONS:
Trace pattern for stockings, and cut shape out with scissors. Pin pattern to folded material, cut two stockings per pair. (Cut pattern on stretch of material from side to side, to allow material to fit legs.) Sew seams up on sewing machine, using tight stitches, turn. Finish tops of stockings with buttonhole stitch. Tops may be crocheted if desired with a simple crocheted edge. Also, tatted flowerettes may be carefully stitched to the stockings and leaves and vines embroidered to give a classic quality stocking.

EMBROIDERY OR NEEDLEWORK ON STOCKINGS:
Glue stocking pattern to thin but firm gray cardboard, cut out and use this to firm shape of stocking. Insert cardboard inside stocking, sketch design for embroidery, or use freehand stitches in design. The cardboard prevents stitches from going to the opposite end of stocking. Embroider one on left side (top) of stocking, and one right side, so the standing finished doll will have outer sections of legs showing embroidery work.

Appliques may be stitched, using the same cardboard to fit stocking. Tiny beadwork, sequins and other ornaments may be used, according to type of costume.

22in (56cm) to 28in (71cm)

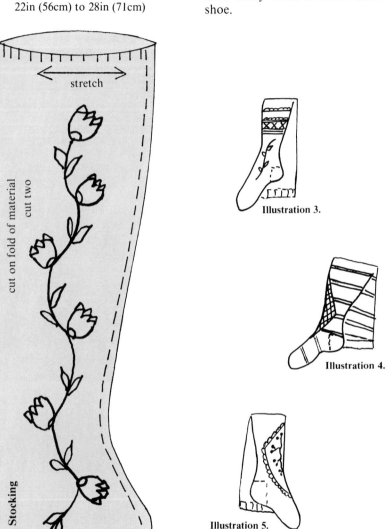

stretch

cut on fold of material
cut two

Stocking

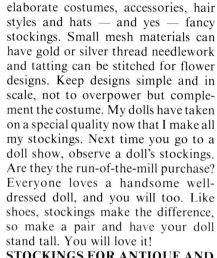

Illustration 3.

Illustration 4.

Illustration 5.

Illustration 6.

DOLL MAKING:

PORCELAIN DOLLS:

Make Your Own Doll Collection: *Princess Elizabeth*
by Artie Seeley

Make Your Own Doll Collection: *Shirley Temple* Doll
by Artie Seeley

How to Model a Doll Head
by Martha Armstrong-Hand

"La plus elegant jeune femme de France"
by Joan Erdman

Royal Heir
by Lauren Welker

How To Make An All-porcelain Doll
by Marie L. Sitton

Cleaning Greenware
by Marie L. Sitton

Make Your Own Doll Collection: *Bye-Lo*
by Artie Seeley

Make Your Own Doll Collection Princess Elizabeth

by **Artie Seeley**

Photographs by **William Seeley**

Many different stories are told about the dolls we are making today. I find the one about this doll most interesting. Supposedly there are very few of the originals and I cannot help wondering how they escaped into the public domain.

You see, this one is called — and very clearly marked on the back of the head — "Princess Elizabeth" (**Illustration 1**), and was made without the permission of the Royal Family of England. I have been told the molds were ordered destroyed. How a few of the finished dolls escaped and got to this country makes me wonder. There could be some interesting stories told!

She is not the prettiest doll I have even seen as the head seems too large for the body. Still I know the head and body mold were both made by Byron Mold Company, since I was with "Elizabeth's" new owner when she bought her. The original doll is on display at American Beauty Ceramics in Willoughby, Ohio. I know this doll we are now making is an exact copy... and oh my, she does grow on you!

The body is cast and all of the necessary holes for stringing are drilled.

Illustration 1.

It is a very simple body to make as there are just two legs, two arms, and one torso, with no knee, wrist or elbow joints.

The porcelain must be cast rather thin or the possibility of cracks, because of the size, are greater. Clean the seam lines and it is ready for the fire. I suggest a slow fire for these pieces, possibly on a bed of silica sand or porcelain prop. They are quite large and the silica sand or porcelain prop makes a good support, allowing the pieces to shrink while in the kiln by apparently floating on the grains of sand. Fire to Cone 6. Personally, I buy composition bodies and save myself all the body work.

You are now ready for the head. Carefully cut the eyes; they are rather small, yet clearly defined. Cut around the inside edge with an X-Acto blade, working on leather-hard clay. Gently tap, and if necessary, cut deeper. This method of pushing the piece out will sometimes break the clay inside the eye in layers. You are lucky if this happens as it helps form the bevel you will need to fit an eye in later.

Using a Kemper tool, cut the bevel inside the eyehole. If your Kemper tool is not the right shape, try bending it into an almost quarter circle, using a very fine file or hone to sharpen both edges of your blade.

My size six brush is a round sable; it does all the smoothing around the eye. I can press it flat with my finger and it will cut a tiny point I want on the inside and outside corners of these

Illustration 2.

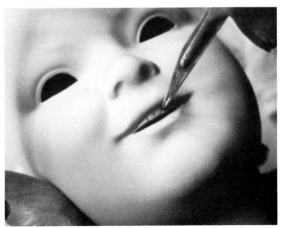

Illustration 3.

Illustration 4.

Illustration 5.

almond-shaped eyes. My other brush is an old size eight water color brush, very floppy and soft. It sweeps around inside the eye and works gently back and forth until I have just the right shape I want.

Try the eyes into the opening for fit; you know that if an 18mm fits now, a 16mm will fit the hole after it has been fired. Try both round or flat; see which gives the best fit.

The mouth is next. It is possible to cut the mouth opening and, I guess, you can buy teeth to put in later, but it is fun to try this. Cut a very small slit along the lower lip (**Illustration 2**). Keep working until you have a fairly good opening. I hope your clay is cast thin, as it makes this work much easier. Now I look inside the head. See the slit you have cut in the mouth? Use your curved Kemper tool to reach inside and cut away some of the thickness. A

little smoothing with a wet floppy brush and now back to the outside; use the damp sable brush (it is a bit stiffer) and poke into the opening back and forth, leaving a ridge under the upper lip for the teeth to be carved in later. Cut the opening to a tiny point on each side of the lip and smooth.

Using the point of an X-Acto blade, cut a center line to separate her two front teeth (**Illustration 3**). On each side cut another line, very gently, and she has two front teeth. Two more cuts and she has four teeth, with one more showing on each side. Using the tip of the sable brush, work gently into the lines, cut deeper if necessary, and see what a lovely smiling mouth you have made!

Finish smoothing all seams and you are ready to sign and date your head and put it into the kiln! Fire to Cone 6.

The next step is china painting. I wish you could all see the larger-than-real photograph of this doll in the picture book, *Originals of Yesteryear*. It is just great to have a large color photograph to work from. The eye shows about 20 upper and lower eyelashes. They are rather short and slanted. The actual color is black and very fine (**Illustration 4**). Try dipping your brush into turpentine, then work it in to the edge of your black china mixture. The turpentine will carry the paint longer and you should get all 20 strokes around the eye without refilling. The lower eyelashes are slanted outward also. After the eyelashes are finished, use a larger brush filled with black and run it around the inside edge of the eye opening. Just a quick swipe and the eyes are done. Add a tiny spot of red at the inside point of the eye and you are ready to paint the eyebrows.

For the eyebrow use capucine brown (red brown). To make them like the original is rather difficult as they are done in long curved strokes. I have to use my little finger as a crutch or my lines would be all over the place.

Let us start the eyebrow by making a dot (with a pencil) at the beginning of the eyebrow and another and another (**Illustration 5**). Now stroke from dot to dot with your china paint. Make the line rather heavy at the center. Use a piece of tissue wrapped around your finger and blot two or three times. Use it as you would a blotter, then wipe off the brow so you have just a shadow of color to use as a guide line for the nice strokes you are now going to make for the finished eyebrow.

There are about three long strokes, then about eight more getting shorter, starting with the bottom strokes. The lines appear to be almost fan-like,

Illustration 6. "Elizabeth" on a commercial composition body.

Illustration 7. "Elizabeth" dressed the way a little princess might have been dressed. Costuming by Marie.

Illustration 8. "Elizabeth" dressed the way a little princess might have been dressed. Costuming by Marie.

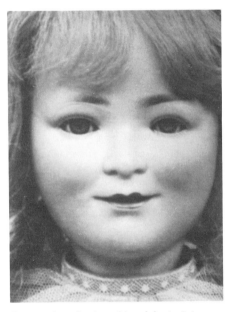

Illustration 9. An old original *Princess Elizabeth.*

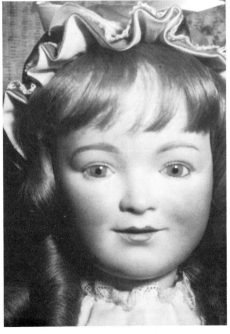

Illustration 10. A reproduction *Princess Elizabeth.*

emanating from the front of the eyebrow line. A few very short faint lines are at the start of the eyebrow, making them very close together (**Illustration 5**). I think it is the eyebrows that give her face so much character...so work at it! I am sure there are other original dolls out there and the eyebrows will be different; so if you make your lines for the eyebrow in your usual way, she will still be lovely.

Her mouth is very thin, the lower lip especially so. The upper lip is elongated. Carry the color right to the edge where the lip is cut to a fine point. Do the same with the lower lip. Be very careful not to get any color on the teeth. Even though the head is cast in flesh and the teeth are the same color, they will appear white (natural) when the lips are painted. Be very careful. Smooth the color on the lips with a small flat brush or a small stipple brush. You can cut an old brush off until the hair is about 1/8in (.31cm) long and it will do a nice job of smoothing for you. Wipe some of the paint off the stipple and touch lightly on the outer edge of each nostril. This will make a very light shadow right where you need it.

Next come the cheeks. Put a small amount of tinting oil on each cheek. Spread it all over the cheeks and wipe it quite dry with your fingertip. Pick up some lip color on a small pounce made of cotton wrapped in a piece of chiffon and, starting quite high on her cheeks, spread the color evenly and naturally. For a true English complexion, add a little more color and blend. She is really quite rosy.

At this time I usually use the pounce to put a faint blush of color on her chin, nose and forehead, and she is ready for her first china fire, Cone 019 — in my kiln I find Cone 018 makes my red color quite dark. The hotter the fire, the darker the red will be.

To finish the head properly, it will need one more fire. I like to wipe a faint shadow over the eyes. Maybe the cheeks need to be a little brighter. Make a tiny partial outline of lip color on the points of the upper lip and across the edge of the lower (**Illustration 4**). Fire again to Cone 019 and she is ready to assemble.

Illustration 6 shows "Elizabeth" on a commercial composition body.

Illustrations 7 and **8** show "Elizabeth" dressed the way anyone's little princess might have been dressed. Costuming by Marie. □

Make Your Own Doll Collection:
A *Shirley Temple* Doll

by **Artie Seeley**
Photographs by **William Seeley**

I do not mean this article to be an apology; somehow making a *Shirley Temple* doll out of porcelain just does not seem right and I have argued with the idea for some time. Then, within the last few months I have seen, of all things, a porcelain *Barbie*® doll. Not only that, but the price was $500.00! Well, my good sense tells me that if a *Barbie* doll made of porcelain is a collectible, then a porcelain *Shirley* would certainly hold her own in the world of collectors! So, for those of you who have asked for her — here is *Shirley*!

Cast the head thin so that the eye and mouth trimming will not be difficult. When the clay (porcelain) is cast

thick, it requires too much work and often the true shape is lost and so is any resemblance to the original doll. Work with wet or leather-hard clay. If your clay is leather hard, it will not change shape when you are working on it. Too much force or pressure, however, will cause it to crack. I find the clay stronger and less apt to crack if I do all the work when it is leather hard. Dry clay seems to be so fragile that I cannot work on it at all; also, there is no dust with damp clay.

This is a dome head and you will have to cut a portion from the top in order to put in the eyes. Make this cut large enough for three fingers; this area will shrink in the firing, but you must

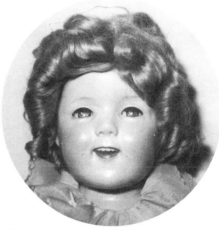

Illustration 1. An "old" *Shirley Temple* doll.

still be able to get two fingers, plus an eyeball through the opening.

Do not make the opening any larger than necessary as the clay is thin and there is no supporting edge; a large opening may cause the head to warp in the fire. This could change the shape of the eyes and might pull the face out of shape, too.

Shirley's mouth is open with a slight smile. The shape of the open mouth makes it impossible to cut teeth. Start by cutting a rounded shape on the lower lip and on the upper and force this football shape out gently,

Illustration 2. Three commercial *Shirley Temple* dolls from the "past."

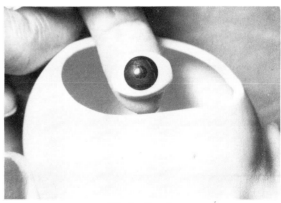

Illustration 3.

thus opening the mouth. Her lips are very thin. Smooth the opening on the outside and scrape some of the clay from the inside. You do not want the teeth set too far back from the opening, as it would not look like *Shirley*. Smooth both the inside and the outside with a swipe of a wet brush and she is ready for teeth.

Illustration 5 shows a scrap that was cut from the eye. Trim the lower edge of this piece, making it straight across. Wet it and reach down inside the head and press this piece where the teeth should be; it should fill the opening a little more than halfway.

Working on this piece from the outside of the mouth, make a center cut, carefully measure a space on each side and then another and you will see six teeth taking shape. Cut gently, each line a bit deeper; wet a pointed sable brush and cut even more deeply. You may even try to separate them. If you should break a tooth or a corner, it is a simple matter to pick up a very wet drop of clay on a tiny brush and rebuild the broken area.

Smooth both back and front. If necessary, bevel behind the teeth, working from the outside of the mouth with a brush so the teeth do not look too thick.

Just as you see the knife blade working to bevel the mouth (see **Illustration 4**) use the same position to bevel the eyes.

Work very carefully at the corners so the eyes stay pointed and almond shaped. Smooth the eye opening with a damp brush; a too wet brush may melt the clay...do be careful!

At this point try an eye into the opening for proper fit. Moisten the tip of your finger so an oval eye will cling to it and reach down into the head opening. If it does not seem to be the

right shape, moisten two fingers to hold a round eye — perhaps it will be a better fit. If not, try trimming some more clay from the inside — wipe a wet brush across the inside for a better shape; carefully...and try again.

The next step is to clean the seam lines and tightly massage the face to remove any rough spots or finger prints. If you wait until the clay is dry, you can rub a piece of nylon hose over the surface to smooth and remove dust. Sign and date the head.

Place the head in the kiln on a bed of white sand and fire to Cone 6.

After the fire, smooth with a very fine grit; I use No. 220 Garnet sandpaper. Wipe free of dust and the head is ready for china paint.

Starting with the eyebrow, make a very fine line. See **Illustration 1**. It may be easier if you make three or four very light dots where the eyebrow is to go

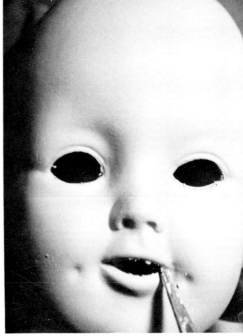

Illustration 4.

Illustration 5.

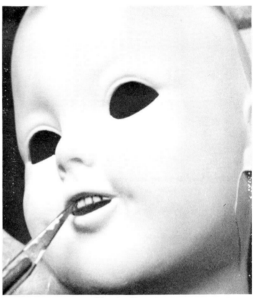

Illustration 6.

and follow the dots. The eyebrows will match better if you do it this way. Use a brown or a red-brown china paint. Be very much aware of the shape of her eyebrow. It follows the line of her eye. The eye is an oval almond shape and the eyebrow will follow this line. After applying the china paint, touch gently with a silk cloth or tissue to remove the heavy color and the eyebrow will be a delicate golden brown after it is fired.

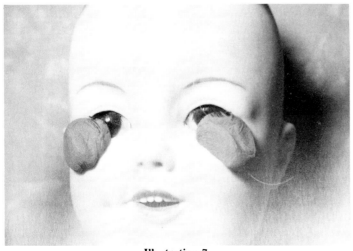

Illustration 7.

Illustration 8. Close-up of completed porcelain *Shirley Temple* doll.

Illustration 9. Porcelain *Shirley Temple* doll in "borrowed" clothes.

For the eyelashes, paint only the lower ones. Use black china paint and make fine lines, straight up and down like you see on most old German dolls. She will have real hair eyelashes attached later so there is no need to paint the upper eyelashes. Be sure to outline the entire eye opening with black china paint.

Her mouth is simple. She does not have full lips. The upper lip is an elongated M and the lower is a curved line joining the upper at the outer edge of the mouth (see **Illustration 1**).

Rouge her cheeks lightly by first touching the cheek area with a dot of tinting oil. Massage into the surface and wipe away any oily residue. Now "pounce" on a bit of color and blend, using either a puff of cotton in a piece of chiffon or blend with your fingertips.

Touch the tinted cloth to the tip of the nose and chin to highlight this area and blend.

Fire to Cone 019. Cone 018 is a slightly higher fire and may make the red darken. I found this out several years ago when my dolls were having almost purple lips and cheeks. Cone 019 seems to have corrected this color problem.

To prepare the head for final assembly...measure a piece of eyelash just a bit shorter than the space to be filled. Push the eyelash in from the outside of the head. A drop of glue will hold it in place. Do not worry about the length of the eyelash as you can trim it to the right length after the eye is set.

Now place the eyeball into the opening, center it and hold it in place with a small piece of modeling clay. Do the other eye the same way. Mix a small amount of plaster...starting with about two spoonfuls of water. Sift in the plaster (I use dental plaster), making a very soft paste (like thick gravy). Drop a bit on each side of the eye and another drop on the eyelash to hold it firmly to the head.

Now you have a porcelain *Shirley Temple* to dress as you wish. □

Barbie® is a registered trademark of Mattel, Inc.

How To Model A Doll Head

by **Martha Armstrong-Hand**

Illustration 1. Martha Armstrong-Hand starting to model a doll.

All sculpting, including sculpting a doll head regardless of the medium of execution, is a highly individual creative process.

Following are questions most asked by students and interested collectors during and after workshops given by the author. The answers come out of personal experiences and reflect her own present understanding.

How do you get started? What is your first consideration when you think of doing a doll?

I make a decision *who* my doll is going to be, then what size — and at that point I decide what my final media (the material of the end product) is going to be so that I can figure in change or shrinkage of material during the sculpture process. Further, I determine at this time what style I see my doll in (simplified, abstract, realistic, or cartoon). All these considerations I work out in paper, with drawings. I develop, more or less, the character of my doll at this time, fortified by research, to strengthen the image I had previously conceived, — be it with my own photographs of a person, magazine scraps or other graphic images. I try to find a model to fit my mental image.

There was a time when I started with a hunk of clay and an image, pushed it around until it began to look like something. Over the years methods have changed, but there always was an image first.

Do you measure your drawings?

I might first draw freely just to get character and proportions on paper — then I make an actual size drawing front and side view, in case I need an armature.

What is an armature?

The armature of sculpture is the skeleton that holds up the soft clay. It is a construct out of any material that would do this job. It could be wood, metal, wire, string, — even a wooden spoon, or a light bulb; most anything could become an armature.

I use a baseboard, a threaded flange screwed to it, pipes and couplings from plumbing. In the case of the head, I make sure the pipe, or rod going into it, is removable from the base for viewing from all sides, and working from different angles than just the stand. In addition, in order to hold the head in place on the pipe, I tie aluminum wire to the top, making sure the construct is smaller than my head.

What material do you work in when you make a doll head?

Now I model in plastilina, an oil clay. I used to use water clay, but it dries out if not covered — for simple forms I might still prefer it, as I did when I made puppet heads. Plastilina enables me to work small detail. There is nothing sacred or "right" about one material or another.

Didn't you say you worked in wax?

Yes, plastilina (or plasticene) is only the first stage of my modeling. Later, I complete my sculpture in wax, which is both carving and modeling.

When you start modeling your head, do you first make a basic shape?

No. I build up the form with malleable bits of (oil) clay. As I get nearer my imaginary form I use smaller and smaller bits to fill out holes. I measure proportions for structure and symmetry, noting relationships of height and width and location of eyes, nose, mouth and ears in proportion to the skull (head) and each other, according to my plan. That plan could be an image of composite impressions, a realistic portrait, or a simplified caricature.

Do you use your hands, or fingers when you model?

I start out with hands and fingers, but very soon I use a wooden spatula — not only to press the clay into place, but also to cut and make marks, as for instance a middle line, or line for eye height, or width, and so on. I work symmetrically, using both hands, and turn my work frequently.

Do you hold the head in your hand, or prop it up?

I usually start on a stand, looking at it at eye level, but have the armature designed in such a way that I can lift the head, with support, off the stand and lay it down, propping it on soft foam so as not to squash my form. I view it from the bottom, and also look at it from the top — and work on it while looking down.

Do you work with daylight, or artificial light?

In my studio, at the moment, I work with both daylight (filling the room) and artificial light - incandescent and fluorescent. When I start modeling, I usually have the artificial light in the middle overhead, but for detail and finishing, I move it around so as to see forms by creating different shadows.

How do you get the surface smooth?

I try to smooth out any form until it is complete. In other words, I complete the form by adding minute particles of clay with a tool that fits the form, and by so doing, my surface loses the holes. On large surfaces, as on the skull or cheeks, I sometimes pull the form together with old smooth sandpaper — small square pieces that fit in between my thumb and forefingers. When I work waterclay, I sometimes use a fine (elephant ear) sponge as used in pottery. All tools used for finishing the form should fit the curves of the form — as inside an ear or mouth, or rim of the eye, and so on.

How do you finish the top of the head — how do you know where the skull is?

I imagine it, drawing from the experience of seeing people's and children's skulls. To see a live child's skull, observe them in the bathtub; books on anatomy help — one can see the skull through the hair, too, sensing it —

feeling it. I sometimes model a portrait with hair first, then take off the hair to where I sense the skull, or head. I study people constantly, even when I am not modeling. I am particularly fascinated as to how the skull changes so rapidly from birth to the first year; the nose and eyes seem to stay in place as the skull and chin grow.

How do you find the size and distance of eyes?

Study and measurement of proportions help, but for a doll there are no rules so long as the eyes are focused. For that they have to have equal curves (from two equal balls) and the balls have to have their highest points touching an imaginary plane parallel to the front of the face. I used to work with actual balls when I was creating dolls with set-in eyes. Now I start with holes — the dark hole helps me to imagine an expression of the doll face. Then I carefully fill the hole symmetrically with eye-curvatures, usually after most

Illustration 3. Finished heads in Plastelline.

of the face is already in place, such as the size, nose, ears and so forth.

How long does it take you to model a head?

When I first started sculpting many years ago, after working three hours, I thought the head completed. Now it takes anywhere from three hours to a week, depending on how subtle or detailed I plan my head. There is no rule; I stop modeling when I like what I have created and there is life in it, and the eyes look at me!

What do you do when you do not like your head, and you do not know what to change?

I take a walk, bake a cake, or wait until the next morning when I am fresh. Usually after intense work, you get so used to seeing the forms that you cannot think or analyze. I find that after a good rest I see with new eyes. Often, looking down from the tip or up from the chin helps detect asymmetry or poor structure. I make myself look at outlines as I slowly turn the head — without naming nose or mouth, trying to see abstract forms, and comparing one side of the face with the other. It also helps to analyze people you like, dolls you like, pictures you like — thinking of imaginary plumb lines, comparative sizes within the face, and location of forms.

How do you know where to put ears, and how big to make them?

Regardless of realistic or simplified sculpture of a human head, there is an underlying structure (in real life, the skull). The ear is housing the balance; it is located on a plumb line from top of the head through the middle of the neck (with the head in an upright position). The top front of the ear is touching this plumb line — the lobe extends over the line. The size depends on the age of the person. Since you cannot see both ears at once, it pays to measure the location from the ground on each side. It is also helpful, when in doubt, to trace one ear on tracing paper — cut out the shape, and compare it to the other ear — making corrections with the cut-out or stencil. I personally make an ear to my liking and worry about mold problems or undercuts later. To model realistic ears takes a lot of practice — it is a complex free form, but we have the freedom to simplify them. Ears on a doll are like personal signatures. No two doll artists make ears alike.

Do you think anybody can learn to model a head?

Yes, The most important thing in modeling a head is to get started. Follow the image that was there at the start, keep it simple and complete the forms before you. If a new image comes to mind, make another head after completing the first one. Be patient. Understanding human heads takes a *lot* of looking, and modeling is a skill that takes practice just like learning to play musical instruments or learning to dance. □

"La plus elegant jeune femme de France"

by Joan Erdman

SUPPLIES:
Swivel head shoulder plate mold
French Antique porcelain slip
Slip thinner
China paint colors:
black matt, pompadour red, dark hair brown matt, fast drying medium, lash and liner oil
Brushes:
6/0 feature brush, 6/0 mini liner, No. 2 shader, No. 10 shader, No. 1 round bristle
Miscellaneous:
Wooden stir stick, plastic bucket, mold bands, mold brush, drill, DCL tool, razor knife, cleanup tool, No. 150 grit rubber scrubber, nylon stocking, 16mm eye sizer, 14mm glass eyes, denatured alcohol, turpentine, palette, palette knife, lint free cloth, popsicle sticks, cloth body, poly-fil, white glue, five minute epoxy, 2¼in (6cm) buckram pate, size seven wig, neck button, cotter pin, needle and thread, earrings.

She is one of the most elegant young women of France. *Renee,* a lovely closed-mouth Jumeau with her swivel neck and tiny pinched waist, is truly a must for the enthusiastic doll maker.

The Jumeau doll is one of the most sought-after by collectors. The originals are priced into the thousands, making it difficult for the collector to obtain. So let us make our own reproduction.

Of all the historic doll makers in the world, the French were unsurpassed with their impeccable taste. Especially Emile Jumeau, who insisted on the paramount of perfection on the creation of his dolls. Jumeau was awarded top honors time and time again for his standard of excellence. Not only were the Jumeau dolls superior in every way, but were dressed in the latest fashions of the day, consisting of rich silks and laces. Under the direction of Jumeau, style and flare were magnifi-

cently created by the couturieres from the house of Jumeau.

We will begin by preparing the French Antique porcelain slip. Use a clean wooden stir stick to mix the slip while it is still in the jug. Empty the contents into a plastic bucket; be sure to remove all of the slip from the jug and again mix very thoroughly. Porcelain slip should be the consistency of light cream If thinning is necessary, slowly add slip thinner until the proper consistency has been achieved. Up to one cap full per gallon is sufficient.

A properly prepared mold is also very important. The mold we are using consists of the head, shoulder plate, lower arms and legs. Open the mold and dust with a soft brush, making sure the mold is absolutely free of dust particles. Reband tightly.

Functional pieces need added strength, particularly doll parts. We are not interested in translucency when making dolls. The head and shoulder plate should be approximately 3/16in (.46cm) in thickness. Arms and legs are cast a little thinner than the head and shoulder plate; do not cast them solid. When the greenware no longer has a sheen, trim with a fettling knife. Open the mold and gently release all parts. Set aside to dry. When the head has firmed enough to handle, cradle it in your hand and drill a small hole in the center of each eye. While you still have the drill handy, drill a hole at each of the four corners of the shoulder plate. Since our little French miss is a lady of fashion, earrings are appropriate. Using a small drill, carefully place a small hole through each earlobe.

When all parts have completely dried, hold the head in the palm of your hand; outline the entire top and bottom eyelid line with a pencil. Using a DCL tool, groove over the pencil mark, going deeper little by little. Do not go all the way through.

With a razor knife, start cutting from the drilled hole in the center of the eye. Cut to the corners and upper and lower eyelid. The groove made previously will help to prevent chipping as you cut. When this has been completed, reach through the eye and bevel inside, both top and bottom with the razor knife.

Using a pair of calipers, measure the eye socket from the inside corner to the outside corner. This will give you the proper measurement for your eye sizer. The measurement for this particular doll is 14mm. Allowance must be made for shrinkage, since porcelain shrinks 15 percent; be sure to use the next larger size eye sizer which is 16mm.

Place a piece of nylon stocking over the ball end of the sizer and secure it with a rubber band. Place the sizer through the top of the head into the socket and with a rotating motion gently size, being careful not to push. A gentle twisting motion is all that is necessary. Use a bristle brush to smooth any rough edges along the lid line.

The best way to obtain a custom fit is to have the proper size eyes at your side while working. As you size, occasionally fit the eyes into the socket. This will give you a true picture as to the fit you are obtaining. You are fitting that particular pair of eyes for that particular head. This is true custom fitting and a very important procedure. When a pair of eyes are fitted into their sockets, they should fit like a glove. There is no room for guess work, as eye sizing is precision work.

With a DCL tool, incise between the upper and lower lips, using short strokes, being careful not to wear through the greenware. This will give definition and added expression which is extremely attractive.

A cleaning tool is used to remove the seam line from the head. Go over

159

the seam line with a No. 150 grit rubber scrubber in a circular motion wherever possible. A piece of nylon hose will remove scratches created by the scrubber. Smooth the entire head with your fingertips and dust lightly with a soft brush. Enlarge the neck hole slightly; remember shrinkage. Go back and recheck the head for blemishes, especially the cheek area.

Unsightly blemishes will interfere with the blending of china paint. Once the greenware has been fired, there is nothing to be done to correct the situation. A magnifying lamp is excellent for checkups. Clean the arms, legs and shoulder plate using the same method. The four corner holes of the shoulder plate should be enlarged to make ample room for attaching the body. The hole at the top of the shoulder plate where the head rests should also be slightly enlarged. Accent the fingers, toes and nails with the DCL tool. It is a good practice to deepen the grooves at the top of each arm and leg; this is where the cloth is attached and the deepened groove gives firm support. After rechecking all pieces for blemishes, fire to cone 6.

Sand the bisque with a No. 150 grit rubber scrubber and wipe all pieces with denatured alcohol.

Prepare your palette with black matt china paint mixed with eyelash and liner oil. Using a No. 1 round brush and working through the top of the head, fill in the sockets that were sized with the eye sizer. Now from the front, apply a fine line on the eyelid edge of both eyes, top and bottom. Be sure the top and bottom line meet at both inside and outside corners of the eye. The eye should be completely enclosed with this fine eyelid line. A helpful hint: load brush; place bristles through eye opening; rest ferrule on edge of eyelid; move brush from corner to corner. The ferrule resting on the eyelid serves as a guide, which keeps the brush steady and makes a tidy straight line of color.

Draw a pencil line as a guide for the eyebrows. Mix dark hair brown matt china paint with eyelash and liner oil. Using a No. 2 shader, place a shaded stroke just above the pencil line.

Mix pompadour red china paint with fast drying medium. Using a 6/0 feature brush, carefully paint in the delicate bow mouth. Do not overload the brush. To get the proper bow effect, keep the corners of the mouth thin. Bring the brush from the corner of the mouth up to form the first bow, dip, then make the second bow, then down to the opposite corner keeping the line thin. Fill the lip in with color. Blot with a lint-free cloth. Blend the color with a dry No. 2 shader. Follow the same procedure for the bottom lip.

With a 6/0 mini liner and pompadour red mixed with fast drying medium, apply a fine line in the crease above each eyelid. Keep the line fine and delicate. Place a dot of pomadour red in each nostril and blend with a No. 2 shader.

Apply fast drying medium to each cheek with a No. 10 shader; blot with a lint-free cloth. The cheeks should have a soft sheen of oil. A very wet look is an indication of too much oil. With a No. 1 round brush, apply dots of pompadour red mixed with fast drying medium to cheek; blend color with a dry shader. The outer edge of the color should be softly blended toward the center; the center will have stronger color. Do the same for the forehead. Using the color that is in your dry shader, blush under the chin and across the bridge of the nose. Oil tops of the hands and the feet; apply dots of color and blend with a dry shader. Color the fingernails and toenails lightly; blot with a lint-free cloth. Fire to cone 018.

Sand all pieces with a No. 150 grit rubber scrubber. Prepare black matt china paint with eyelash and liner oil and apply eyelashes with a 6/0 mini liner. To successfully complete eyelashes as authentically as possible, they should slant from the corner of the nose to the ear. French eyelashes are rather long but delicate, with long graceful tips. The eye should have the same amount of eyelashes for balance and be completely enclosed with eyelashes.

Pull a little black matt china paint into dark hair brown matt china paint and mix with eyelash and liner oil. Apply individual feathered strokes to the eyebrows. The feathered strokes go directly over the earlier applied shaded stroke. The French eyebrow is rather bold with many individual strokes.

Using pompadour red that is slightly thicker than a blushing mix, apply the little lip accents, one at the top of each bow on the top lip and two on the bottom lip, using a 6/0 feature brush. Bring up the cheek color with additional blushing at this time. Fire to cone 019.

After the pieces have been fired, lightly sand with a No. 150 grit rubber scrubber.

Just a note pertaining to the brushes used in this project. Always use one brush to apply color and a separate brush for blending. Keep the blending brush dry at all times.

Squeeze some glue from a double tube of five minute epoxy into a small container; mix well. Reach down through the head with a popsicle stick and apply epoxy to the eye socket. Holding the head in the palm of the hand, face up, reach down through the top of the head with a 14mm glass eye and fit into place. There will be a few minutes to make adjustments. Make sure the eye is looking straight on, hold securely until glue firms and eye locks into position. Do the same with the other eye. When the eyes are firmly fixed, soak a cotton ball with acetone and place one on each eyeball. This will soften any excess glue that has seeped through onto the eyeball. Use the DCL tool to scrape off glue making sure to remove the excess that has filled in between the eyeball and eyelid line.

Assemble the head onto the shoulder plate by placing a cotter pin through a neck button; place the unit down through the head with the cotter pin protruding out through the neck hole. Place the head on the shoulder plate allowing the cotter pin to go through the neck hole in the shoulder plate; turn upside down; place another neck button onto the protruding cotter pin and bend the ends of the pin with a pair of pliers. The head and shoulder plate are firmly attached; the head now moves freely.

Sew the cloth body and two cloth arms. Pass the bisque leg down through the neck opening in the body. Slide the leg all the way down into the cloth leg. Cloth is then attached to the leg groove with glue and heavy thread. Do the other leg the same way. After the glue has dried, turn the body right side out, bringing the feet through neck opening, one leg at a time. Very firmly stuff the legs to the bottom of the seat line. Stitch the legs closed, going straight across the bottom.

Stuff the body firmly with poly-fil. Insert a popsicle stick in the middle of the body to make the waist rigid. Be sure to pack the poly-fil firmly around the stick. Close neck and sew.

Place the bisque arm down through the cloth with the seam running down the palm. Slide the arm through the cloth to the groove at the top of the bisque arm. Apply glue to the cloth, wrap heavy thread around the groove and secure tightly. Do the other arm the same way. When the glue has dried, turn the arm right side out. Stuff the arms, leaving the top portion of the arms free of stuffing. Place the unstuffed portion of the arms on the top of the body, wrapping slightly around the shoulder in a natural curve. Arms will then hang down gracefully. Whipstitch into place.

Place piece of bias tape through each of the four holes on the corners of the shoulder plate; place the shoulder plate onto the body. Using straight pins, secure tape and sew to the body.

The shoulder plate is securely fastened to the body and completely covers the top portion of arms that were whipstitched into place. The arms are hanging from under the bisque shoulder plate.

Attach the earrings by inserting wire end of the earrings through the earlobes; position carefully. From inside the head, press the wire firmly against bisque. A little epoxy may be applied to hold the wire securely in place.

Using white glue, attach a 2¼in (6cm) buckram pate to the top of the head. Place a rubber band over the head and under the chin; when the glue dries, remove the rubber band.

Place beads of glue around pate; attach a size seven wig. It is important to select a wig that has been appropriately styled according to the motif of the doll.

An elegant French lady dressed in the finest satin and lace. A beautiful bustle and fru-fru hat reminiscent of days gone by. What more could you want? A lovely creation to enhance the collection of the most discriminating doll collector. □

Editor's Note: Mold, china paint and porcelain are by Bell Ceramics, Inc. Body and dress pattern are also available from Bell Ceramics, Inc.

Illustration 1. An elegant French lady dressed in the finest satin and lace.

Royal Heir

by **Lauren Welker**

Photographs by **Kervin Welker**

There is a certain magic in the birth of a royal baby. Perhaps it is the idea that this baby is set aside from all others by his special future, or perhaps it is the stream of "blue blood" flowing from the past connecting this child with history.

The birth of Prince William of England caught my imagination making me want to do something special to mark this event and so the idea formed of making a doll that would, for me, capture the idea of a royal child.

I quickly decided that my doll would be an all-bisque toddler. A baby in a christening gown would be old hat before I finished my doll. I also decided to add the tongue-in-cheek touches of a gold crown and rattle. My *Royal Heir* would have a five-piece body and be produced in a limited edition.

STEP ONE...THE MODEL

I used Sculpey for my original sculpture. My husband, Kervin, is my mold maker and he prefers working with a model that has been baked and is "set."

STEP TWO...THE WASTE MOLD

As I finished each piece I handed it over to "the master plaster caster" and he produced a set of waste molds.

The first set of molds will produce a usable doll, but generally the greenware taken from the first mold demands quite a bit of cleaning. Therefore, if an artist wishes to produce a number of dolls from a mold she will use the first mold to produce a refined working model from which a working mold is produced.

STEP THREE...WORKING MODEL

Porcelain makes an excellent working model but the shrinkage from the clay model to the fired porcelain model can be as much as 20 percent. To eliminate much of the shrinkage we decided to use ceramic clay for our next model.

Ceramic slip not only shrinks less, but it is also much easier to work with than porcelain. Although it does not have the smooth vitrified surface that is characteristic of porcelain, I find it very satisfactory for this step.

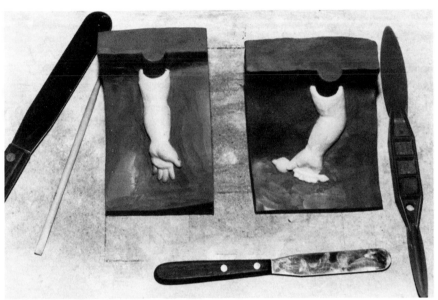

Illustration 1. The Sculpey arms are blocked in with soft clay before they go in the mold box.

Illustration 2. The arms in the mold box. Plaster is being poured in through a funnel. A mold piece will be formed in the area not blocked out by clay. Kervin decided to make separate molds for each arm on the working molds so the rattle would release.

STEP FOUR...WORKING MOLD

The refined and fired ceramic model is used to make the final plaster molds. Kervin has determined while making the waste molds just where the separation lines should be on each body part and how many pieces there will be in each mold in order for the greenware to release properly. It takes a set of six molds to produce this doll. The crown is a separate mold.

STEP FIVE..GREENWARE

Porcelain slip is poured into the molds. The mold must be very dry to absorb the liquid from the slip in order to form the shell that becomes the doll. After the liquid left in the center is poured out of the mold the greenware doll is removed and left to dry to the still-damp "leather" stage. The crown is then applied to the head using porcelain slip for "glue," the openings for the arms and legs are cut in the body, and the pour hole in the lower body is patched.

The pieces are set aside for a few days to dry. Then they are smoothed with a nylon stocking and the details are enhanced using various tools. Both in the original sculpting and in this step I find ordinary orange sticks (used for manicures) and round toothpicks invaluable. When all the pieces are properly cleaned they are signed, numbered and fired to cone 6.

STEP SIX...PREPARING TO PAINT

When you open your kiln after the first porcelain firing you find that a bit of wizardry has taken place. The dry fragile chalky parts have become hard beautiful porcelain. The surface is rough to the touch and must be sanded smooth before paint can be applied. This job usually goes to our son, Peter.

Since I will be using gold on this doll a special surface must be prepared. Where the gold will go, porcelain glaze must be applied and these parts must be fired to cone 2.

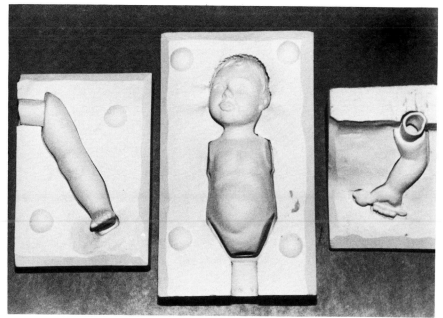

ABOVE: Illustration 3. Using a humble melon baller, we cut keys into the first mold piece before making the second. The keys will insure that the molds always fit together the same way.

MIDDLE: Illustration 4. Halves of three of the final molds showing the keys and how the pieces set in the molds.

BELOW: Illustration 5. The final step in painting.

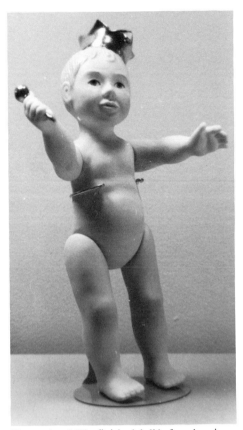

Illustration 6. The finished doll before dressing.

Illustration 7. The *Royal Heir.*

Illustration 8. *Little Princess* stands 8½in (22cm) tall without her hat.

STEPS SEVEN, EIGHT, AND NINE...PAINTING

I first apply blush to the tummy, elbows, hands, knees and cheeks (both sets!) and paint the lips, fingernails and whites of the eyes. The doll is then fired to cone 018.

I then paint the blue of the eyes, the eye crease, hair, add more blush, where needed, and fire again to cone 018.

For the final firing I add the pupils and eye detail, the eyebrows, and the gold crown and rattle, and fire to cone 018.

Many times I have read that you must fire each color separately. I do not find this to be true in an adequately vented kiln. I never crowd my pieces in the kiln and always leave the top peep hole open on an 018 firing.

STEP TEN...FINISHING

Doll putty is mixed and hooks are set in the arms and the legs. When the putty is thoroughly dry, the doll may be strung and dressed.

It was ten months from the time I started my first clay model until the first doll was completed. Of course, this is not the only project we worked on during that time. Shortly after I started *Royal Heir,* I felt that he should have a friend so I designed a girl friend for him. *Little Princess* is the same size, all-bisque, and dressed as an all-American cowgirl. I also designed a limited edition *Royal Heir* paper doll.

What next? Our current projects include a limited edition line of storybook characters in 1in (2cm) equals 1ft (30cm) scale. Completed are *Cinderella* and the *Wicked Witch.* We will try to add two more characters each year.

For people who want to read more about doll artists and how they work I recommend *Petite Portraits* by Carol-Lynn Rössel Waugh, Hobby House Press, Inc.

Anyone considering mold making can find a wealth of information in *The Complete Book of Pottery Making* by John B. Kenney, Chilton Book Co. Although this is not a book specifically for doll makers, the instructions on making a mold box and mixing plaster are very good.

Another interesting book is *Making Original Dolls and Molds* by Mildred and Vernon Seeley. □

How To Make An All-Porcelain Doll

by **Marie L. Sitton**

Illustration 1. Left to right: A *Gibson Girl*, Marque, Googly and a Jumeau.

Illustration 2. Supplies for pouring.

The first thing you need to consider is what kind of a doll you will want to make. If you want a good one for a collection try and pick a rare doll that is not commonly found on the market. Some good choices might be an early Jumeau, the Gibson Girl, a Googly or one of the Marques. If you are going to make more than 25 I would advise you to invest in more than one mold so the pouring could go faster.

You will need some equipment to get started. Have a box filled with shredded paper to put the finished pieces into. You will need a clean pitcher, doll flesh porcelain, multipurpose tool, detail tool, long handled spoon, large rubber bands, strainer, sable brush and, of course, your mold. Have a clean large flat surface to work on. I prefer to work outside when the weather is nice. Remember, you will not be able to pour on a rainy day. The molds have a hard time setting up and they will not release.

Before you start pouring your mold make sure it is clean and free of dust. Band your mold tightly closed with three or four rubber bands that are used expressly for banding molds. If your mold has a plug be sure one of the bands is holding it securely in place so the slip will not move the plug and spill out on to the table top.

Begin by mixing your porcelain right in its container with a long handled spoon. When it is well mixed, pour it through a strainer into your pitcher. Continue stirring until it is a good pouring consistency. If it seems a little thick you can add a little distilled water. Only add a tablespoon at a time so you can control the thickness. I like it the consistency of thick pancake batter.

You are ready now to pour your mold. Pour the pitcher of slip directly into the mold in a steady stream so as not to create any rings in the greenware. As it begins to recede, continue adding more slip until it fills to the top. This should take only a few minutes for a small mold. Leave the slip inside the mold for about five minutes. A large mold will require more time so be sure to check the walls of the mold for 1/8in (.31cm) thickness. (If I am pouring a *Hilda* body, I always leave it in longer so I have a heavier body to support the large arms and legs.) When the desired thickness is reached pour the slip back into the pitcher. Do not let the slip pour out too fast as it may cause a large casting to collapse. Let it set with the

Illustration 3. Band securely around plug.

pour hole down for a few minutes and then turn it right side up for about an hour.

Before removing the bands, take your multipurpose tool and remove the spare porcelain around the mouth of the mold. This will give you an indication of whether or not the mold is ready to open. It should be dry and remove easily. Remove the bands and lift the mold straight up. If it is ready it will open easily. Never force the mold open.

Let the greenware sit in the open mold while you check for holes and scratches. If you need to smooth anything out do so with distilled water and a soft sable brush. If you find an air hole fill it with a dab of porcelain slip. Be sure to smooth it out with a damp brush.

Sometimes a finger is broken when the hand is removed from the mold. This can be easily repaired by wetting each piece and, using the liquid slip as glue, stick it back on. Smooth it with a damp sable brush and it is as good as new. You can remove some of the seam line with your multipurpose tool also. This will make it easier to clean later on. Be sure to smooth it with your damp brush.

The arms and the legs have rims that protrude inside the body. Make sure there is enough rim there to extend inside the arm opening to insure that the doll's arm can stay in place and not slip out of its socket. If part of the rim was broken off when the mold was opened this must be repaired before it has had a chance to dry. Use the same method you used in repairing the finger. When repairs are done properly at this stage there is no harm done to the greenware.

After the pieces have been allowed to dry for a day they reach a stage called "leather hard." It is at this stage you can do the cutting out of the porcelain pieces without damaging effects. When you look at the top of the doll's head you will see markings where the head is to be cut out. To avoid warping in firing you may cut it out perfectly round instead of the half circle as shown. Either way is acceptable.

This is a good time to remove the open portion of the mouth and carve in the porcelain teeth. Be sure to smooth the area with your damp brush. If your doll has a chest plate or pierced ears you should now open the holes with a broom straw. Anything you can do at

Illustration 4. Straining the porcelain slip.

Illustration 5. Pouring a mold.

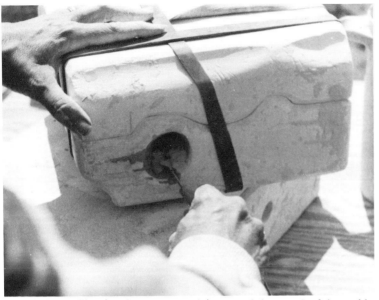

Illustration 6. Cleaning the spare porcelain around the mouth of the mold.

Illustration 9. Repairing a rim on an arm.

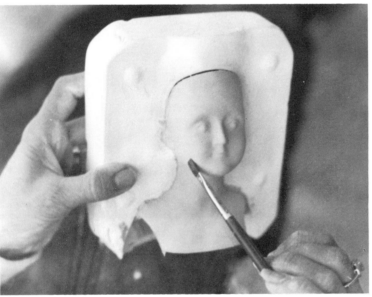

Illustration 7. Smoothing a scratch in greenware.

Illustration 10. Removing the head cut out.

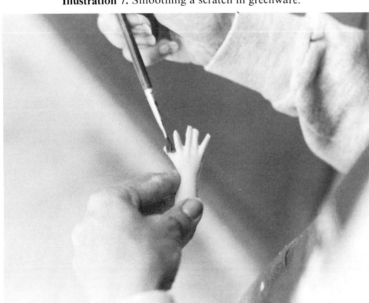

Illustration 8. Repairing a finger.

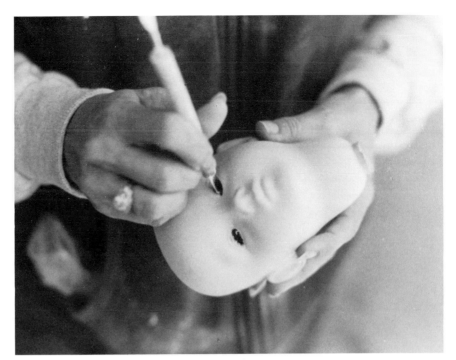

Illustration 12. Opening up the eyes.

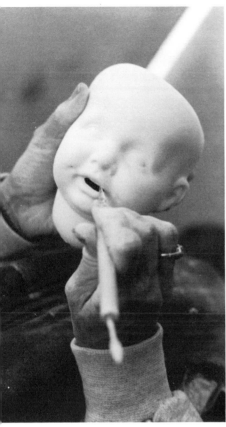

Illustration 11. Cutting in porcelain teeth in the greenware.

Illustration 13. Cushion your greenware.

this stage will cut down the time it takes to clean the greenware. Be careful not to squeeze the greenware.

If your doll is to have glass eyes take your detail tool and draw around the eyes where you want them opened. Now with your multipurpose tool carefully cut out the eye. (Some doll makers prefer an *X-Acto*® knife because it is sharper.) Try to make it almond shaped and be especially careful in the corners. When you have removed the center portion, take a damp brush and lightly smooth the edges.

Place all your pieces in a box cushioned with shredded paper and place it in a safe place that is warm and dry. Drying usually takes three or four days depending on the weather. Now take a little time out to clean out any particles of slip left in your mold. Reband the mold and put them away. If you take care of your molds they will last longer. □

Cleaning Greenware

by **Marie L. Sitton**

One of the most important steps in making a quality reproduction doll is cleaning the greenware. You cannot have a perfect doll if the seam lines are still visible and the roughness on its cheeks make the blushing blotchy. It is sometimes hard for a beginner to understand the importance of this, but after trial and error the determined doll maker will settle down and perfect these techniques. When you are cleaning your dolls take your time and enjoy what you are doing. Do not try to rush through. You will only be sorry later on.

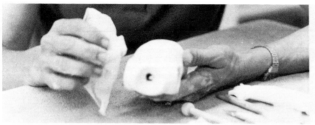

Illustration 1. Cleaning greenware.

Illustration 2. Beveling the eye socket.

Illustration 3. Opening the eyes.

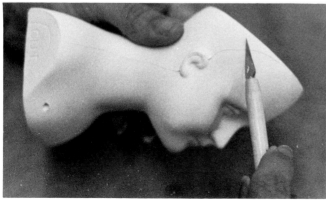

Illustration 4. Removing the seam line.

1. When your greenware is perfectly dry it is ready to be cleaned. The greenware should be separated in a box cushioned with shredded paper. Have a cleared table to work on with a bath towel to cushion your work. It will also keep down the dust. There should be no eating or smoking in the room, and you should have good ventilation. I recommend wearing a face mask to protect yourself from the porcelain dust while you work. If it is a nice day, and there is no dampness in the air, try to work outside. The light is better and you will not have to breathe the dust.

2. The first piece to start on is the head. This will take the most time so you want to be fresh when you start. The eyes are the most delicate so your attention should go to them first. They have already been opened so take out the correct eye sizer and start by beveling out the back of the eye. Choose a sizer one size larger than the glass eye you will be using. This will allow for shrinkage. Remember, greenware breaks easily so "cradle" it in the palm of your hand. Do not squeeze or grip it too tight. Secure a piece of nylon hose around the eye sizer with a rubber band. Rotating the eye sizer, clean out the back of the eye making a pocket for the glass eye to sit in. When it has been cleaned enough you will have a very thin ledge between the eye sizer and the eyelid. Do this before you work on making the eyes the same size in case you accidentally chip the eyelid. This would be disastrous if the eyelids were already finished. If a chip does occur at this stage you can usually even it out when you are opening the eyes and evening them out.

3. When the eyes are properly sized, work on the outside of the head making the eyes the same size. Measure the eyes and mark them with a pencil where the correct size is. Be sure to leave the lids on if the original doll (like a Marque) calls for eyelids. Take your X-acto® knife, hold it perfectly level and carefully remove the eyelid area until they are exactly the same size. Carefully take your bristle brush and smooth the edges. Now take a soft sable brush and smooth them so they are perfectly clean and smooth.

4. Now you are ready for the face. Remove any seam lines using a scraping motion with your cleaning tool. Take a piece of nylon tulle wrapped around a cotton ball and smooth over the area. Make sure the head is open enough to insert the glass eyes. Smooth the edges of the opening. Take a damp brush and go around the edge of the opening. This helps prevent cracking in the cone 6 firing. When you have removed all of the nicks and scratches, go over the entire head with a cotton ball. Use a magnifying glass to check for any imperfections. To clean inside the nose, ears and lips, you can use a cotton swab. You will be blushing the forehead and cheeks so check these areas very carefully. Incise the head with your name and date.

5. The hands are of next importance so start on the fingers. (If you have to repair one it can be drying while you are working on the rest of the body.) Use an LFM Kemper tool to open the fingers. It is a little saw that really makes cleaning between the fingers a lot easier. Do be careful not to cut too deeply, in case the hand was poured thin and you cut into the hollow inside. Use a flat bristle brush to sand the fingers. You will have a lot more control over the amount of pressure you apply. Fingers break very easy so go slowly and be very careful. Remove all seam lines, nicks and scratches the same as you did on the head. When the fingers are perfectly smoothed and shaped, redefine the fingernails. Go up under the fingernail and redefine where the nail separates from the finger. You will be blushing the hands so make sure there are no nicks and scratches. Use your magnifying glass.

6. Completely finish the arms and legs before you do the body so you will be able to fit them into the sockets. Finish the feet the same as the hands but do not try to separate the toes. Redefine the toenails, remove any seam lines and go over the piece with nylon tulle and a cotton ball. If the ears are pierced, make sure the holes are open. If you are doing a shoulder plate doll, make sure the sew holes are open enough to accommodate a needle and thread after firing.

7. When you are ready to clean the body have the arms and legs handy so you can make the body openings big enough to accept the body parts. The arms and legs should be able to move freely. When the openings are satisfactory, clean the edges with your bristle brush. Remove all seam lines, nicks and scratches the same as you did on the head and body parts. You will be blushing the tummy, breast and back so make sure these areas are perfectly smooth.

8. Now lay the complete doll out and make sure all body parts fit perfectly and move smoothly. Go over again with your magnifying glass and recheck all seam lines. Remember if you can feel the seam lines they are not removed properly. Take a small damp sable brush and go over the inside rim of the eyes. This will help set the eyes and prevent cracking. If you have followed all of these directions carefully, your doll will be a joy to paint. Load in the kiln immediately to protect pieces from breakage. Cushion all parts on kiln prop inside the kiln. Place prop in the opening of the body and head. Be sure they are free of any dust. Fire the pieces to cone 6. □

Illustration 5. Using a saw to open the fingers.

Illustration 6. Cleaning the feet.

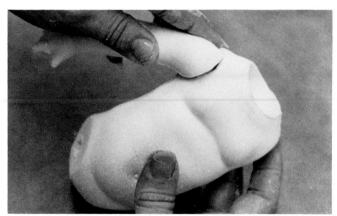

Illustration 7. Fitting arms and legs into the body socket.

Illustration 8. Load doll on kiln prop in kiln.

Make Your Own Doll Collection:
Bye-Lo

by **Artie Seeley**

Photographs by **William Seeley**

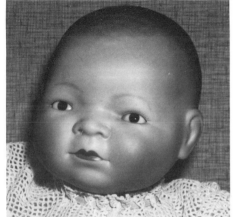

Illustration 1. Old *Bye-Lo* with 17in (43cm) head circumference.

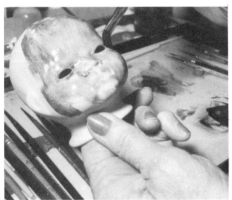

Illustration 2. Old doll in hand-crocheted gown from 1915 (ten years older than the doll).

Illustration 3. Applying stain.

The *Bye-Lo*, the newborn baby by Grace S. Putnam, is one of the most popular dolls in a collection today. Since I have given you all so much information in previous articles on "How To," there does not seem to be too much to say. However, it is very difficult for me not to find something to share, so here is the *Bye-Lo*, made in Germany in 1924. This head circumference is 17in (43cm); the one we are going to make is only 9in (23cm).

The eyes must be cut tiny, almost as though the daylight was too much; after all, she is only a few days old. Be sure there is no strain or stretch or crack showing on the seam line. Clean and fire to Cone 6.

Most of the old *Bye-Los* I have seen are quite ruddy (what new baby is not?). It really takes time to paint the whole head a baby hue; and, if you brush and smooth you can really make a big job of it. So here is how to do it the easy way. Mix about a quarter teaspoon of pompadour china paint with a non-dry oil. Pick up a floppy water color brush about size eight; dip it in the non-dry oil and stir it around in the paint until well loaded; now just (the only expression I can think of is) "slop" it on — all over the head; what a mess! (**Illustration 3.**) Pick up a soft cloth or tissue and wipe; wipe off all the color you can and wipe as dry as possible. You will find that the color you put on has stained the entire head a nice even shade. Compare heads in **Illustration 4.** If you think it is too dark, put a few drops of oil on a clean cloth and wipe all over again — satisfied? Fire to Cone 018 or 019. Earlier I mentioned to watch for pull or strain on the head when you remove it from the mold; obviously I did not and **Illustration 5** shares with you one of the heartbreaks of doll making, as this head had to be destroyed.

Now to china paint the features — short fine eyelashes are painted with a bit more oil or pull the color away from the original mass and it will be a lighter tone than pure black. (**Illustration 6.**) The eyebrows are rather close to the eyes; follow the bone structure and the shape of the eye; use light pencil dots to make sure the eyebrows match each other. Paint over the dots with brown paint; use a tissue to pat off the excess paint (**Illustration 7.**), press gently, do not smear; then rub until no more paint will come off and the eyebrow will look right. They show up very faintly and that is as it should be. (See **Illustration 1.**) Before you paint the lips, study the close-up. (**Illustration 8.**) The *Bye-Lo* mouth is like no one else's. If you paint a pretty mouth or full lips, you lose the whole *Bye-Lo* look; every time you see a real *Bye-Lo*, study the mouth. The lower lip is thin, sometimes almost square on the lower edge, and the upper lip rounds ever so little and comes out to long thin lines on the sides, making an elongated M. (See **Illustration 8.**)

Pat color on the cheeks and blend with your fingers or a puff of cotton wrapped in a chiffon or silk cloth. Then paint the hair; make an oily mixture of brown; spread all over where the hair grows; then carefully wipe off, using a clean area of cloth with each swipe. You will have a nicely stained area that is very pale and looks usually just like the old *Bye-Lo* hair. Hair on the old doll was air-brushed. Fire to Cone 018 or 019.

Make the body according to directions and stuff lightly. (**Illustration 9.**) □

Illustration 4. Stained and unstained.

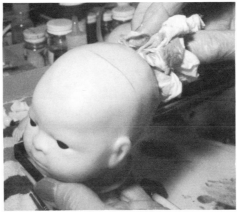

Illustration 5. Fracture shown.

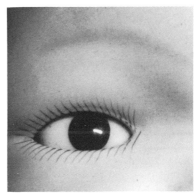

Illustration 6. Eyebrow and eyelashes of the old doll.

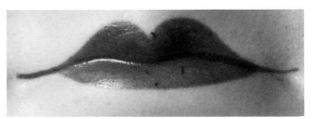

Illustration 8. Mouth detail of the old doll.

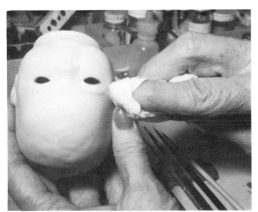

Illustration 7. Eyebrow shaping.

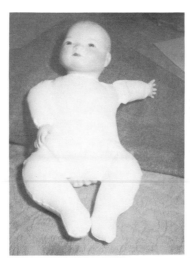

Illustration 9. Head on assembled body.

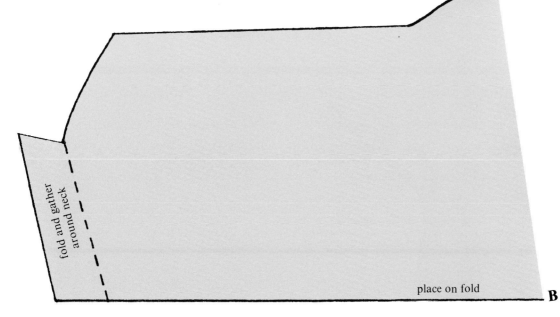

A

fold and gather around neck

place on fold

B

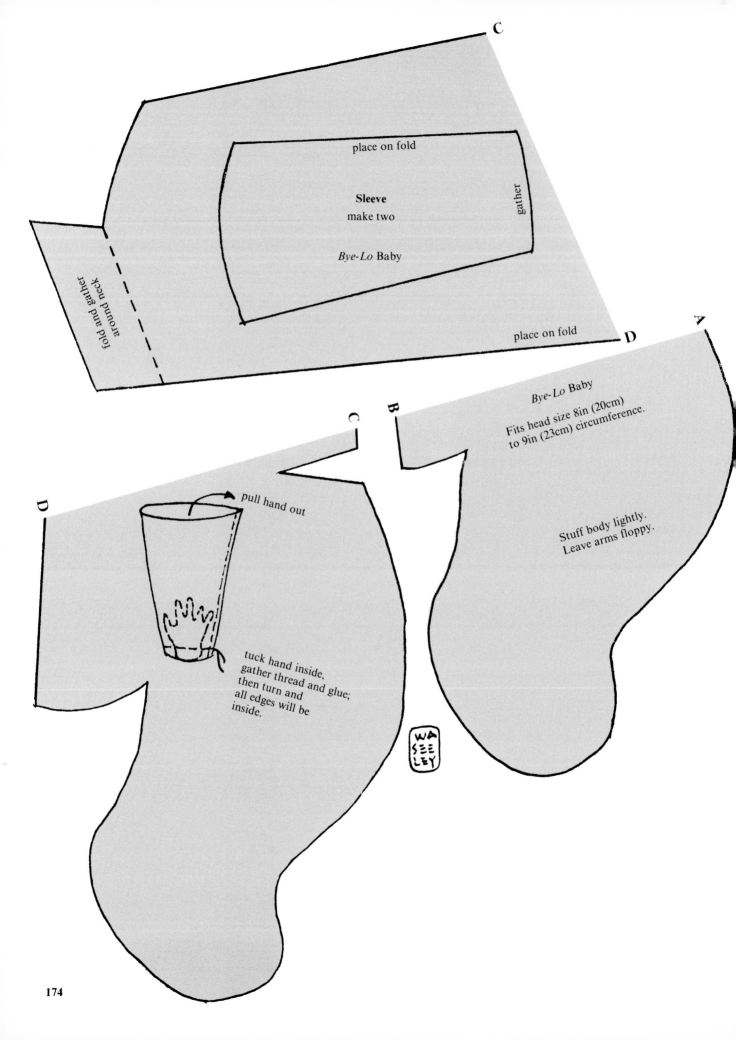

C

place on fold

Sleeve

make two

Bye-Lo Baby

gather

fold and gather around neck

place on fold

D

A

Bye-Lo Baby

Fits head size 8in (20cm) to 9in (23cm) circumference.

Stuff body lightly. Leave arms floppy.

B

C

D

pull hand out

tuck hand inside, gather thread and glue; then turn and all edges will be inside.

WA SEE LEY

174

DOLL MAKING:

CLOTH DOLLS:

Queen Elizabeth I — **A Cloth Doll**
   by Bette Wells

Christopher, **A Googlie-eyed Little Sailor Doll**
   by Doris Rockwell Gottilly

A Flapper of the Twenties
   by Bette Wells

Pincushion Dolls
   by Janet Carija Brandt

Gabriella, **A Painted-face Cloth Doll**
   by Patricia Wilks

OTHER MEDIA:

Pincushion Needlework Companion Doll
   by Doris Rockwell Gottilly

Queen Elizabeth I — A Cloth Doll

by **Bette Wells**

©Bette Wells — 1983

This doll takes a different approach to portrait doll making. The inspiration for this doll comes from an anonymous portrait of the Queen, circa 1593. Some of the areas of her clothing such as the skirt, parts of the bodice and facial features and hands are drawn on the fabric.

Other areas I have chosen to do more realistically such as the real feather fan, pearls at the neck, ears and head decoration. Others fall in between such as the beading done on the stuffed sleeves of her gown.

This method of keeping the outlines flat while building up others can be applied to any of your favorite portraits of kings, queens or even family ancestors.

If you wish, have the portrait enlarged by a photographer or perhaps less expensively — have a photocopy made of your favorite photograph; then have a printer enlarge the photocopy for you. The grid method could be used, too, to enlarge a photocopy.

Elizabeth has a very simple but effective wig method. The tight head-hugging curly wig that Elizabeth wore is reproduced in smaller form by embroidery floss in the French knot stitch.

MATERIALS NEEDED: unbleached muslin; black, yellow, brown and red markers with fine tips; yellow embroidery floss; stuffing; cardboard for base and neck; wide and narrow scalloped lace; eight medium beads; tiny beads of crystal yellow; beading needle and thread; narrow ribbon; small string of pearl roping and four small white fluffy feathers.

Transfer all pattern pieces to un-bleached muslin. I prefer to pin my pattern on the underside of the fabric. Then the whole is placed over a "light box." This is a box with a frosted glass top. A light bulb is turned on under the glass, thus making the pattern clearly visible through the fabric. If you do not have a light box, place fabric with pattern on a pane of glass during the day. Pattern will be visible through the fabric. With a fine black-tipped marker, outline all pattern pieces, including the broken cutting lines.

FACE: Eyebrows and eyes are brown. Eyelids, eye lines, pupils and line outlining nose are black. Upper lip is red. Lower lip is pink. When mouth colors are dry, draw a narrow black line through the lips to separate them. Add a white dot to eyes for sparkle. The hair is marked with yellow dots.

HAIR: Embroider hair in medium yellow French knots. Use three strands

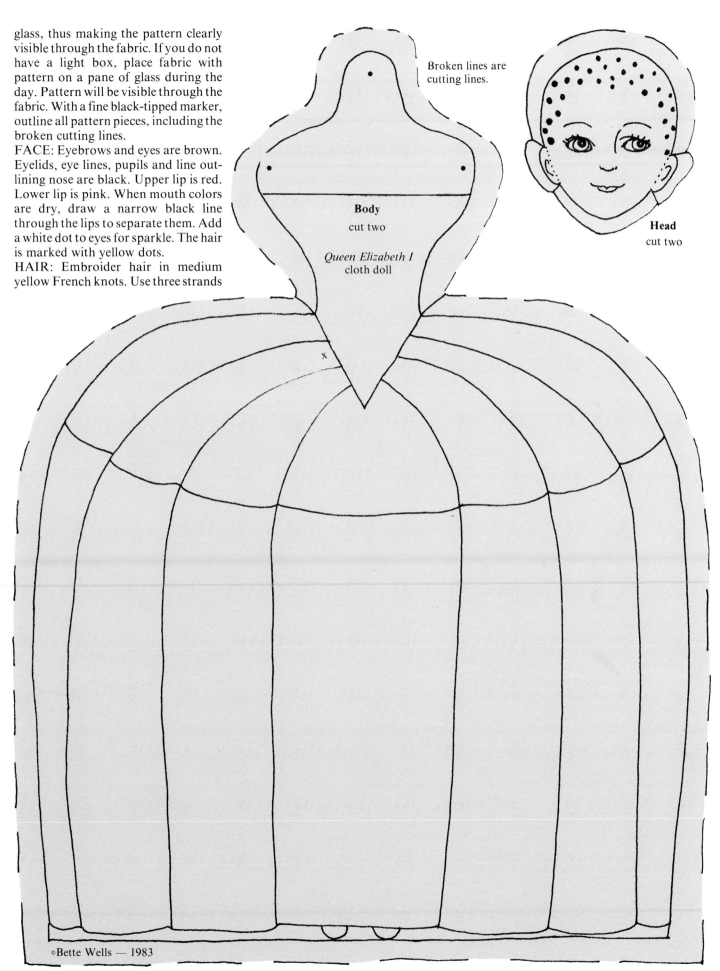

Broken lines are cutting lines.

Body
cut two

Queen Elizabeth I
cloth doll

Head
cut two

©Bette Wells — 1983

of embroidery floss. French knots should be worked closely together.

ARMS: Sew small beads to sleeves as indicated by dots on sleeves. I chose yellow but green or a mixture of red, green and crystal could be used.

Cut out all pattern pieces. Back of doll is blank. Adjust pressure foot on sewing machine so that little pressure is used when sewing the sleeves. Otherwise beads sewn to sleeves will be crushed.

Neck brace is cut from white cardboard. Do not forget to cut a blank back for arms, body and head.

Join all pattern pieces except bottom to skirt bottom. Leave an opening for turning and stuffing. Clip all curves. Turn right side out.

Stuff all body parts. Before stuffing neck, insert cardboard neck; then proceed as usual with stuffing.

BOTTOM OF DOLL: Cut out of white card, a bottom liner. Insert flat into bottom of doll. Hand sew bottom to doll's hemline.

CUFFS: Hand sew 1in (2cm) wide lace just above hands for cuffs. Choose a white lace that has a fancy scalloped edge.

FAN: Cut a piece of narrow red ribbon 16in (41cm) long. Loop ribbon in half. Sew raw ends of ribbon to queen's waist at X. Loop ribbon in half and tie in a loose knot. This way the queen could hold her fan and when she wanted to fan herself, she loosened the knot.

At end of ribbon — the end she will hold in her hand — sew several short white fluffy feathers. Sew hand so she is holding fan.

BODICE: Sew white or pale beige narrow ribbon to doll's bodice top and around waist following the V of her waist. At regular intervals, sew medium size beads to ribbon. Do not extend ribbon or beads to the back of doll.

RUFF: Cut scalloped edged lace 34in (86cm) long. Fold in half. Gather unscalloped edge to fit from shoulder to shoulder. Start at top of bodice, bringing around back and end at opposite side of bodice.

Several strings of pearls go around queen's neck and hang down front of bodice to the waist. More pearls and "jewels" are sewn to her hair, ears and fingers for rings. A small pink or red rose is sewn to left ruff front. □

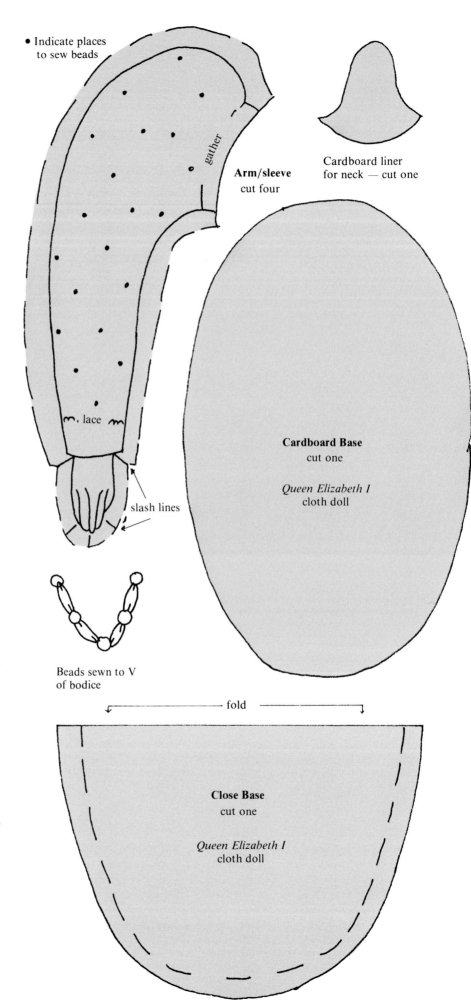

• Indicate places to sew beads

Arm/sleeve cut four

Cardboard liner for neck — cut one

Cardboard Base cut one

Queen Elizabeth I cloth doll

Beads sewn to V of bodice

fold

Close Base cut one

Queen Elizabeth I cloth doll

slash lines

lace

Christopher, A Googlie-eyed Little Sailor Doll

by **Doris Rockwell Gottilly**

Googlie-eyed dolls like Grace Drayton's *Dolly Dingles,* Rose O'Neill's *Kewpies* and *Scootles* and Horsman's *Campbell Kids* are favorites of many collectors. They all have in common a cute impish look with large round eyes glancing sideways. *Christopher,* the little sock doll, now joins this famous group. *Christopher* has large blue eyes, flaming red hair and an impish grin. He is yours to make, as easy as one, two, three, and add to your collection or to give as a gift, a soft cuddly doll in a winsome sailor suit of red plaid. Add a paper sword and a small wooden sailboat and he is ready for all sorts of sea adventures.

Read the instructions carefully and study the drawings and illustrations before beginning.

MATERIALS NEEDED:

Man's cotton work sock.

Red acrylic yarn for hair.

Needle, thread, scissors, glue, empty thread spool.

Dacron stuffing.

For costume: Piece of plaid fabric 21in (53cm) by 24in (61cm).

White cotton for collar and belt 10in (25cm) by 12in (30cm).

Black felt, 5in (13cm) by 4in (10cm).

Paints: Acrylic paints for face and hands — flesh, red, blue, black.

Two brushes, sizes No. 1 and No. 4.

Small piece of poster board, and pine board 12in (30cm) by 6in (15cm) by lin (2cm), 14in (36cm) dowel, white cotton sailcloth 12in (30cm) by 6in (15cm) by 2in (5cm).

The above materials can be found in department stores, art and craft shops and fabric shops.

MAN'S WORK SOCK:

1. Cut out arms, legs, body. Sew; turn; stuff arms and legs.

2. Stuff the head about 4in (10cm) down from top; slip in empty spool for

Illustration 1. 17in (43cm) *Christopher,* an original sailor doll with flaming red hair and a red and blue sailor suit by Doris Rockwell Gottilly.

LEFT: Illustration 2. *Christopher* showing body construction and pieces to his sailor suit costume.

neck. Tie with thread before painting head with acrylics.

3. Paint head and hands (three coats of flesh paint).

4. Attach arms and legs.

5. Make wig (see illustration). Glue to top of head.

HOW TO MAKE WIG.

1. Wrap red yarn 45 times round a piece of poster board 3in (8cm) by 9in (23cm).

2. Cut at both ends keeping the yarn smooth.

3. Put a piece of wax paper under the yarn and sew down the center for center part. Use red thread on machine.

4. Glue to the top and sides of *Christopher's* head. Trim as in illustration, allowing for bangs.

HOW TO MAKE BODY:

1. Stuff head until 9in (23cm) in circumference.

2. Measure approximately 4½in (11cm) down from top of head for neck. Using needle and thread and starting from back of head, stitch, using tiny basting stitches and gather gently, all around neck, finishing at the back. The neck should be about 5in (13cm) in circumference.

3. Insert empty spool into body, after head has been stuffed. Wrap thread around spool for neck.

4. Stuff rest of body until waist measures 10in (25cm) in circumference.

5. Paint face and hands with flesh paint (three coats).

6. Paint on features.

7. Apply matte varnish to face and hands.

8. Make wig and glue to top of head. Hold on with rubberband till glue is dry. Trim yarn like illustration.

9. Make costume (paper sword, and wooden boat, optional).

10. Make black felt shoes (see pattern).

COSTUME

Use a pretty red and blue cotton plaid.

Cut out patterns pieces, and assemble and *sew using 1/4in (.65cm) seams and 1/2in (1.3cm) hems at legs, wrists and neck.*

Attach snap to back neck opening.

Sew collar and turn and press.

Sew belt, turn right side out and press.

Topstitch with red thread using a straight stitch or decorative stitch.

Cut out felt shoes and sew.

Paper Sword and Wooden Sailboat

Cut sword from poster board.

Paint and decorate with acrylic paints.

Tuck into *Christopher's* belt.

Boat

Cut pine board to shape in drawing.

Glue a 14in (36cm) dowel as shown.

Glue and wrap sail to dowel.

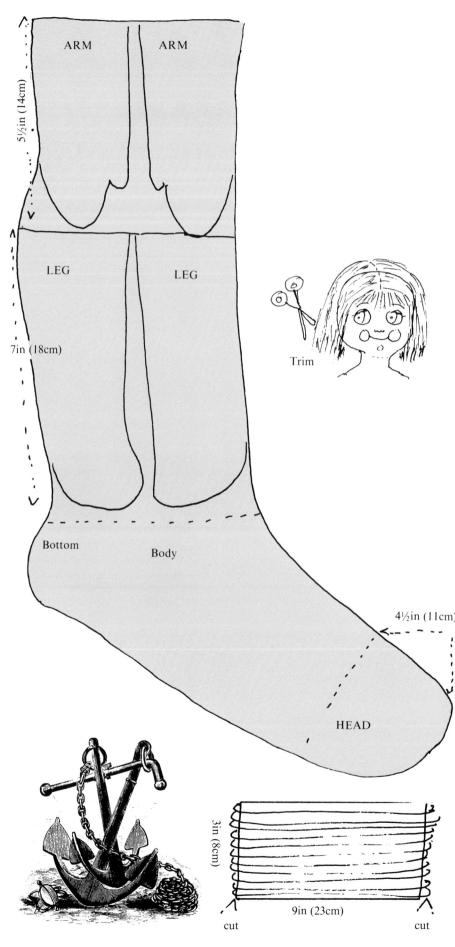

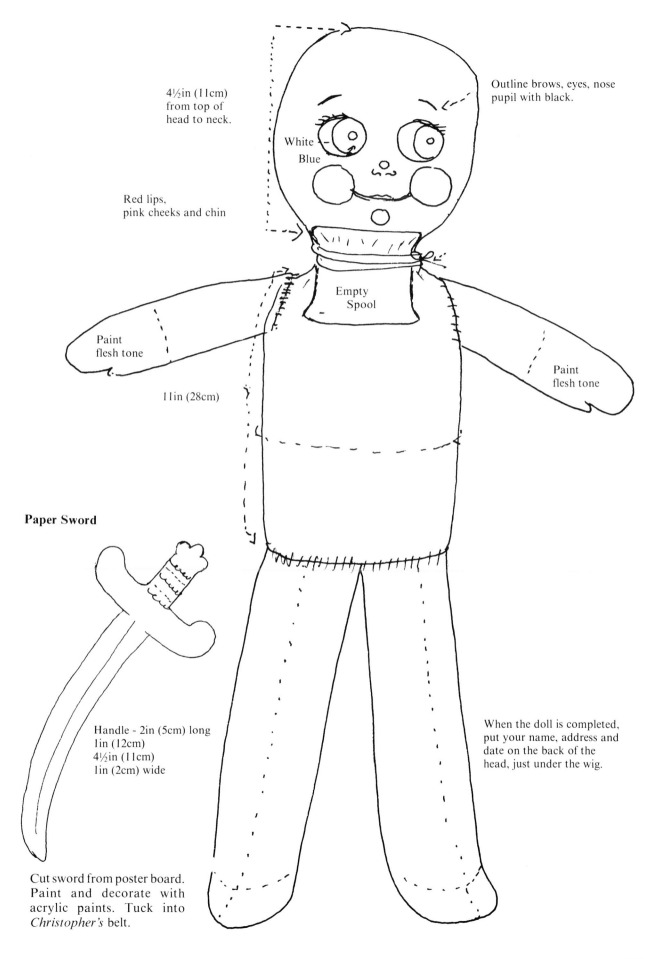

4½in (11cm) from top of head to neck.

Outline brows, eyes, nose pupil with black.

White
Blue

Red lips, pink cheeks and chin

Empty Spool

Paint flesh tone

Paint flesh tone

11in (28cm)

Paper Sword

Handle - 2in (5cm) long
1in (12cm)
4½in (11cm)
1in (2cm) wide

When the doll is completed, put your name, address and date on the back of the head, just under the wig.

Cut sword from poster board. Paint and decorate with acrylic paints. Tuck into *Christopher's* belt.

COSTUME
Use a pretty red and blue cotton plaid.

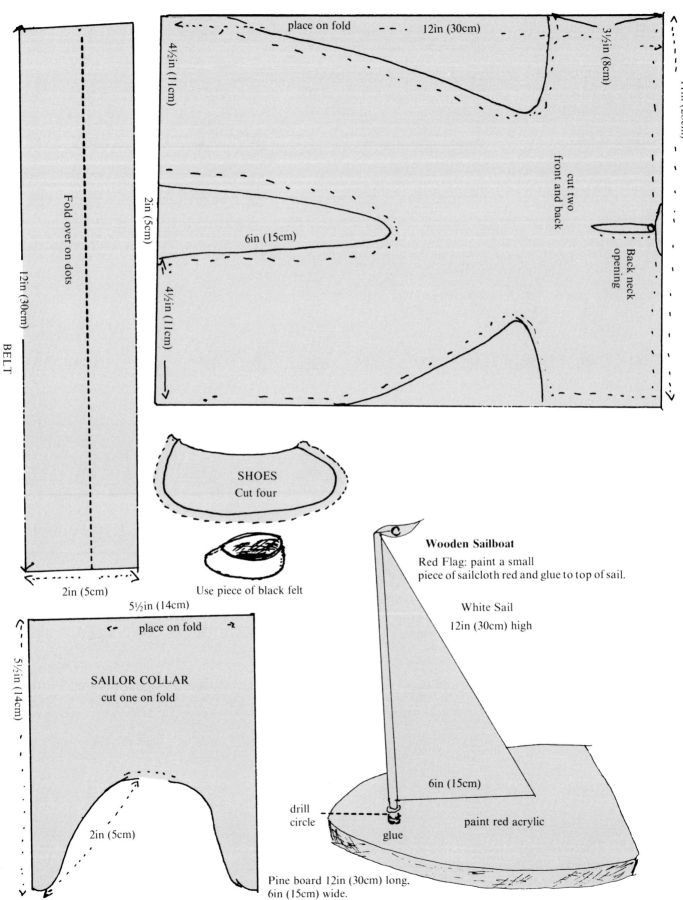

BELT

Fold over on dots

12in (30cm)

2in (5cm)

place on fold

12in (30cm)

4½in (11cm)

6in (15cm)

4½in (11cm)

3½in (8cm)

11in (28cm)

cut two
front and back

Back neck
opening

SHOES
Cut four

5½in (14cm)

Use piece of black felt

SAILOR COLLAR
cut one on fold

place on fold

5½in (14cm)

2in (5cm)

Wooden Sailboat

Red Flag: paint a small
piece of sailcloth red and glue to top of sail.

White Sail
12in (30cm) high

6in (15cm)

drill
circle

glue

paint red acrylic

Pine board 12in (30cm) long,
6in (15cm) wide.

182

A Flapper of the Twenties

by Bette Wells

Illustration 1. A cloth Flapper doll from the 1920s. This doll was inspired by a doll at the Museum of the City of New York, New York. The original doll is commercially made; from the 1920s; has a pressed cloth face with painted features; ostrich plumes decorate her hair and make up her fan; wears a neck collar; dress consists of several rows of fringe; body is pink sateen fabric and hair is mohair. This doll wears satin and lace tap pants, nylons with garters and high heels and is shown wearing her "shimmy" dress.

This Flapper doll is ready to Charleston from her satin and lace tap pants, nylons with ribbon garters and fringed dress, to her headband and feather fan.

The Flapper represented the changing roles of women. Clothing became shorter, unstructured, flashy and revealing. The restraining corset was done away with while women began smoking and added short hemlines to their wardrobes. A great deal of clothing would be right in style today. Lounging pajamas, evening gowns, even silky teddys would be just as "right" today as they were in the 1920s.

To make doll, cut all body pieces from muslin.

Face is colored with marking pens, pencils and Craypas, a type of pastel crayon.

Eyebrows, eyelids, eyelashes and eye crease and nose are marked with a black marking pen. The iris of eye is outlined in a clear blue marking pen. Eye is filled in with a paler blue pencil called "Sky Blue." This produces a very luminous, lively eye. The pupil is black marking pen. A dot is left uncolored for eye sparkle.

Lips are a bright red, colored with pen. Note area on upper and lower lip has been left uncolored. As a result, lips will look shiny and lush. When red is dry, stroke a narrow black line between lips to separate them. Allow face to dry before assembling.

Join all body pieces. Turn right side out. Lightly stuff face. Insert cardboard insert into neck and tightly stuff rest of body. Sew arms to body at X. Legs are slipped into hips and stitched in place.

Rub pink pastel crayon on a clean sponge. I use clean eye makeup sponges that come on little sticks. These are sold at makeup counters. Stroke on Flapper's face for cheek bones. Brown pastel is stroked over eyes. Refer to face pattern and illustration.

Illustration 2. Shown here from left to right: Construction of doll's tap pants; nylons on doll's leg, back view of leg; basic doll's body; "shimmy" dress; headband with feathers.

TAP PANTS: Cut from satin or similar fabric. Hem waistline and leg openings.

Join inner leg seam. Cut lace trimming 2½in (6cm) wide and 4in (10cm) long to fit leg opening. Sew lace to leg opening, both front and back pieces. Hand finish raw edge of lace. Join side seams. Sew a gathering stitch around tap pants waistline. Put on doll. Pull up gathers to fit doll's waist. Tie off thread.

NYLONS: Cut from lady's nylon hose. Lay pattern on folded nylon leg; do not pin. Cut out. Starting at toe, roll edges of nylons together. With matching thread, sew rolled nylon seam while on doll's leg. Do not sew nylons to leg. When seam is finished, roll down top of nylons. Place a narrow ribbon or narrow rolled elastic around doll's leg for garter. Cover ends in a tiny bow, pearl or other small decoration.

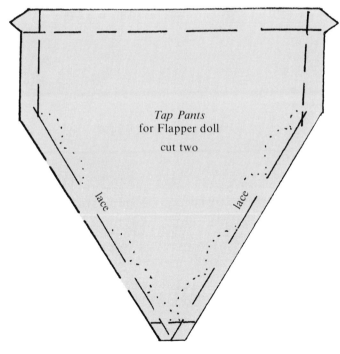

Tap Pants
for Flapper doll
cut two

lace   lace

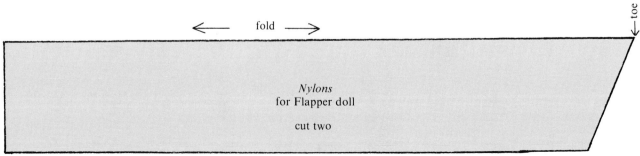

← fold →   toe →

Nylons
for Flapper doll

cut two

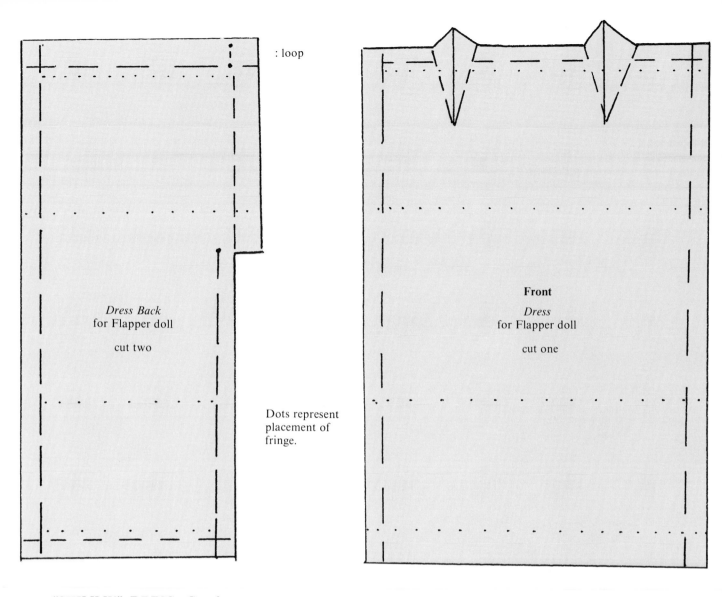

: loop

Front
Dress
for Flapper doll

cut one

Dress Back
for Flapper doll

cut two

Dots represent
placement of
fringe.

"SHIMMY" DRESS: Cut from satin or similar fabric.

With right sides together, join side seams. Join back center seam to dot. Turn back opening at back and sew seam formed. Sew front darts.

Sew a loop of narrow, rolled elastic to dress top at back opening as indicated on pattern. Turn under top hem of dress allowing loop to stick out.

Turn under hem; sew in place.

Starting at bottom, sew fringe to dress following dots as indicated on pattern. Sew two bead straps to doll bodice at X. To do this, string tiny colored beads on thread. Bead-covered thread is then sewn to doll's dress for straps. Sew a small button with a shank opposite of loop at back opening.

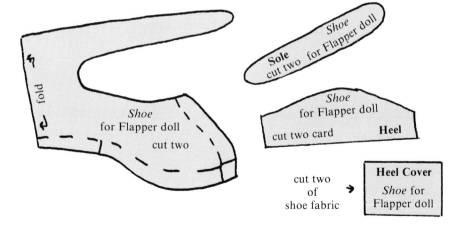

fold

Shoe
for Flapper doll

cut two

Sole
cut two
Shoe for Flapper doll

Shoe
for Flapper doll

cut two card   **Heel**

cut two
of
shoe fabric → **Heel Cover**
Shoe for
Flapper doll

SHOES: Cut from shiny plastic "leather," glove leather or black felt. Sew front shoe seam, then bottom seam. Glue sole, cut from heavy card, to bottom of shoe. Shape the sole to the bottom of the arch of shoe. Cut heel from white card. Lightly spread glue over card. Roll up. Glue heel cover around white card to cover heel. Glue to sole of shoe. Allow glue to dry. Place shoe on doll's foot. Tie shoe around ankle. Trim ties so that only a small bit of tie is visible.

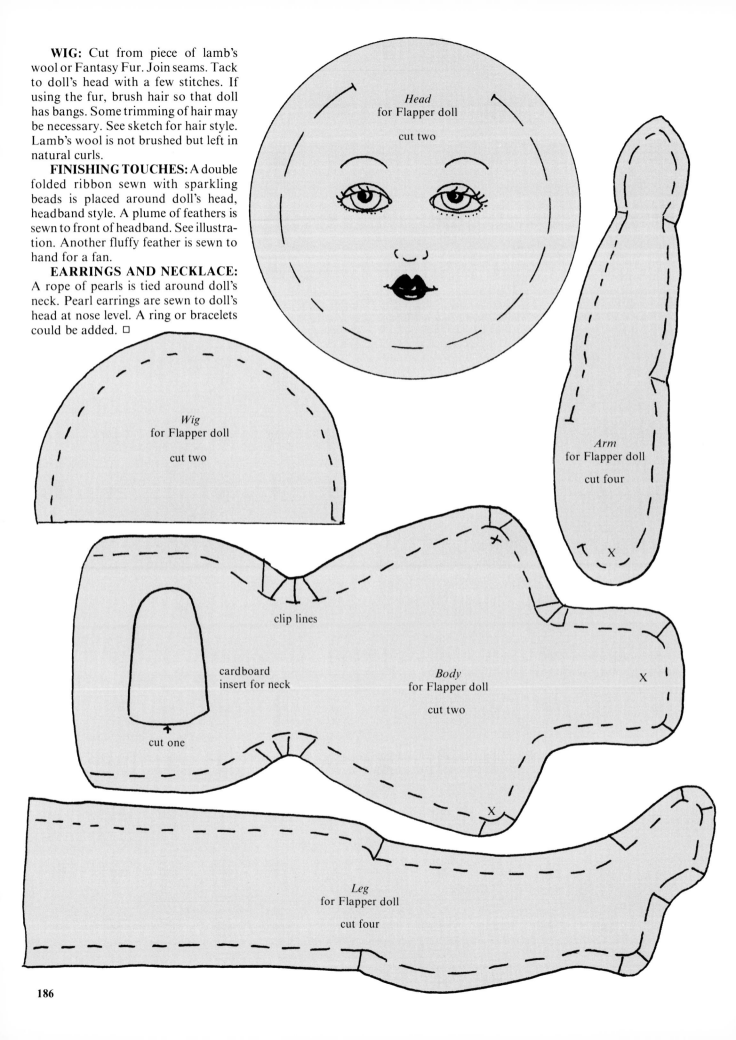

WIG: Cut from piece of lamb's wool or Fantasy Fur. Join seams. Tack to doll's head with a few stitches. If using the fur, brush hair so that doll has bangs. Some trimming of hair may be necessary. See sketch for hair style. Lamb's wool is not brushed but left in natural curls.

FINISHING TOUCHES: A double folded ribbon sewn with sparkling beads is placed around doll's head, headband style. A plume of feathers is sewn to front of headband. See illustration. Another fluffy feather is sewn to hand for a fan.

EARRINGS AND NECKLACE: A rope of pearls is tied around doll's neck. Pearl earrings are sewn to doll's head at nose level. A ring or bracelets could be added. □

Head
for Flapper doll

cut two

Wig
for Flapper doll

cut two

Arm
for Flapper doll

cut four

X

clip lines

cardboard
insert for neck

Body
for Flapper doll

cut two

X

cut one

X

X

Leg
for Flapper doll

cut four

Pincushion Dolls

BY JANET CARIJA BRANDT

Pincushion dolls are roly-poly tabletop dolls to use in the sewing room, bedroom, powder room or kitchen. In fact, anywhere in your home, office or studio that you need to keep needles and pins handy, these happy-faced dolls will do the job. They can also be decorated for use as a child's toy, (minus the needles and pins of course!).

MATERIALS:

Body, head and hat: velour, velvet, cotton, lightweight wool, felt.

Holly leaves: felt.

Collars: assorted colors of felt.

Trims: 10mm or 12mm size jingle bells, ribbons, rackrack, braids, embroidery floss, sequins, beads, crayons.

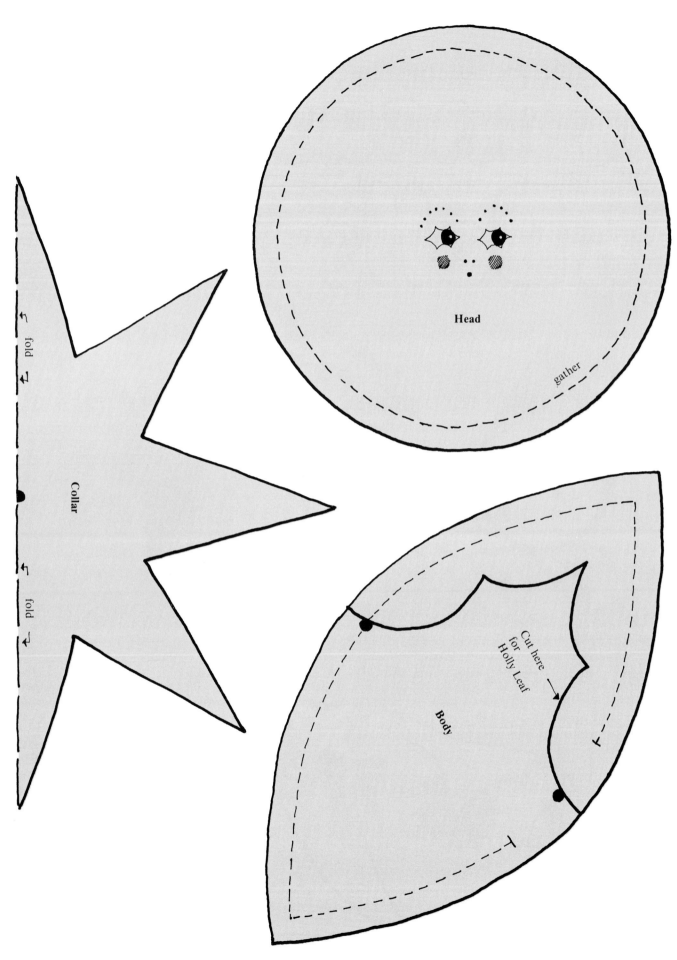

Head

gather

Collar

fold

fold

Body

Cut here
for
Holly Leaf

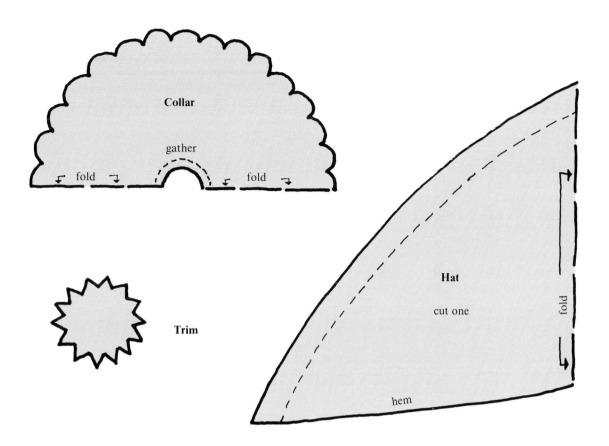

Collar

gather

fold   fold

Trim

Hat

cut one

fold

hem

DIRECTIONS:
BODY:

For Ribbons and Bells doll cut three dark body pieces and three light color body pieces. For Holly Eyes pincushion doll cut five body pieces of one color and five holly leaf pieces of a contrasting color.

With right sides together sew the body pieces together, alternating colors for the Ribbons and Bells doll and leaving an opening in the last seam to turn and stuff. Slip stitch the opening after the ball shaped body is stuffed. For the Holly Eyes doll sew five holly leaf pieces together from the bottom point to the large dot on the pattern. Turn right side out and put the stuffed solid round body inside the holly leaf shell. Slip stitch the two together.

HEAD:

For both dolls begin by sewing a gathering stitch around the circumference of circle as indicated on the pattern. Pull up on gathering stitches,

stuff and shape into a ball. Sew the back of the ball closed. The back of this ball is the back of the doll's head. Using embroidery floss sew the eyes, nose and mouth, following the drawing as a guide. Shade in the cheeks with a crayon or colored pencil.

Once the basic bodies are completed, decorating your pincushion doll is only limited by your imagination and the odds and ends around your sewing table.

HAT:

With right sides together fold hat on the fold line indicated on the pattern. Sew the long edge, turn the hat right side out and hem the bottom edge. Place the hat on the head of the doll with the seam centered in back. The hat should cover the entire back of the head extending down to the neck. With felt, beads, pearls or ribbons decorate the hat and sew the decorations in place.

COLLARS:

Cut the collars from felt so the cut edges will not ravel. The scalloped edge collar is gathered in the center to give it a soft ruffled look on the doll. Attach the collars to the top of the body and decorate with lengths of knotted ribbon, jingle bells or beads. When the collar is completed attach the head, sewing through the collar to anchor the head to the body.

FINISHING:

For the Holly Eyes doll the holly leaves at the base of the body are turned back and the points sewn down over the trim piece with a small bead or pearl on the top. Buttons can be sewn down the front of the body.

A CHILD'S TOY:

To decorate the pincushion dolls as toys for children do not use sequins, beads, jingle bells or anything small and easily swallowed. Ribbons or felt decorations very securely sewn in place would be appropriate. □

Gabriella, A Painted-face Cloth Doll

by **Patricia Wilks**

Gabriella is about 23in (58cm) long. She is easily fashioned of broadcloth, dressed in cotton and has fine hair of cotton warp. She has the serene expression of a refined young lady.

MATERIALS FOR THE DOLL:

Flesh-colored broadcloth, 1yd (.91m).

Cotton print for dress, 1/2yd (.46m).

Small amounts of white cotton or muslin for pantaloons.

Small amount of black faille or lining weight fabric for boots.

Small amounts of laces, ribbons, rosettes and so forth, for trims.

Thread and heavy duty thread or topstitching thread.

Snaps, elastic.

Cotton warp (weaver's warp) or perhaps Knit-Cro-Sheen.

MATERIALS:

Face painting: pencil, acrylic pointed-tip brush no. 5, acrylic pointed-tip brush no. 1. Acrylic tube paints: titanium white, ultramarine blue, yellow ochre, napthol crimson, bright aqua green, black, burnt sienna, (or colors of your choice).

Procedure: Painting the doll face will result in an original look for you as each person will paint a bit differently. If you have not painted before this will take some practice and patience. You may not like your first few efforts. You will need to acquire a feel for the way to move the brush and the amount of paint to carry along. Since you will be painting on fabric you must be careful to not get the fabric too wet or the colors may run. Once you do get the idea you will find the painting enjoyable.

Begin by carefully tracing the facial features through the fabric with a pencil. Instead of cutting the face out with a sewing selvage leave an ample amount of fabric around the piece so you can maneuver it while you are painting.

Lay a small amount of all the paint colors out on a sheet of paper or palette. Have a cup of clean water handy. Leave room on the palette for mixing colors. Begin painting the eyes. Using the no. 1 brush carefully, fill in the pupil area with a combination of colors which have been only "loosely" mixed on the brush, possibly ochre/sienna or ultramarine/ochre. Avoid a flat one-color look. Next fill in the eyelids and eyelashes keeping the brush well pointed with just enough water and paint for flowing on a thin line. Use a darker combination color for the top eyelid. Paint the eyebrows in a similar fashion. The paint will lighten as it dries so most likely you will want to fill in or go over some or all of the color a second time. When the eyes are finished to your liking, and dry, place a thin dot of white paint in the center for the pupil. Paint two nose dots with the burnt sienna. The lips are filled in with a combination of either ultramarine and crimson for a darker look, or crimson and burnt sienna for a lighter look. Swirl some white in with your colors for shading. When the lips are dry you may, again, prefer to go over the color. Let the face dry completely. Finish the face by blushing on the eyeshadow and cheek color. Wet the entire facial area with clear water and the larger brush. Lay the aqua or ultramarine or a combination on the eyelids slowly. It will run in the area. If it looks too dark, blot some away. Blush the cheeks the same way. You may paint on a sealer although this will tend to stiffen the fabric somewhat. The paint should be fairly permanent used alone, barring careless handling.

CONSTRUCTING THE DOLL:

1. Cut out the face pieces. Sew seams, turn right side out and stuff.

2. Cut remainder of pieces. Sew and stuff each piece. Stuff body cavity to top firmly. Limbs: Sew seams, stuff lower part, arms to elbow; then stitch

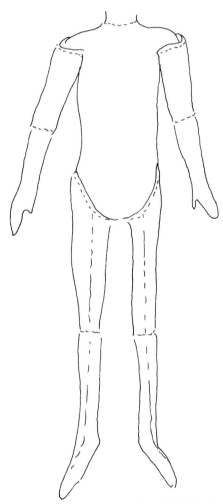

Illustration 1. Construction of doll body.

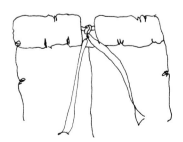

Illustration 2. Pantaloon waist construction.

Illustration 3. Boot construction.

Illustration 4. Coiled hairdo.

across for "bend" and continue stuffing to within 1in (2cm) of shoulder. Legs: Sew seams, turn right side out, stuff to knee; stitch across for "bend" and stuff to top of leg leaving 1in (2cm) for turning under and sewing to body.

3. Hand-stitch arms and legs to body with topstitching thread. Use a whip or buttonhole stitch. Arms are stitched in a circle to shoulder, legs are stitched to side edge of body.

4. Stitch head to body securely. Be certain it is stuffed evenly and firmly so head will be supported. You may insert a small cardboard tube in neck for more stability if desired.

5. Hairdo: Wrap 300 rounds of cotton warp around a 12in (30cm) book or cardboard piece. Cut off at top edge when wrapping is done. Lay the strands neatly along the center of the doll's head (in the middle of the strands). Spread it from forehead to center back of head just under crown area. Tack these strands down with close stitches. When hair is secured, separate into three sections: a back and two side sections. Braid one side section keeping braid close to front of face but still at side area. Coil the braid, taking care to tuck all the loose ends under coil. Tack closely all around the coil and inside it, to the head. You may pin the braid in place, first with straight pins. If the doll is for a collector you may leave a pin or two in, but for a child they must be removed. Prepare the other two coils in the same manner. You may want to fluff the strands a bit so that the hair looks natural. The warp is not especially heavy but it is not so light and must be tacked at several points. Sew on the side hair ribbons.

FASHIONING THE DRESS AND PANTALOONS:

1. Cut out front and back of dress.

2. Cut out pocket. Sew lace and ribbon on pocket top which you have turned with a small hem. Turn to inside about 1/4in (.65cm) on remaining three sides of pocket and stitch to center dress front at about underarm level.

3. Seam sides and shoulder arm of dress: Slash an opening at center back to just under waist level. Turn in 1/2in (1.3cm) and seam. Make a facing for neck edge of same or contrasting fabric. You may prefer to use bias tape for the neck facing. Sew facing to inside, turn to right side and hand-stitch around front side. Sew snaps at back edges. Hem sleeves and dress bottom. Press.

CONSTRUCTING PANTALOONS:

1. Cut out four pieces. Seam at center and sides. Turn in a small hem at bottom edge. Add 2½in (6cm) lace and ribbon or rosettes or trim of your own choice.

For waistband: Cut a piece 3in (8cm) wide and longer than waist measurement. Pin piece to inside waist (wrong side of pantaloons) at a little to the side of center front and around. Stitch waistband on just short of center front. Turn ends of waistband to right side of

Illustration 5. *Gabriella.*

Illustration 6. Another version of *Gabriella.*

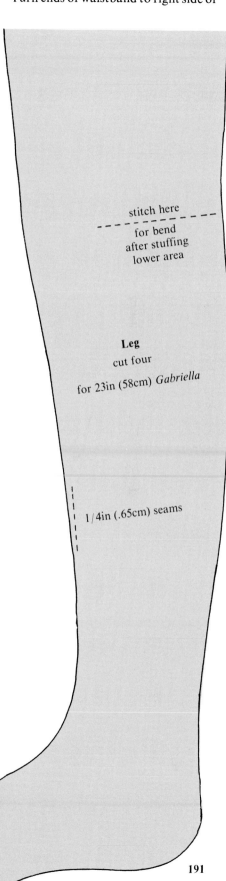

stitch here
for bend
after stuffing
lower area

Leg
cut four
for 23in (58cm) *Gabriella*

1/4in (.65cm) seams

191

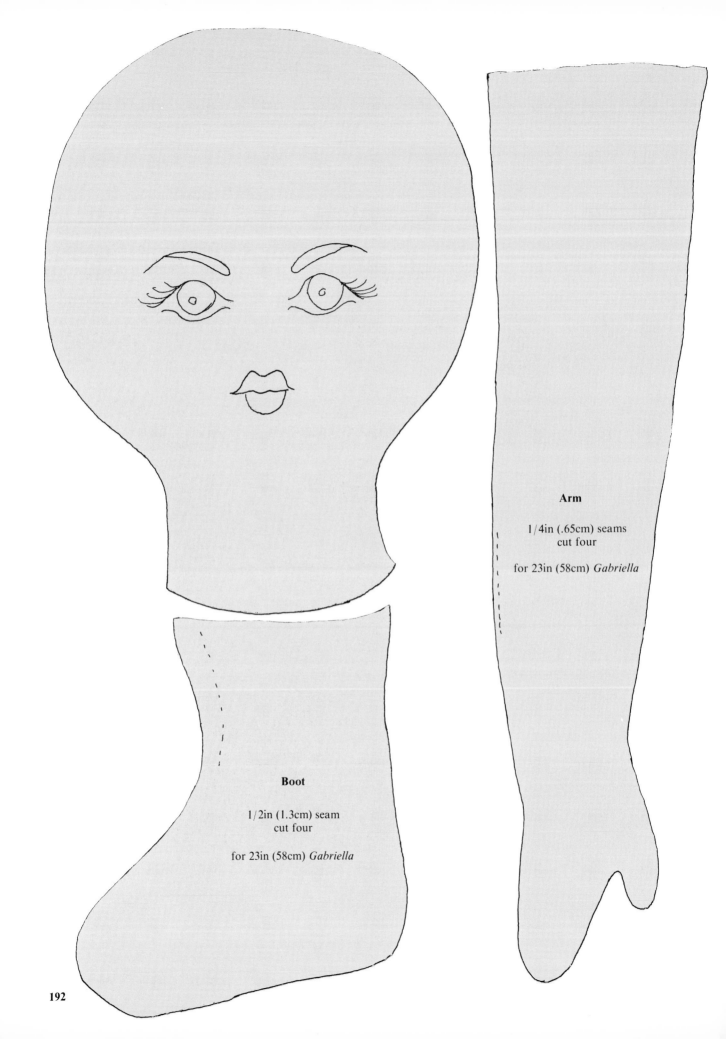

Arm

1/4in (.65cm) seams
cut four

for 23in (58cm) *Gabriella*

Boot

1/2in (1.3cm) seam
cut four

for 23in (58cm) *Gabriella*

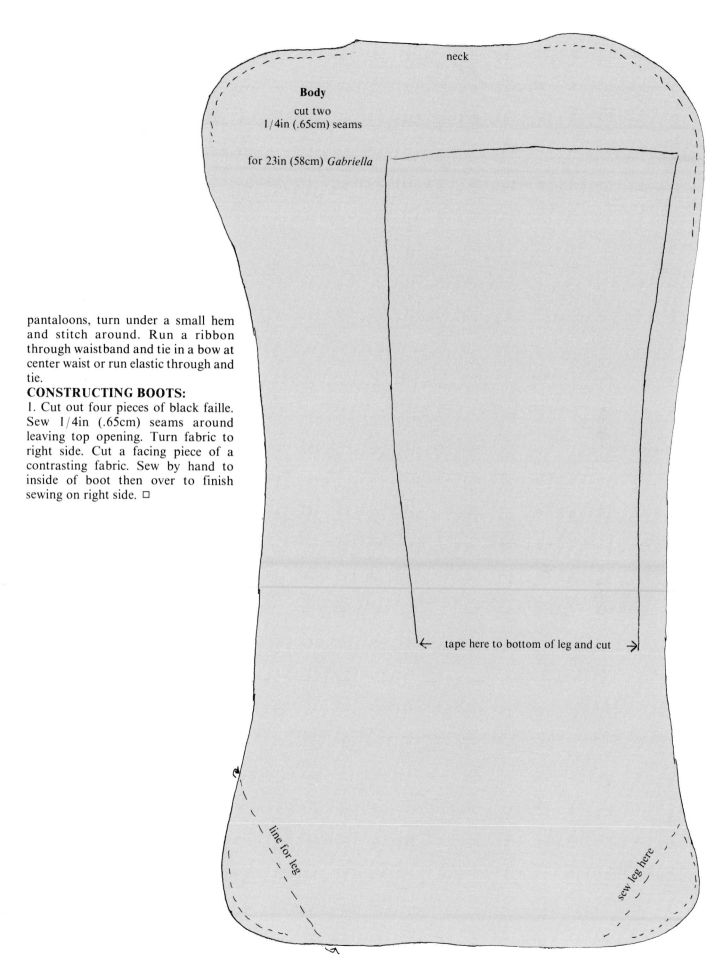

Body
cut two
1/4in (.65cm) seams

neck

for 23in (58cm) *Gabriella*

pantaloons, turn under a small hem and stitch around. Run a ribbon through waistband and tie in a bow at center waist or run elastic through and tie.

CONSTRUCTING BOOTS:
1. Cut out four pieces of black faille. Sew 1/4in (.65cm) seams around leaving top opening. Turn fabric to right side. Cut a facing piece of a contrasting fabric. Sew by hand to inside of boot then over to finish sewing on right side. □

← tape here to bottom of leg and cut →

line for leg

sew leg here

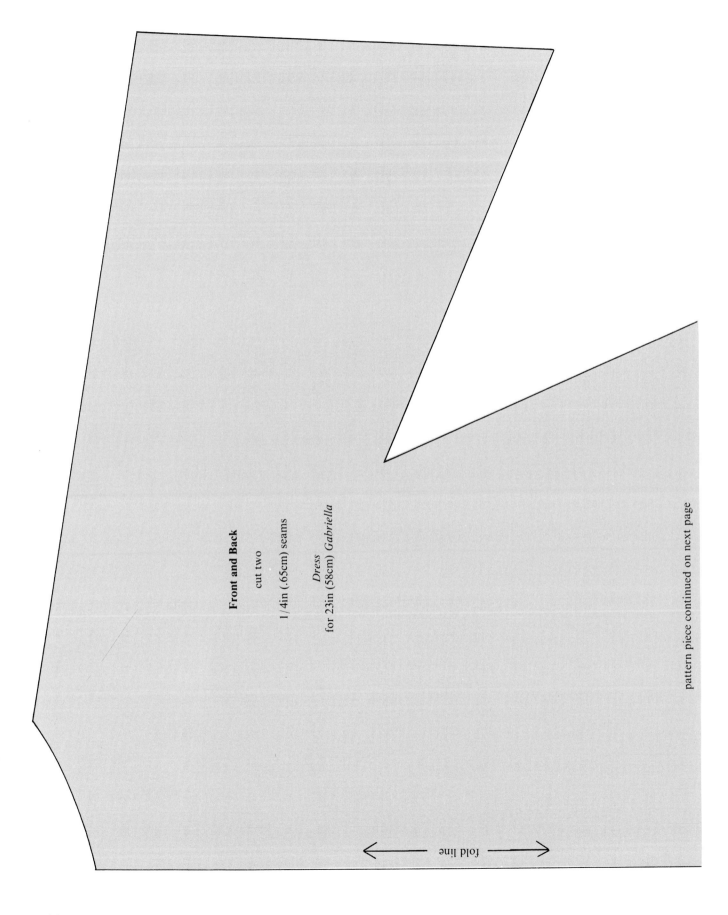

Front and Back

cut two

1/4in (.65cm) seams

Dress
for 23in (58cm) *Gabriella*

pattern piece continued on next page

← fold line →

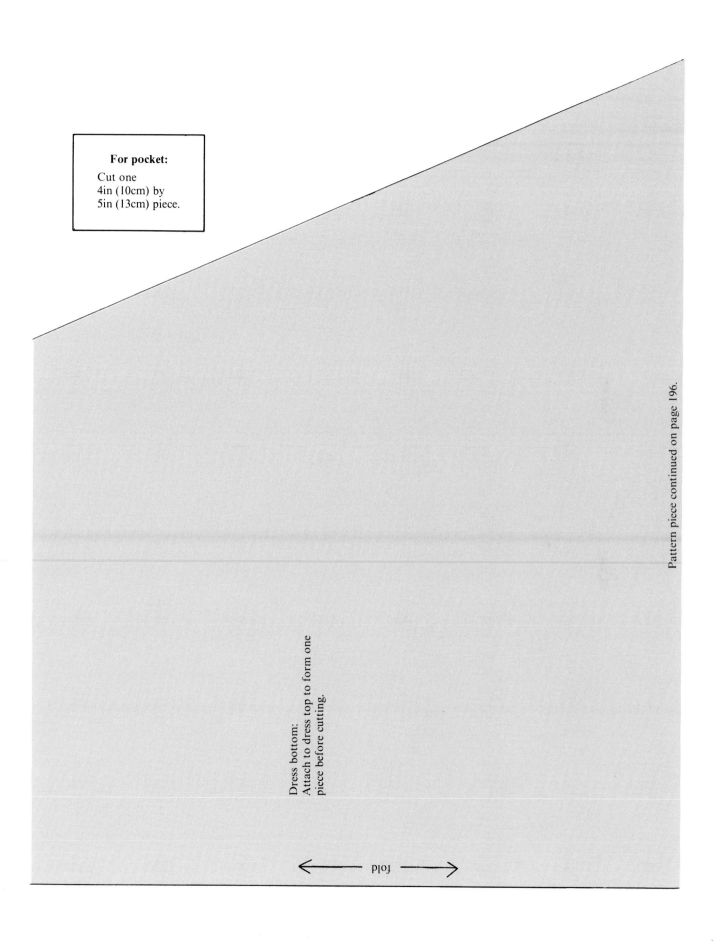

For pocket:

Cut one
4in (10cm) by
5in (13cm) piece.

Dress bottom:
Attach to dress top to form one
piece before cutting.

Pattern piece continued on page 196.

fold

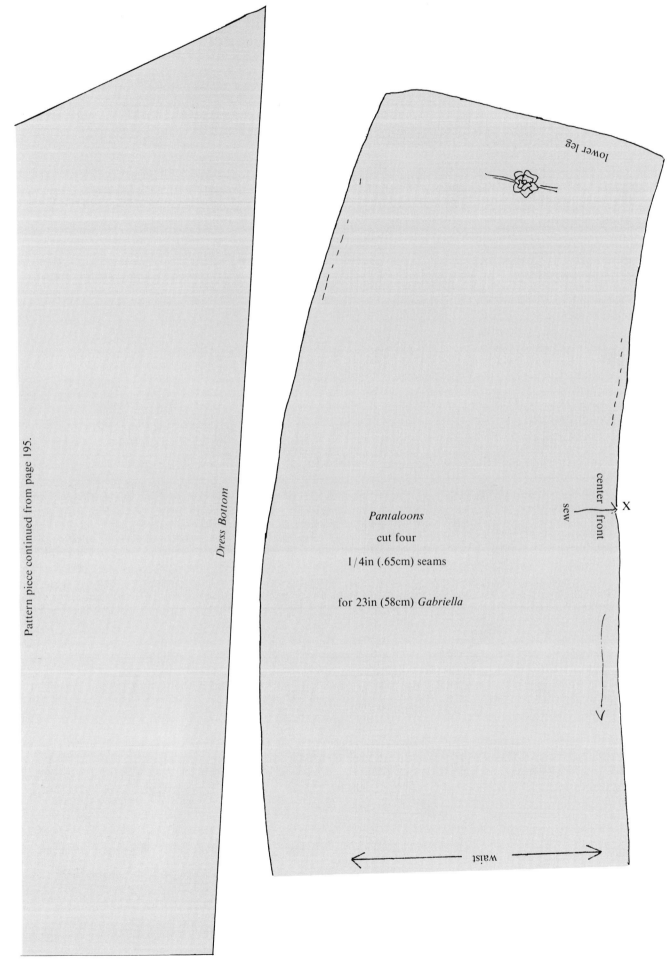

Pattern piece continued from page 195.

Dress Bottom

Pantaloons

cut four

1/4in (.65cm) seams

for 23in (58cm) *Gabriella*

lower leg

center front

sew

X

waist

Pincushion Needlework Companion Doll

by **Doris Rockwell Gottilly**

Pincushion dolls have been made from the beginning of the 1800s. Pins were expensive and it was necessary to protect and save them. Bags were filled with sawdust or emery powder to keep the pins rust free. The bags were formed over circular wood or cardboard which provided a firm base and the top was gathered in to fit the waist of the doll. Any type of doll head could be used and most pincushion dolls were homemade. These dolls were made to serve a purpose, to preserve expensive pins.

Their popularity continues to the present day.

I have designed a *Pincushion Needlework Companion Doll* for you to make and use, or to add to your collection. It is made of wood macrame beads and a sturdy cloth base stuffed with sawdust. Some of the same features are used that made the pincushion doll of the 1800s and early 1900s so popular. There are three pockets on her base pincushion skirt to hold a packet of needles, snaps and small buttons, or a small pair of scissors. At the base of the doll are seven elastic holders for spools of thread or other items you need to have handy.

MATERIALS NEEDED FOR DOLL:
Wooden macrame beads (painted white)
Two large round beads, 5in (13cm) circumference, 1¾in (4cm) long
Four oval beads, 2¼in (6cm) circumference 1in (2cm) long
Seven small beads, 2in (5cm) circumference 5/8in (1.6cm) long
20in (51cm) pajama elastic, 1¼in (3cm)
1 yd. (.91m) elastic thread for stringing beads
Two large white buttons, 1⅛in (2.8cm)
Two small flat white buttons, 7/16in (1cm)
Yarn or mohair for wig, 10in (25cm) by 2in (5cm)
White glue

Illustration 1. Pincushion Needlework Companion Doll showing the wood bead upper body and the cloth base.

Illustration 2. Pincushion Needlework Companion Doll shown completed, with her pincushion hat at her feet. She is dressed in a tiny floral cotton print in soft shades of yellow, lavender and green with a lavender felt vest.

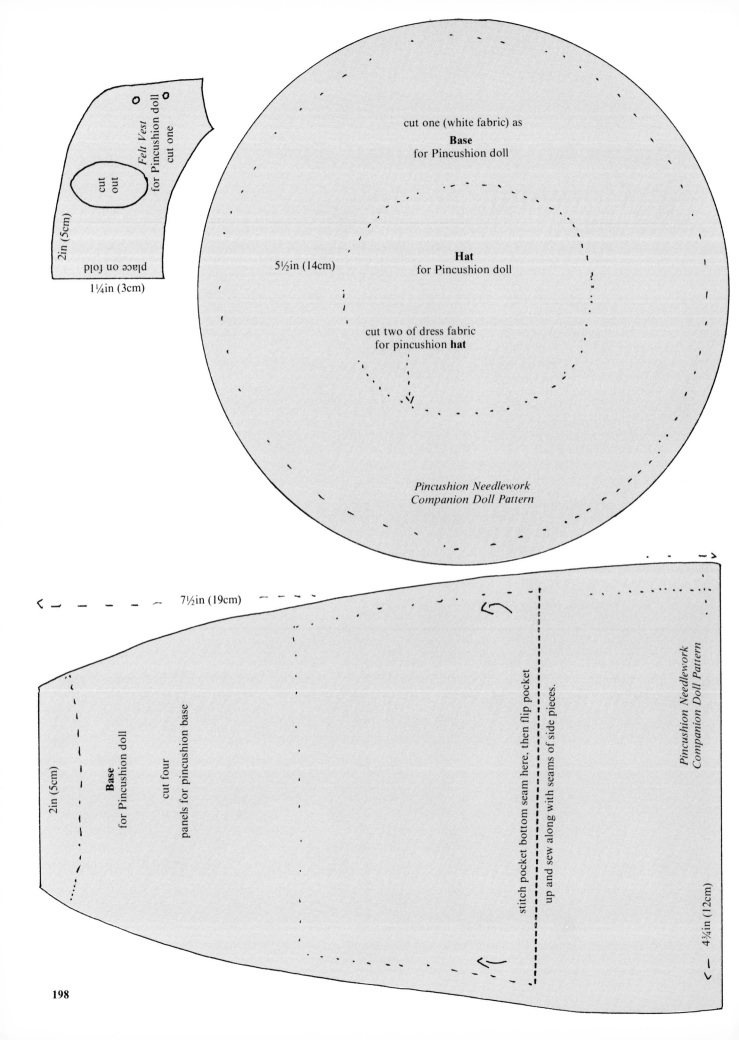

Felt Vest
for Pincushion doll
cut one

cut out

2in (5cm)

place on fold

1¼in (3cm)

cut one (white fabric) as
Base
for Pincushion doll

Hat
for Pincushion doll

5½in (14cm)

cut two of dress fabric
for pincushion **hat**

*Pincushion Needlework
Companion Doll Pattern*

7½in (19cm)

2in (5cm)

Base
for Pincushion doll

cut four
panels for pincushion base

stitch pocket bottom seam here, then flip pocket
up and sew along with seams of side pieces.

*Pincushion Needlework
Companion Doll Pattern*

4¾in (12cm)

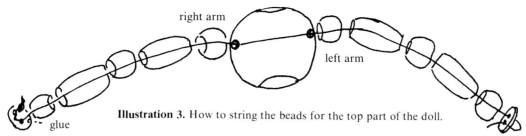

right arm

left arm

glue

Illustration 3. How to string the beads for the top part of the doll.

Acrylic paints: black - to outline eyes
               blue - eyes
               red - lips

Small paint brush, No. 1

Sawdust, about five cups - for base of doll (can use cotton stuffing if sawdust is not available)

Five small spools of thread, (assorted colors)

Sturdy white fabric for base, 1/4 yd. (.23m) (50% polyester, 50% cotton)

White thread, scissors, needles, straight pins

Hair spray (to style wig)

Nylon upholstery thread, white

INSTRUCTIONS:

HOW TO STRING WOOD BEADS FOR TOP PART OF DOLL.

1. The first thing to do is have two holes drilled through the wood bodice head. The holes should be about 1/8in (.31cm) across. This is necessary for inserting the elastic thread through the bodice so the arms are strung properly.

2. String the arms:

Cut a piece of elastic thread 10in (25cm) long. Take the small flat button and insert the elastic through two holes. Pull the elastic to the inside of the button and tie a small knot. Put a drop of glue on the knot so it will be permanent. Put a small bead over the button, next an oval bead, small bead, oval bead, small bead. Now that you have strung the right arm, take the elastic end, insert into the right hole in the bodice bead; go all the way through to opposite hole and pull the elastic through. You are now ready to put the beads on for the left arm. Put on a small bead first, oval bead next, small bed, oval bead, small bead and finish the arm with the other small flat button. Insert the elastic through two holes, pulling the elastic taut on the inside of the button and tying a firm knot. Put on a drop of glue and the arms are finished.

HOW TO STRING THE HEAD, NECK AND BODICE:

1. Start with the large button, bodice wood bead, small neck bead, large wood head bead and last, on top of the "head," place a large flat button. Cut a piece of elastic thread 12in (30cm) long. String from the bottom up,

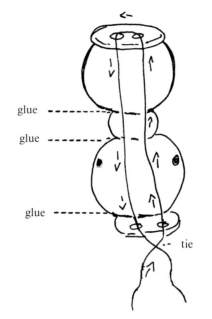

glue

glue

glue

tie

Illustration 4. How to string the head, neck and bodice.

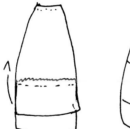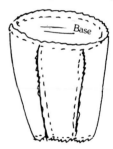

Base

Illustration 5. How to assemble the pincushion base for the doll.

through the left hole in the button with the elastic, through the large bead, the small neck head, into the head bead, and the left hole in the button on top; now bring the elastic down through the right button hole and go back down through all the beads to the right hole in the button at the bottom. There should be two ends of the elastic protruding from the button. Pull each end down tightly and tie in a firm knot. The square knot is a good knot to use. A drop of glue on the knot makes it permanent. Let dry. Put a bit of glue on the neck bead, where it attaches to the head and the bodice; it keeps the head from being wobbly.

HOW TO ASSEMBLE PINCUSHION BASE FOR DOLL.

Trace pattern pieces and cut out.

There should be eight pieces: four sides, one base and three pockets. Allow 3/8in (.9cm) seams. Ease pieces together. Sew pockets on each piece before assembling. The front and the two side pieces will have pockets. Sew the bottom of the pocket about 2in (5cm) up from bottom of the side piece. Flip up and pin in place and the sides of the pocket are sewn along with the seams of the side pieces when you join them together. After attaching each pocket, sew all four sides together. Now with seam side out, sew the sides to the base, easing the pieces together. (You might want to pin first to make sure the pieces fit properly.)

Cut the pajama elastic and pin around base of doll. The base of the finished doll is about 16in (41cm). Allow 2in (5cm) for overlapping in back. Sew with **firm, tight stitches,** catching the elastic and sewing through the base fabric. Measure and pin off every 2¼in

(6cm). Next, using the nylon upholstery thread, sew the elastic firmly to the base and remove pins. You can now stuff the base. I have used sawdust, but if that is not available, use cotton stuffing.

Now that the base is stuffed firmly, using nylon upholstery thread, **gather the waist** using small stitches. Sew about 1/2in (1.3cm), tucking the cut edge inside; pull thread tight to fit around the waist of the top part of doll. Put glue on the bead, the button and around the edge of the fabric and pull together at waist, Apply a bit more glue around the stitches and let dry. The basic pincushion doll form is now complete.

PAINT THE FACE:

Paint the face as shown in the illustra-

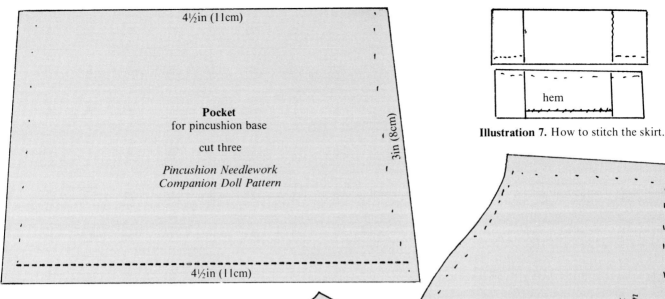

Pocket

for pincushion base

cut three

*Pincushion Needlework
Companion Doll Pattern*

4½in (11cm) [top]

3in (8cm) [right side]

4½in (11cm) [bottom]

Illustration 7. How to stitch the skirt.

hem

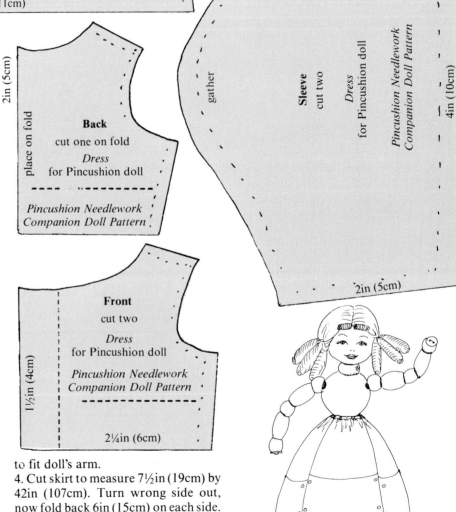

Back
cut one on fold
*Dress
for Pincushion doll*

*Pincushion Needlework
Companion Doll Pattern*

2in (5cm)

place on fold

Sleeve
cut two
*Dress
for Pincushion doll*

*Pincushion Needlework
Companion Doll Pattern*

gather

4in (10cm)

2in (5cm)

Front
cut two
*Dress
for Pincushion doll*

*Pincushion Needlework
Companion Doll Pattern*

1½in (4cm)

2¼in (6cm)

Illustration 6. A drawing of the doll showing construction.

tions. Draw the features first with a pencil before painting. This way you can change them if you are not satisfied. Outline the eyes with black, paint the eye blue and the lips red.

MAKE THE WIG:
Measure your yarn or mohair 2in (5cm) wide and 10in (25cm) long. Sew down middle for the center part. Glue top and sides of bead (head) and place yarn on head. Hold in place with a rubber band until glue dries.
Style: Section off wig in thirds. Pull one section of hair over to the right side, the other to the left and one down the back. Tie each section at hairline with thread the same color as the yarn. Each section will have three long curls. Spray with extra hold hair spray and, using the handle of your small paint brush, roll the curls. Insert a straight pin in the center of each curl until dry. Roll two tiny curls on the forehead (either side of the part). Now give final spray with hair spray. Remove pins when curls are dry.

MATERIALS FOR DOLL'S DRESS AND HAT:
1/2 yd. (46cm) cotton fabric with a tiny print
1/2 yd. (46cm) lace to trim cuffs and neck of bodice)
Thread to match fabric
Felt - for vest (choose color to contrast with dress fabric), 1½in (4cm) by 6in (15cm)

HOW TO ASSEMBLE DRESS AND HAT:
1. Trace patterns. Cut out dress and hat pattern pieces.
2. Sew front and back shoulder seams of bodice together.
3. Hem sleeve 5/8in (1.6cm) and sew lace to cuff. Gather top of sleeve to fit armhole and sew sleeve to bodice. Sew up under arm and sleeve. Gather sleeve

to fit doll's arm.
4. Cut skirt to measure 7½in (19cm) by 42in (107cm). Turn wrong side out, now fold back 6in (15cm) on each side. This will be the skirt interfacing. Stitch along bottom 1/2in (1.3cm) up.
5. Turn right side out and press; press in hem of skirt. Now gather the waist to fit bodice top (to fit waist of doll). Sew bodice and skirt together, leaving a 1in (2cm) overlap on left side of skirt. Attach small snap at neck and at waist.
6. Cut out the felt vest as shown on the pattern; no sewing required.
7. Cut out two circles of dress fabric for hat. Use base circle as pattern. With wrong sides out, stitch all around

circle, leaving a 1in (2cm) opening for turning right side out. Press and sew a small circle in center (see pattern); stuff this for the pincushion hat. Trim with a band of felt to match the vest. □

DOLL MAKING:
DOLL BODIES:
German Kid Body
by Elizabeth Andrews Fisher
Make Your Own Doll Collection: Costuming a Lady of the 1890s
by Artie Seeley

German Kid Body

by **Elizabeth Andrews Fisher**

Trace the body front on paper, on the fold. That will give you the full pattern for the body front top. It is better to make the first body from unbleached muslin before tackling the kid. The dotted line down the leg shows you the center of the leg and will help you to fit the back legs for seaming. BEFORE any seaming, put in the knee gusset. Take care when you slash. It is far better to slash NOT QUITE ENOUGH. It is easy to cut a bit more, easier than trying to sew the slash up to fit.

After you put in the gusset in the knee, sew the back seam. Be sure the seam is on the correct side. Now are you alert to the fact that the hip slash goes across the back on each side of the seam? Remember, it is easier to cut the slash a bit more than it is to sew up the slash when you have cut too far

OOOO on the bottom of body front fits on OOO on the leg top. Body back, marked ⓍⓍⓍ fits on leg top back ⓍⓍⓍⓍ

Sew sections marked ZZZZ together; that is the crotch. Match toe top marked X; sew it in. Be sure the long side is toward the outside of the foot. Sew on the sole. Seam the sides of the body together and turn right side out.

The top of body front and back may be pinked or scalloped. If you are making a kid body, use this unbleached muslin body to line the kid. Just put the muslin body inside the kid. Stuff with sawdust.

You already know that after you cut out one piece of the pattern when it calls for two, turn the pattern over and trace on the wrong side of the kid and cut each piece separately. If you fail to turn the pattern over, when cutting from kid, you will end up with two left legs.

This pattern makes a neat body; have fun, and be proud of your good work.

Sew by hand. □

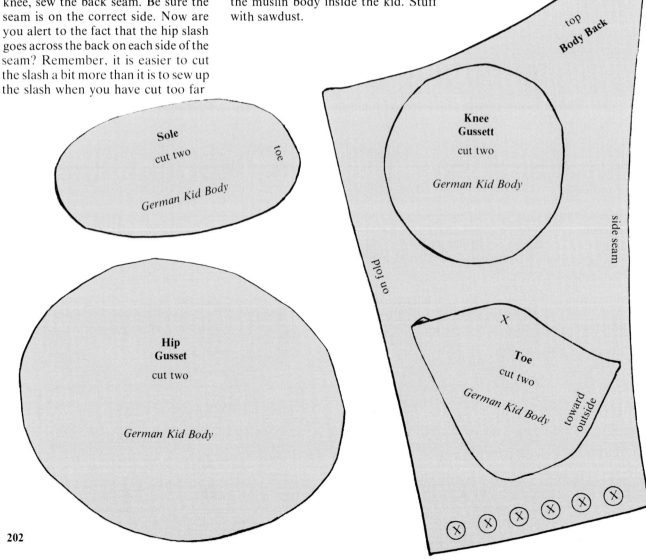

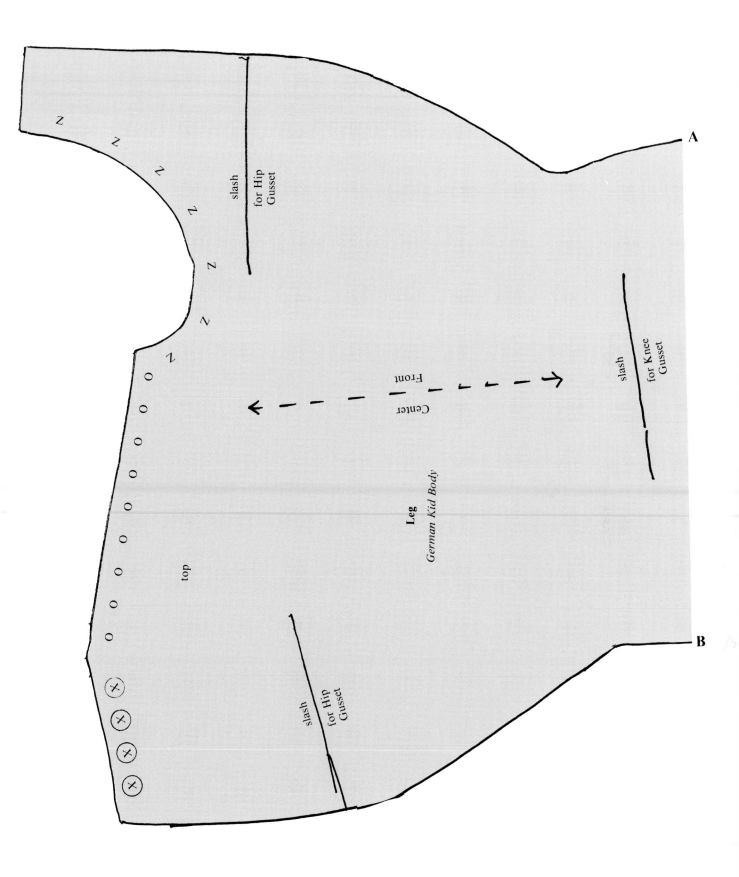

A

B

Z Z Z Z Z Z Z Z Z Z

slash
for Hip
Gusset

slash
for Knee
Gusset

Front
Center

Leg
German Kid Body

top

slash
for Hip
Gusset

203

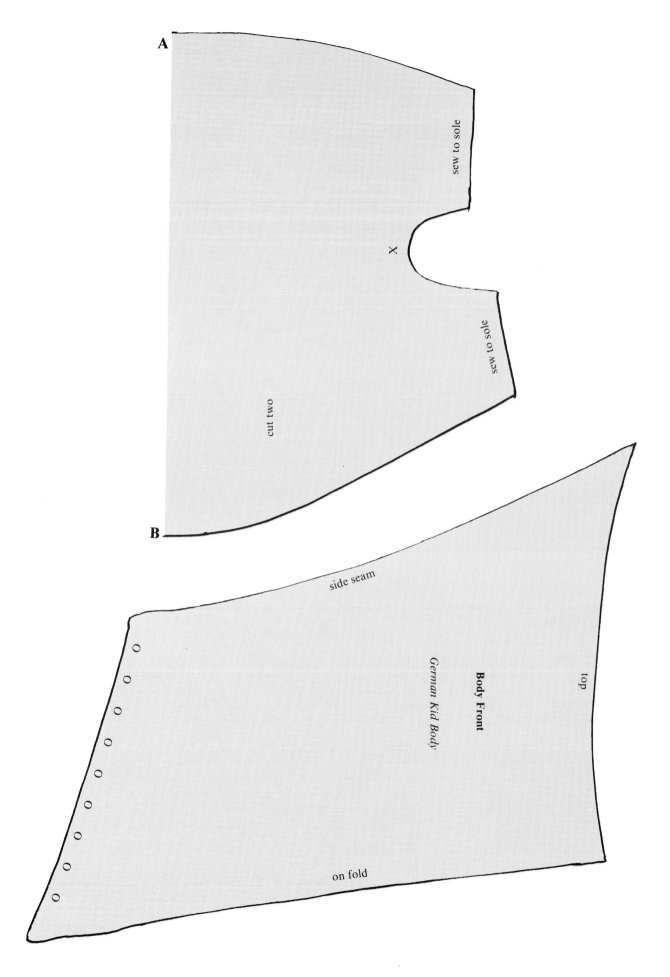

A

sew to sole

X

sew to sole

cut two

B

side seam

German Kid Body

Body Front

top

on fold

Make Your Own Doll Collection: Costuming a Lady of the 1890s

by **Artie Seeley**

Photographs by **William Seeley**

Illustration 1. Close-up of the Gibson Girl.

Illustration 2. Side view of the Gibson Girl.

This will be a trip down memory lane — a walk back in time. For some of you it will be where your grandmother walked; for most of you it will be in the time of your great-grandmother.

We will take the years encompassing the 1890s and use the doll portrayed in the drawings of Charles Dana Gibson. She is the epitome of serene beauty, who came along about 1910. Kestner called her the Queen of Hearts.

Her head is lifted proudly, her dress long, her sleeves are long, too; and heaven forbid that any one should see her elbows! The parasol was a real necessity for no woman in her right mind would dream of getting suntanned.

Getting dressed in those days was not the simple trick of stepping into pantyhose, pulling on a blouse and going anywhere and everywhere in a pair of blue jeans; far from it. First, the pantalettes and then the corset. Help was usually needed to lace it up. "Now hold on to the bedpost while I pull it tight!" was a very familiar line of the time. The waist must be drawn into a mere 18in (46cm) or 20in (51cm). Over the corset, the corset cover; but if mother nature had not endowed her with the proper shape, a well-padded pillow (bras had not been invented) helped to shape the bust line. Next a half-moon shaped "pillow" tied snugly around the waist will give the hourglass figure so necessary for the fashionable lady. And now the corset cover goes on. In reality this padded form was taking the place of the bustle of an earlier age. The old ones were formed over a heavy metal base and were most uncomfortable to wear. The bustle of great-grandma's day might have been

Illustration 3. Undergarments for the Gibson Girl.

FAR RIGHT: Illustration 4. Blouse with leg-of-mutton sleeves, parasol, hat and fully lined skirt with eight gores.

Illustration 5. Detail of the pointed, laced, high-heeled two-toned shoes.

made of almost any material native to where the lady lived. It might be filled with cotton or feathers or, if she was a farm girl, it could be filled with oats, wheat or bran.

Shoes of that day were pointed, laced, high-heeled and, of course, two-toned.

Back to the clothes of the lady of fashion. There were at least two petticoats with many flounces, rows of lace insertion and dainty ribbons, interspersed with rows of tucks which allowed for shortening or lengthening of the garment, guaranteeing many years of wear. Fancy eyelet was often used on one of the petticoats because it was much more economical than lace.

The blouse follows, usually made with a very modest high neck trimmed with lace and a bow tie. The stand-up collar on the jacket is exceptionally good styling. The leg-of-mutton sleeves are an absolute must on the blouse or jacket. A snug fitting waist on the skirt or jacket will enhance the hour-glass shape. The skirt has eight gores and is fully lined to give it the proper weight.

Note that the hats, seen in **Illustrations 1, 2, 4, 6** and **7**, are covered with flowers, ribbon and net. In the winter they might have had feathers, artificial

Illustration 6. Two Gibson Girls modeling their fashions.

Illustration 7. Back view of the Gibson Girls shown in **Illustration 6**.

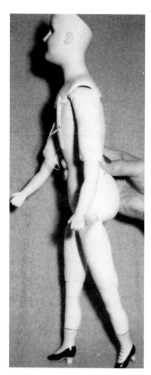

Illustration 8. A view of the Gibson Girl's body.

Illustration 9. Attach leg as shown here.

fruit, or birds with wings spread, perhaps even a bird's nest, or vegetables, or almost anything that struck her fancy.

Winter also would have called for a fitted coat with cape collar and fur muff.

Missing from our friends' hands are the drawstring purses of this time, called reticules. A lady could twirl it in her hand and along with a carefully dropped handkerchief she could attract the attention of the gentleman of her choice and still be a "lady."

If you intend to paint one of these dolls for your collection, pay close attention to **Illustration 1.** The eyebrows are one-stroke; I find I can make the line with a pencil and follow it very carefully. When painting, start with a very fine line, let it thicken in the middle, then end with a very fine line. It is easy if done in two fires. When the first line is fired and you do not have to

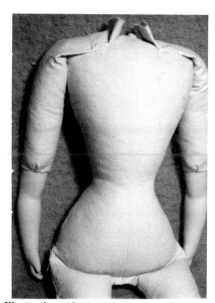

Illustration 10. Attach arms to body as shown.

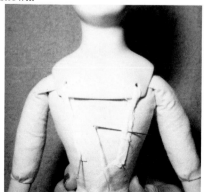

Illustration 11. Attach head to body as shown.

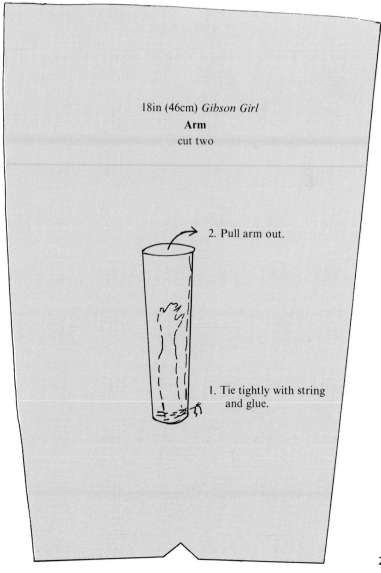

18in (46cm) *Gibson Girl*
Arm
cut two

2. Pull arm out.

1. Tie tightly with string and glue.

worry about smearing, it is real easy to go over with a firm stroke and thicken it a bit in the middle. Some of the old dolls are found with brows made in several strokes. I have a very good photograph to work from and this is how she is painted. Note that beautiful bone structure above the eyes; in the photograph the eyebrows follow this line; too high or too low and you will lose the austere look of the Gibson Girl. Painted eyelashes are only on the lower part of the eye and they are made straight up and down. Real hair eye-lashes must be added to the finished doll. These can be glued in place and allowed to dry before the blown glass eyes are installed.

Paint the lips a delicate rose and do not increase their size. Any makeup used at this time had to be very modest. A girl might pinch her cheeks or bite her lips to add color, but never must she have a painted look.

The Gibson doll head is a Byron mold. The accompanying body pattern should be a perfect fit. The doll is about 18in (46cm) tall.

BODY ASSEMBLY:

Fold body both back and front and stitch down middle as marked. Clip on fold; this will give the body a tiny waist. Back section: lay upper and lower body together; match A to A and B to B, and stitch across. This forms the derrière. Next sew back and side seams together. Stitch outer leg seam as shown on pattern (leaving opening on outside seam). Sew inside leg seams and cut apart. Turn body right side out and stitch again from A to B, this time with a downward curve as shown in this

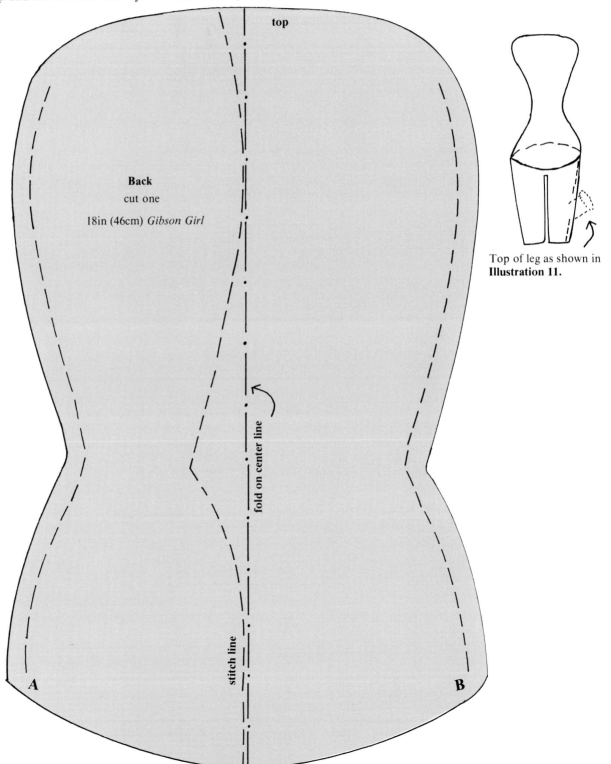

Back

cut one

18in (46cm) *Gibson Girl*

top

fold on center line

stitch line

A

B

Top of leg as shown in **Illustration 11.**

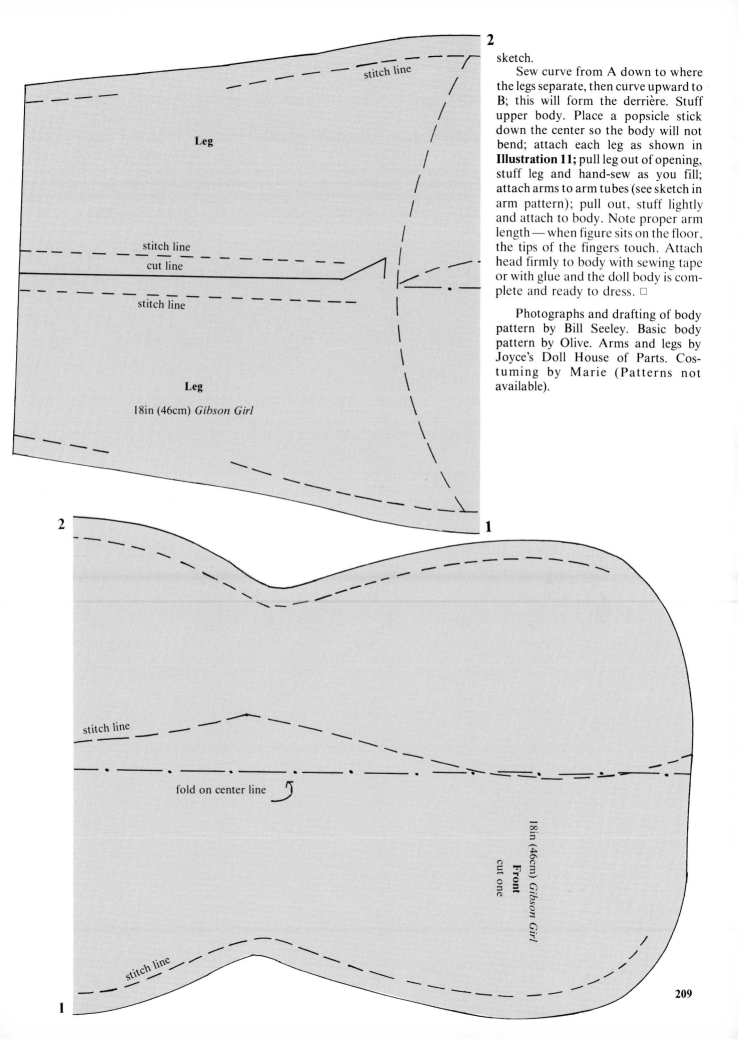

sketch.

Sew curve from A down to where the legs separate, then curve upward to B; this will form the derrière. Stuff upper body. Place a popsicle stick down the center so the body will not bend; attach each leg as shown in **Illustration 11;** pull leg out of opening, stuff leg and hand-sew as you fill; attach arms to arm tubes (see sketch in arm pattern); pull out, stuff lightly and attach to body. Note proper arm length — when figure sits on the floor, the tips of the fingers touch. Attach head firmly to body with sewing tape or with glue and the doll body is complete and ready to dress. □

Photographs and drafting of body pattern by Bill Seeley. Basic body pattern by Olive. Arms and legs by Joyce's Doll House of Parts. Costuming by Marie (Patterns not available).

2

stitch line

Leg

stitch line
cut line
stitch line

Leg

18in (46cm) *Gibson Girl*

1

2

stitch line

fold on center line

stitch line

18in (46cm) *Gibson Girl*
Front
cut one

1

209

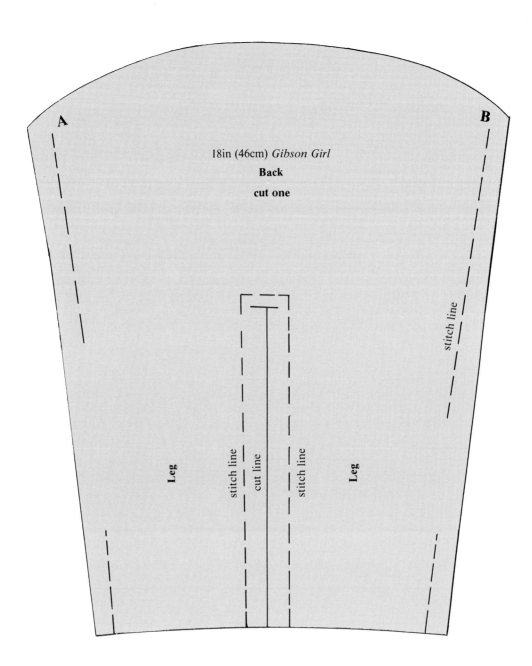

18in (46cm) *Gibson Girl*

Back

cut one

A

B

Leg

Leg

stitch line

cut line

stitch line

stitch line

stitch line

DOLL REPAIR/RESTORATION:

Care of a Doll Collection
   by Robert & Karin MacDowell
Stringing Without Tears
   by G. P. Jones
Dolling Discoveries
   by Elizabeth Andrews Fisher
The Hazards of Being a Doll Doctor and Doll Maker — A Personal Account
   by Linda Greenfield
Notes on Preventing Avoidable Damage to Fine Antique Dolls
   by Robert & Karin MacDowell

Care of a Doll Collection

by **Robert & Karin MacDowell**

Photographs by the **Authors**

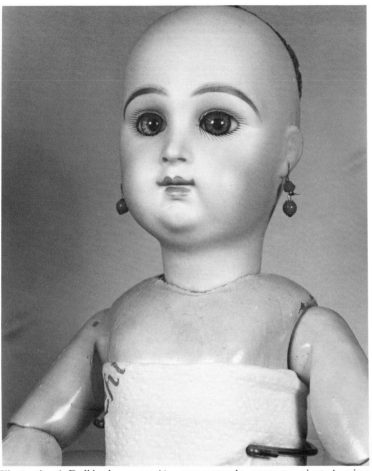

Illustration 1. Doll body wrapped in a paper towel to protect against abrasion by the stand. Other means can be used such as placing soft plastic tubing over stand and wire.

GENERAL

Dolls, especially the antique, require careful consideration regarding methods for safe display or storage, and for preventing deterioration. All who own or handle dolls should make every reasonable effort to pass them along to future owners in as close to original condition as is possible.

Proper care need not detract from the pleasure of ownership; indeed, thoughtful maintenance is an interesting pursuit, as well as being of great benefit in terms of preserving historic material, and also maintaining the value of the collection.

FUNDAMENTAL STEPS

The following should always be accomplished:
1. Make certain all newly acquired material is properly examined and treated before being placed in the collection.
2. Inspect all objects in the collection periodically.
3. Maintain a suitable, constant and physically safe environment at all times. Shelves and tables must be strong and stable.
4. Provide treatment for observed deterioration if facilities are available.
5. Avoid unnecessary handling.

Fortunately, dolls given reasonable care do not deteriorate rapidly, nor is the degree of care required as demanding as for many other types of collectible material.

MAJOR FACTORS IN CONTROLING DETERIORATION

The following are the agents over which we generally have control, and which can cause serious and rapid deterioration if not kept within reasonable limits.

HUMIDITY. Water vapor in the air and liquid water which condenses from it form a known hazard to objects in nearly all collections. When the humidity is too low, moisture is lost from specimens, causing glue, paste and paint to dry out and lose their adhesive power; paint, fabrics, leather (kid) and paper become brittle; wood cracks and warps.

When relative humidity is too high, many materials absorb water which accelerates other forms of degradation such as corrosion (rust) and growth of fungi which consume and stain materials. Adhesives soften; wood swells, warps and checks.

Rapid changes in humidity are especially harmful as most specimens cannot accommodate change quickly.

A fairly constant relative humidity of 40 to 60 percent is generally acceptable; the more constant, the better.

TEMPERATURE. As with humidity, try to keep temperature reasonably constant, preferably below 70 deg.F. (21 deg.C) but not below 60 deg.F. (16 deg.C.) Higher temperatures promote the growth of microorganisms and may also speed the reproductive patterns of destructive insects.

Be especially mindful that rapid drops in temperature can cause moisture to condense in the form of droplets which can be quite harmful.

LIGHT. Generally, a doll collection will fare best when displayed under fairly subdued light. Sunlight or bright light from windows should be avoided, as should light from nearby hot lamps or fluorescent tubes. Light in the red to infra-red spectrum causes heating, while the violet to ultra-violet spectrum causes fading.

Not only does intense light cause fading and color shifts, but it can actually weaken some materials structurally. Silk, when exposed to sunlight for a month, may lose as much as half its strength.

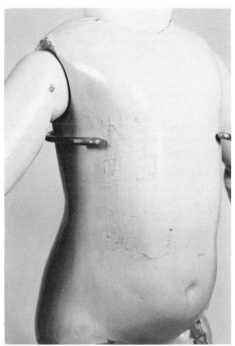

Illustration 2. Paris Bébé body showing superficial paint damage cáused by rubbing against metal stand.

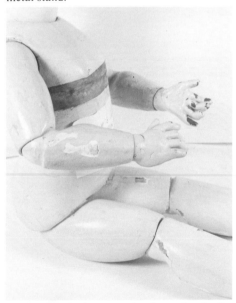

Illustration 3. An example of a rather badly deteriorated Jumeau body. Paint and underlying prime layers have chipped and peeled, glue joints securing wood parts to composition parts have cracked. Since most Jumeau bodies of similar age are found in much better condition, this one has obviously suffered the effects of improper moisture control, temperature variations, or both.

Ideally, the collection should be kept in the dark when not on view. Otherwise, try to limit light levels as much as is practicable.

MOLD. Aside from unsightliness, mold can be very destructive, as it feeds on specimens by dissolving and absorbing elements of their composition. When discovered, try to eliminate both the mold and the conditions which allowed it to flourish.

SMOKING AND WOODBURNING STOVES. Any device which emits smoke or products of combustion is a severe hazard.

DISPLAY CASES AND ENCLOSURES. These should be ventilated and should not contain lights. Objects in cases should be frequently inspected.

DUST. Dust is abrasive and can combine with excess moisture to form chemically harmful agents, as well as being much more difficult to safely remove.

INSECTS. There are numerous insects which can be hazardous to your doll collection. Among these are the dermestids, the most common being the carpet beetle, a small, inconspicuous insect about 1/8in (.31cm) to 3/16in (.32cm) long. Carpet beetles attack fabrics, some compositions, especially wool, fur, feathers and hair. Evidence is usually seen as holes in garments or loose or missing hair in wigs. The cast-off larval skins are often found, especially inside the heads, hollow arms and bodies of dolls.

Other insects which cause problems include:

1. Powder-post beetles: Woodboring insects which bore round or oval holes in wooden objects, usually leaving telltale accumulation of fine, light powder near or under the holes.
2. Clothes moths: Adult has narrow buff-colored wings spreading about 1/2in (1.3cm). Larvae feed on fur, fabric, wool, feathers and other animal fibres. They spin a light-colored case or web covering their bodies which may be more easily seen than the actual larvae.
3. Silverfish: Generally, these are best seen when a light is first turned on. They are a gray-colored insect about 1/2in (1.3cm) long, with three prominent caudal "bristles." Silverfish are a special hazard to paper, bookbindings, rayon textiles and the starch in cloth.
4. Cockroaches: As is the case with silverfish, these are best detected when a light is first turned on. They are brownish, oval-shaped, and range from barely visible to as much as 2in (5cm) in length. They are a particular hazard to paper specimens, and will consume glue, size and sometimes the actual printed surfaces of documents, including the ink.

A collection should be checked frequently for signs of infestation. New specimens should be kept separate from the established collection until it is determined they are not brining unwelcome visitors.

Problem specimens may be placed in air-tight containers with para-dichlorobenzene crystals or moth-balls; however, do not allow the substance to contact the specimen. After a week or longer, check to see if control has been achieved. If not, seek the services of a professional. Your local museum may be able to recommend a known person or firm in this field.

RODENTS. Make certain your display and storage areas are free of mice, squirrels, rats and other small rodents. All can do extreme damage in short order. Be alert for signs of gnawing or telltale droppings.

FIRE. Even a minor, smoky fire can do great harm to a doll collection. There are numerous steps which can be taken to reduce the risk of fire. Start by eliminating hazards which occur to you, then check to see whether your local fire department or insurance company have inspection programs and, if so, utilize them.

Illustration 4. Heavy dolls often cannot be safely supported with normal doll stands unless extra precautions are taken. Here the stand base is weighted with building brick wrapped in fabric. Stands may be screwed to shelves or to large wooden bases such as plywood sheets. Whatever means is used, make certain the spot-welds which attach the stand base to the vertical support are secure.

Keep all records and photographs, insurance inventories and other important papers in a fire-resisting safe or container designed for the purpose. Keep extra copies with your insurance company or in a bank safe-deposit box. Do not buy a safe without good advice from your insurance agent or police department; safes are graded by nationally recognized testing laboratories (such as UL), and will be properly labeled if they meet the requirements.

Automatic fire alarm systems which notify the fire department are well within the reach of most collectors. If properly installed and maintained by qualified personnel, such a system may qualify for a reduction in fire insurance premiums; it can also save your life and all that you keep in your home.

INTRUDERS. Thieves, vandals and other trespassers are to be considered extreme hazards to life and property; this problem is becoming increasingly intense, and it deserves careful attention.

Check with your insurance company and police department to see if they offer inspection programs and other ideas along the lines of improving your security. Take whatever steps are feasible to make entry into your premises as difficult as possible; this will discourage most would-be intruders, as they are not known generally for wishing to work very hard at their trade.

AUTOMATIC BURGLAR AND FIRE ALARMS

Electronic alarms offer excellent protection if installed professionally and properly maintained. A comprehensive system will detect intruders and automatically summon the police. Having a visible alarm system in the premises is a very strong deterrent to would-be intruders, and may also qualify for reductions in insurance premiums.

It is generally much more economical to have fire and burglary protective systems installed at the same time.

If desired, alarm systems which automatically report to fire and police departments can be expanded to report other conditions such as duress (panic, ambush, holdup), equipment failure (heating, air conditioning), flooding and/or medical emergency; any condition which can be arranged to open or close an electrical circuit.

INSURANCE

Having a responsive, understanding, professional insurance agent is one of the most important factors in managing the "risk" factors which accompany property ownership. An independent agent able to offer coverage by different companies can offer flexibility.

Since most readers will have their doll collections in their homes, they should be able to properly insure their doll collections under the homeowners policy by writing an endorsement for Scheduled Personal Property. Dolls are generally listed as Fine Arts, and they will have to be documented according to the requirements of the particular company involved. How troublesome this becomes will be influenced by your personal/business relationship with your agent.

Most policies will not cover dolls for breakage, unless you have the endorsement written to specifically include breakage. The normal policy covers you against the usual hazards: fire, theft, vandalism and so on.

You may have some flexibility in being able to select a fairly high deductible amount on such a policy. You would, then, be covered for any loss which exceeded the fixed deductible amount.

REFERENCE

We would suggest the following book for serious collectors, curators and owners, as it provides many valid and interesting perspectives on the management of collections, as well as many references to other allied works: Manual for Museums, Ralph H. Lewis, National Park Service, U. S. Department of the Interior, Washington, 1976. For sale by Government Printing Office, Washington, DC 20402, Stock No. 024-005-00643-5 $4.70 (Paper). □

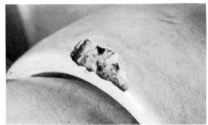

Illustration 6. The lower edge of the upper leg section of Kestner No. 14 shows typical insect damage. Note the dark hole which penetrates completely into the leg interior, probably the work of a powder-post beetle. This body was extensively eaten away on the inside, probably by carpet beetles, as the inside of body and head contained thousands of identifiable carpet beetle larval skins.

Illustration 7. Part of the electronic security system, this heat/fire detector responds to a rapid rise in temperature, making it much more sensitive than a regular heat detector. This rate-of-rise sensor is not as expensive as a system smoke detector, and it provides valuable protection for areas not covered by smoke detectors. The entire premises are protected by the fire system which, in the event of smoke or fire, will automatically summon the fire department.

LEFT: Illustration 5. An example of a display area suitable for antique dolls. Wooden shelves are painted light gray and adjustable metal shelf supports can be set at any convenient height along the vertical metal support members. Vertical supports are screwed into the building framing, not simply attached to the drywall. Also shown is a combination temperature/relative humidity indicator, showing the temperature to be 60 deg.F. (15.5 deg.C.) and the relative humidity to be an ideal 50 percent.

RIGHT: Illustration 8. This passive infra-red detector senses the presense of intruders by responding to the heat radiating from moving bodies. It covers a large area and provides excellent protection in addition to the usual magnetic switches protecting the doors and windows. The intrusion system automatically summons the sheriff in the event of an unauthorized entry.

Stringing Without Tears

by G. P. Jones

I have heard horror stories from some of my customers who have attempted to string their own dolls, only to end up smashing the heads when the elastic slipped and the heads shot across the room.

Here is a method of stringing bodies, without the heads, so that there is no danger of turning the bodies into giant slingshots.

There are two general types of lower leg designs, one in which the elastic comes directly out of the lower leg socket, the other in which the lower leg has a hook. The design of your lower leg determines the method in which the doll will be strung.

Some torsos, especially in larger dolls, have a bar inside the torso at the shoulders over which one of the legs is strung. Directions will be given for stringing a doll of this type. If your torso has no such bar, both legs are strung in the same manner, and **both loops** will be hooked to the head to complete the stringing of the doll.

For both methods, determine the size of elastic needed. The larger the doll, the thicker the elastic must be. Do not use plain rubber loops. If plain rubber is not absolutely fresh, it will snap under tension and put your doll in danger. Also, do not use dressmaking elastic. It is not strong enough to achieve the correct tension. Elastic especially for stringing dolls is available from most doll supply houses.

Method for Legs Without Hooks

1. Cut a piece of elastic which will reach easily, without stretching, from one lower leg, up through other leg parts, through torso to neck hole, and back again, plus a couple of inches. This is more elastic than you need, but will make your task easier.
2. Tie a knot in one end of the elastic. Insert a small tack into the knot, and pull the knot as tightly as you can. Stuff the knot and the tack into the hole in the lower leg. The tack will serve as a bar inside the hole to keep the knot from slipping out.
3. Thread the ball joint and the upper leg onto the cut end of the elastic.
4. Pass the cut end of the elastic through the proper leg hole in the torso and out through the neck hole in the torso.
5. Get a stick, short pencil or similar object to use at the outside of the neck hole in the torso to secure the elastic loop until you are ready to attach the head.

6. Loop the cut end of your elastic over the stick or pencil; then pass the end back down through the torso and out the other leg hole, then through upper leg and ball joint.
7. You are now ready to stretch the elastic for the proper tension. Tension should be taut enough to keep the legs straight without buckling, but not so tight as to damage the sockets. When the tension is correct, tie a knot in the elastic, insert a tack as you did for the first leg, and cut off the excess elastic.
8. Stuff the knot and tack into the hole in the second lower leg.

Stringing One Leg Over a Bar

If one leg is to be strung over a bar inside the torso, do this leg first.
1. Cut a piece of elastic that will reach from the neck hole, down through the leg hole, upper leg and ball joint and back again, plus a few inches. This is more elastic than you need but will be simpler to handle.
2. Fold the elastic in half and hook one lower leg at the fold.
3. Thread both cut ends of elastic through the ball joint and upper leg.
4. With your stringing tool reach down through the torso through the neck hole and, one at a time, pull the cut ends of the elastic up through the torso and out the neck hole, making sure that you get one cut end of the elastic on either side of the bar.
5. Tie the first half of your knot in the ends of the elastic and pull up as tightly as possible. Remember, when the knot is completed, it will drop inside the body, over the bar, so the tension must be much tighter than necessary.
6. Complete your knot, and cut off the excess elastic. Let the knot drop into the body over the bar. String second leg as described below.

Method for Legs With Hooks

1. Measure your elastic twice the length of the torso and cut.
2. Tie an overhand knot in the ends of the elastic to form a loop. Pull tightly on both sides of the knot to get it as tight as possible. To test, separate the two ends on the loop side of the knot and pull. When the knot no longer moves, it is tight enough.
3. Fold the loop so that, when stretched, the knot will be about at the location of the navel and will not interfere with the arms or hooking on the head.
4. Hook on one lower leg. String on the ball joint and upper leg.
5. With a stringing hook, reach down through the body from the neck hole

and out the proper leg hole. Hook on the leg elastic and pull it up through the body.
6. Check your tension. It should be slightly tighter than you want it, but not enough to damage the torso sockets.
7. On the outside of the neck hole, insert a pencil or stick under the loop to secure the loop until it is time to attach the head.

String the other leg in the same manner unless the bar method, as described above, has been used.

Stringing Arms

Arms for both body styles are strung in the same way.
1. Measure from ball joint in one elbow, up through the upper arm, across chest, and down to the other elbow joint. Double this measurement and cut the elastic.
2. Tie a knot in the ends, testing for tightness as instructed above.
3. Fold the elastic loop so that, when stretched, the knot will be in the center of the chest.
4. Hook one hand into the fold in the elastic. String on the forearm, ball joint and upper arm.
5. Reach into the body with your stringing tool from the opposite arm-hole to which you are stringing. Hook the stringing tool into the elastic and pull it through the body. Secure the loop, if necessary, to keep it from snapping back into the body. Use a pencil or stick.
6. On your stringing tool, thread on the forearm, ball joint and upper arm in that order.
7. Hook the stringing tool, with parts on it, into the elastic loop, and pull through all the parts.
8. Hook on the hand.

If you do not have a stringing tool, you can make one from a strong wire coathanger. Make a loop in one end to serve as a handle and bend a hook in the other end with a pair of pliers. Pinch the hook part so that it will fit easily through your doll parts.

To attach your head, simply lift the stick at the neck hole, keeping the tension of the stick. Hook on the head, transferring the tension from the stick to the head, and remove the stick. It is nice if you have someone to help you at this point, as sometimes the hook in the head is short and a bit difficult to push around the elastic, at the same time keeping the tension on the elastic.

One more thought. If you are just learning to string dolls, or if you want to be extra cautious, hook your head on while sitting in the center of your bed, surrounded by pillows. □

Dolling Discoveries

by **Elizabeth Andrews Fisher**

Here are a few discoveries to help you do some minor repairs to your dolls so that you can collect and display them better. Pleasure comes with sharing.

MARBLE DUST

Did you hear about marble dust? To repair porcelain chips, mix white marble dust with Weldbond glue to make a paste to the consistency of thick cream. Apply to a chipped porcelain in layers. Apply a thin coat and wait for it to set; then apply another layer and keep on until you have the chipped area built up level with the surrounding area. Paint to match with Testors or Pactra paints.

REPLACEMENT HANDS

You need a left hand and have the right one. Coat the right hand with shortening. Plan what to do to hold the right hand to drip dry before you get involved with the wet molding material. Please do not think you can hold it in your hand, since it takes a little more than an hour. Dip the shortening-coated hand into MOLD-IT. One dip is enough. Hold the dipped hand over the can of MOLD-IT while the first heavy run-off takes place, then close the can. If you find that drops are forming on the tips of the fingers, take them off by touching lightly with a tissue or cotton ball.

The mold rubber changes color from a chalky opaque white to a transparent cream color.

When you touch the mold and your finger comes away clean, and there are no wet spots, sprinkle generously with talcum powder, preferably with Johnson's Baby Powder, and roll the mold off the hand. Make sure that the mold turns inside out. If you were *reproducing* the right hand, you would be sure it did NOT turn inside out.

If you have trouble turning the fingers well, slash the length of each finger, turn the fingers, then dip your finger into the MOLD-IT, and seal the fingers where you cut them. Put a pin hole in the end of each finger to let the air out when you fill the mold, either with plaster of paris mixed with water or Durham Cold Water Putty mixed with water.

Since the mold is soft and flexible, it should be "nested" in sand or sawdust, and can be nested in salt, sugar or cornmeal to help it to keep the correct shape if the mold is large. A small mold will not need it.

Mix plaster of paris with water to make a thin-cream consistency. Pour the mixture into the mold. Be sure there are no bubbles or air pockets in the hand. Let harden, then roll off the mold. The new hand may be painted to match when it is absolutely dry, and attached to waiting arm. Durham Cold Water Putty may be mixed to thin-cream consistency and the mold filled with it.

To fill a mold, use a big soda straw and suck up the putty a short distance, and blow into each finger.

DOLL SOCKS

If you are always searching for socks for your dolls, drug stores sell cotton finger tubing in three sizes, and all you have to do is measure off the length and sew one end together. Sometimes the stores have tan or flesh, too.

TO ATTACH PLASTIC HANDS

To attach plastic hands or feet to cloth arms or legs, heat a darning needle (big) in a candle flame. Push the needle right through arm top from one side to the other. Heat the needle again and push it through in another section. Pull the arm tube, wrong side out, over the hand to be attached, sew through the holes you made, then wrap the thread around the arm end twice and finish it with a knot. Turn right side out, fill with sawdust, fiberfill and you are in business.

BISQUE HEAD REPAIR

To repair a broken bisque head, clean the broken edges carefully. Moisten the edges, sprinkle on cleanser, leave for a few minutes, rinse off. Dry the parts. Fit two parts carefully. Put a drop or less of Krazy Glue in one spot, fit the two pieces together with quick care. Mix Epoxy Putty, and press a thin strip of putty along the mending crack which covers the crack and extend about 1/4in (.65cm) beyond on both sides. Take your time. The putty goes inside the head, of course. If the edges are smooth and not chipped, you

will be able to repair with no cracks showing.

SOFTEN FAKE HAIR

Many modern dolls have rough, tough stiff hair that defies combing. Dilute Downey: water 40 percent, Downey 60 percent. Dip your hand into the bowl with the Downey and water, smooth the hair and pat the hair with your damp hand. Soon the hair will become manageable.

SHINE THE BODY

Ball-jointed bodies need help, sometimes, to shine and be beautiful. Rub the body and limbs with NEUTRAL paste shoe polish with a soft cloth. Let stand for a few minutes and rub with a dry soft cloth until the soft desired shine appears.

COMPOSITION HEAD REPAIR

When a composition doll has the misfortune to lose the back of his head, blow up a balloon and fit it into the head. Fit heavy paper gummed tape into the missing head. The balloon will support the tape. Cover the paper with Durham Cold Water Putty mixed with Weldbond glue or Franklin Hide Glue. Smooth the putty area with your finger, wet on your tongue. Use a different finger each time and when the fingers are all used up, wash your hands and start over. When the putty is dry, puncture the balloon and remove. Paint the head back.

GOUACHE

Sometimes you may need to "save" the painted eyes and mouth on a composition doll. To be sure of doing a neat job, get some white Gouache paint. Paint the eyes and mouth with it. Then, using your flesh paint, paint the rest of the head and even over Gouache paint. When paint is dry, wash off the Gouache with a damp cloth.

Have fun. □

EDITOR'S NOTE: Before making any repairs to a doll make sure whatever repair being attempted can be corrected or does not ruin "originality" of doll, if repair does not come out satisfactory.

The Hazards of Being a Doll Doctor and Doll Maker — A Personal Account

by **Linda Greenfield, "D.D.", Chili Doll Hospital**

©1984 Linda Greenfield

We have all read these words, **"Use with adequate ventilation, vapor harmful, avoid prolonged contact with skin."** However, have we actually paid attention, or **understood** the grave importance and meaning of these words? Whether you are a mere hobbyist, or deeply

own boss!" If they only knew the great responsibilities involved and how seriously one should regard their work. Yes, it **is** fun to work on dolls, but complete consideration and thought should be given to all aspects, especially occupational safety which, sad to say,

used in making composition dolls in the 1920s and later? And the painted surfaces of many of these dolls contained lead which was commonly used in the paint pigments during that time period?

*Sawdust Compositions
(Cheap Compound)
20 parts of liquid glue
20 parts of sifted pine sawdust
6 parts of white-lead
1 part litharge
2 parts of plaster-of-paris
1 part whiting

*Other Favored
Sawdust Compositions
10 parts hardwood sawdust
10 parts of liquid glue
5 parts of plaster-of-paris
1 part of resin
1 part of litharge
2 parts of white-lead

*These formulas are from the book, *Doll-Making and Repairing,* circa 1920, formulas for making composition. Excerpts from two books, *Toy Manufacture and Toy Making* by J. T. Makinson. ©1979 Hobby House Press, Inc.

Illustration 1. Painting with an airbrush in Ventilating Filter Booth. Note the face mask, gloves and bib-apron.

involved in doll restoration or doll making to the point of production type methods, doll work **is** serious business. If not taken seriously, it can be **deadly!** It is easy to say, "Oh, not me. I don't do **that** much sanding or painting." The point is, you are at risk, especially if you are not adequately protecting yourself against the dust and chemicals you work with.

When physical fitness and health awareness seems to be at its peak, the same alertness should be applied to artist safety. Unfortunately, the mere mention of being a doll doctor or doll maker conjures up thoughts of fun, fantasy and a departure from the restraints of the more practiced professions. I am often told, "What fun it must be to work with dolls and be your

has been greatly lacking in the arts.

There are numerous "How To" repair and doll making books on the market today, but little or no mention is made about personal safety and how many of the repair materials should properly be used. Whereas, many industrial companies have developed hazardous materials control programs that are designed to ensure that employees are aware of the hazardous properties of materials they work with, as well as proper procedures and protective measures required for safe handling and usage. You are probably wondering how this applies to doll work.

Did you know that white-lead, formaldehyde, silica, litharge (lead monoxide) and possibly asbestos were some of the ingredients commonly

These facts should be of greatest concern to restorers who work with these materials full-time. Being a doll doctor myself for the past 16 years, I have done my share of work on restoring composition dolls. I began this venture as a hobby, but upon completion of high school, decided to make this my vocation. I graduated from a mail order doll repair course and read as many repair books as I could find. I was enthused and eager to "save" dolls! Many times the kitchen table was used as my worktable. Painting either by brush or airbrush was done either in the garage or outside during the warm months. (I live in the East.)

A local doll hospital abruptly closed when the owner suddenly died of multiple brain tumors. Many of her clients then became mine. It was a sad time as

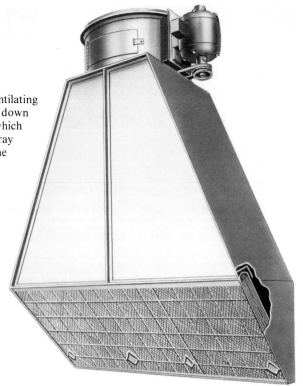

Illustration 2. Wall Duct Ventilating Unit with Filters creates a down draft movement of air which exhausts fumes and over-spray instantly. As with any of the illustrated Ventilation Units, replacement air is needed and one should know where it will come from. You should also be aware that because these units evacuate so much air that it could cause a back draft down the chimneys of fireplaces, wood stoves and gas water heaters and furnaces. *Photograph courtesy of Passche Airbrush Co.*

we had been friends and, although I missed her, one learns to accept death, not question it. I did not stop to think that her exposure to repairing dolls could have caused her fatal condition.

Time passed. My business grew and 13 years ago I moved into a building which is now the home for my doll hospital and museum. The trickle of dolls to repair became a steady and ever increasing stream. Day after day I spent repairing dolls. To save time, I learned to schedule similar types of repairs at one time. It was not uncommon for me to sand and refinish dolls' parts and heads for a two or three day period. Likewise, all painting was done the same way. It is such a slow transition from being a dabbler to becoming a full-time restorer that one does not always know at what point it happens.

My exposure to the sanding dust and paint was rapidly increasing. My workroom measured 10ft square. I had one window for ventilation which faced my worktable. My paint bottles and other supplies were stored on open shelving in the same room. The most frequently used supplies such as glue and plastic wood remained right on my worktable at all times. Small painting procedures were also performed on my worktable, and I would open the window for "ventilation."

I began to notice, after a day or two of sanding, a break or eruption of the skin on my fingers which became consistent with each time I sanded. I also began to develop frequent headaches, a feeling of loss of appetite; I had trouble sleeping at night and had a general tired feeling. I became quite concerned and began to suspect a connection between my work with my health malaises. (If you are currently experiencing some of these problems, I urge you to heed my suggestions.)

After I had my annual physical which indicated no noticeable health problems, I contacted a local representative of an airbrush company. After his visual inspection of my workshop and how I was ventilating it, he determined that, indeed, I was in peril. My greatest mistake was the lack of adequate ventilation. The window which faced my worktable was not any help. Suppose, for example, the wind direction blew **in** outside air? Then I was not only failing to properly ventilate, it was also pushing the air contaminants further into the workroom or into other areas of the building. And on cold snowy days the window was not opened at all.

Storage of paints and other chemical supplies on open shelving in the same room was another mistake. After a container's seal has been broken, small amounts of fumes are released into the air. The more containers, the more leakage. Together we worked out the size of my workroom in volume cubic feet and determined that for the quantity of sanding and painting I was performing, a professional ventilating unit-bench type filter booth, would serve both needs. I work directly on and into this unit. (See **Illustration 1**.) I am happy to say that all my previous health problems are no longer present.

I suggest that you begin examining **all** your repair supplies: glues, cements, fillers, paints, china repair solutions, refinishers, brush cleaners and glazes. **Know what you are using.** Read the

Illustration 3. Single Exhaust Bench Type Filter Booth with disposable filters, which trap practically all coating solids as they are drawn through the working area of the spray booth. *Photograph courtesy of Paasche Airbrush Co.*

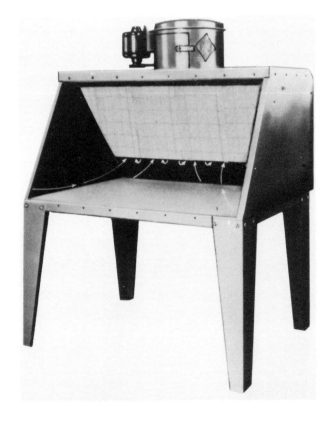

label which appears on each item for the following:

1. What are the ingredients?
2. For what purpose/use is it intended?
3. Does it say: FOR INDUSTRIAL USE ONLY?
4. What are the listed cautions/warnings?
5. Does it warn of harmful vapors/spray mist?
6. Does it warn of prolonged contact with the skin?
7. Is it highly flammable?
8. Does it tell what to do in case of emergency?
9. Does it tell where to store item or at what temperature?

You may even wish to make a card file on each item you use, along with answers to the above questions. I think that you will be as surprised as I was to learn that one can actually use potentially harmful materials without realizing **how** harmful they can be. It is not until the death of someone you knew, or when your own health begins to fail, that you suspect a correlation. The impact is overwhelming.

I made copies of my repair supplies and solvents lists and sent them to a locally renowned toxicologist who works at our local Environmental Health and Safety Department. Listed below are known, verified hazards found with the use of, or exposure to these supplies, if adequate protection and ventilation is not followed. See how many you work with.

Xylene, toluene and mineral spirits (found in many popular hobby paints and Plastic Wood® filler) are moderately toxic. All evaporate at a fairly slow rate. Ventilation control is easily achieved, given proper ventilation is maintained. A ventilation rate of 250 cubic feet per minute is adequate to handle an evaporation rate of half-pint per hour of xylene, according to OSHA standards. For toluene the ventilation rate could be about half as much. However, noticeable health problems are common at lower levels, where it is less a question of "how long" this chemical is used than "how much" is used. This becomes of concern as concentrations become higher. *Side effects to watch for:* Headaches; loss of appetite; trouble sleeping; listlessness.

Ketone (found in Plastic Wood® filler) is of increasing concern. It evaporates rapidly so high concentrations are easily achieved. It presents a fire hazard and is highly volatile and flammable. It should only be used in a ventilating

Illustration 4. Airbrushing a doll head. I use the Economy Bench Type Filter Booth on legs, manufactured by the Paasche Airbrush Co. This booth is ideal where space is at a premium. I also wear a face mask to protect against possible paint over-spray.

cabinet. Some evidence suggests that some ketones may be carcinogenic (cause cancer). Prolonged exposure results in dizziness and mental confusion.

Acetone (found in popularly used glues/cements) is a ketone; therefore the same hazards listed above under *Ketone* would apply.

Refinishers or Strippers (with methylene chloride as an ingredient) are highly volatile. Good ventilation control is important. The ingredient behaves like carbon monoxide in the blood on inhalation, interfering with oxygen transport.

Laquer thinners have a very damaging effect on skin. Acetone, one of the ingredients, can defat skin surfaces within a few minutes. Whereas, for example, rubbing alcohol has only a minor capacity to do so.

Ceramic Glazes and Overglazes: (Unless they are lead safe and are labeled as such on the container, or are lead free). Almost all other glazes contain lead. Even the fritted glazes present some risk if ingested. The porcelain materials are essentially inert, although some of them have free silica.

Sanding, Refinishing Doll Parts, Sanding Greenware: Breathable particles, which are so small that they are not trapped in the upper respiratory tract and deposit in the lungs, are too small to be seen with the naked eye so that dangerous quantities of airborne dust could be present in what appears to be clean air. A ventilation cabinet should

be used for all operations which generate airborne contaminants. This is particularly important for airborne particles, especially those containing lead, cadmium, chromium VI and other metals commonly used in older pigments — like paint. This takes on added significance in that often the composition of pigments would be unknown, as well as the unknown composition of the sanding dust. Recent information suggests that some hardwood dusts may cause nasal and/or pharyngial (throat) cancer on inhalation. Contact dermatitis can result from direct physical contact with the dust. Dusty lungs is an extreme example as is silicosis, diseases which result from exposure to high concentrations of dust, or silica dust for a long period of time. Silica was listed as an ingredient in some composition doll making formulas.

Benzene, Carbon Tetrachloride and Chloroform: These should only be in a ventilating cabinet as these chemicals are just too dangerous otherwise. Benzene is an active substance, found in many paint removers and varnish removers, and also is contained in cleaning agents and rubber cement. Since 1928, exposure to benzene has been linked with leukemia.

Many of the toxic chemicals have a cumulative action and buildup in the body and remain there. They are not filtered out. Some of the health hazards resulting from unprotected exposure take years to show up. Health problems caused by asbestos exposure, now being brought to light, is one example. For many of those unfortunate people the reality of their exposure has developed some 30 years later, others sooner. Another example is when it became recognized that the bone marrow may be susceptible to many volatile inhalable chemicals as well as those that may enter through the skin. Industry now demands toxicologic studies on all chemicals before introducing them into their processes. Unfortunately, hobbyists and other non-industrial, or self-employed people in business, are responsible for their own use, proper or improper as the case may be, of various chemicals, without realizing the great risk involved.

I, myself, had difficulty in making my own physician aware that I was **restoring** dolls, not just sewing up *Raggedy Ann* dolls and dabbing a little glue here and there; that I work with potentially harmful chemicals and repair substances. The stereotype of the little old lady with white hair and nimble fingers is difficult to change. As you know collecting, making and repairing dolls is a very active and growing field among all age groups and more people than ever are getting involved, most, unaware of the dangers of unprotected exposure.

It is my hope that we can all benefit from the tragic mistakes of others and that you will be inspired to make the

Illustration 5. Large size pull drawer storage files. Dolls awaiting repair are kept in these and the customer's name and claim check number is posted on the outside of each box, for easy reference.

hobby work areas not only a fun place to be, but also a healthy one.

Coupled with the known risks, the expanding base of knowledge continually brings to light new ones. My personal library of books, illustrations and related reference material brings to mind the feeling of outrage and anger every time I see a picture of a doll doctor or doll maker performing a task with potentially harmful substances, without **any** kind of protective garments, gloves or face masks. Several books caption the picture by saying "Note the open window." As I have mentioned earlier, this is not adequate for getting rid of the fumes or other airborne contaminants and in some instances, when the wind direction causes breezes to come in, this only spreads the particles further into the work area or beyond.

Some mail order doll repair courses need to amend their advice, too. The course I took listed various locations which would be suitable for a repair workshop within the home. These included the basement, garage and spare bedroom, with a notation that most people began on a kitchen table! At the time I took this course, I lived in a rather small house, so the idea of the kitchen table appealed to me for its convenience. Now that I have the years of experience behind me and I know better, the thought of someone refinishing dolls and painting them on the kitchen table, without much ventilation, then covering all the paint bottles and putting them away to start preparations for the family dinner absolutely revolts me! Many of the popularly used hobby paints today leave "substances in suspension," lingering in the air until/unless they are vented out by means of swift removal of that contaminated air.

THE WORK AREA

My first important suggestion is to have a specific work area which is not used for any other purpose, like where food consumption would take place or where young children play. Make sure you install some type of ventilation system. Windows are really inadequate for proper and sufficient ventilation, unless you position them so they are wide open **with** a fan blowing the inside room air **out**. Preferably, you should install a ventilation hood, a wall duct ventilating unit (**Illustration 2**) or a bench type filter booth (**Illustration 3**). If a person is suspicious of the cleanness of the air brought in by these units as

make-up air, a face mask or respirator could additionally be worn when working in the ventilating units, filter booth or when using a ventilation hood. It is a good idea to keep ventilating the work area after all work has been completed, to rid the room of accumulated or built-up fumes, caused by items left to dry thoroughly. It would also insure that the more dangerous breathable dust particles, too small to be seen, would be removed from the air. (See **Illustration 4**.)

If you intend to use paints, cements, fillers and so forth, which contain potentially harmful substances, as previously mentioned, it would be a good idea to install a metal storage cabinet with doors, or use a ventilating type solvent cabinet. Keep containers closed except during use.

If you plan to work on a sturdy worktable, be sure it is covered with a washable or disposable cover.

Be sure to have an appropriate fire extinguisher within easy reach. (Note that a CO_2 extinguisher does not stain or damage adjacent material.)

Dolls awaiting repair or other supplies such as wigs, elastic or material, could be kept in storage drawer containers or boxes (**Illustration 5**). This keeps the workroom not only organized, but also maintains a low-dust condition. A dusty work place is not inherently a hazardous one, although it certainly is evidence of poor practice.

GARMENTS

It would be best if you had a specific outfit you wore when you work, similar to that of a gas station attendant or delivery person. If you prefer your comfortable jeans, select a pair to wear only when you are working, and do not wear them at any other time. A bib-apron or work apron should additionally be worn over your jeans and top. If you have long hair, tie it up, or otherwise get it out of the way of your work. A hair net would be fine. Be sure after a day's work involving sanding, painting or cleaning dolls, you wash your garment (unless it is disposable) separately from your other wash. Be sure to bathe and wash your hair.

EYE PROTECTION

Wear safety glasses or painters' goggles when drilling into bisque or china, cutting wire, chipping old paint off doll parts, or when using motorized power tools or electric grinding wheels, buffers or sanders.

RESPIRATORY PROTECTION

Wear a protective face mask, a dust mask, allergy or pollen filter mask, or filter respirator, for protection against non-toxic dust, powders or other airborne irritants.

When using many of the repair supplies previously mentioned, such as glue, cement, fillers, or when brush or spray painting, where **toxic vapors** are present, a cartridge respirator, or similar type approved for industrial use should be worn. However, a ventilating cabinet should be used for all operations which might generate airborne contaminants as encountered in working with these materials. To increase your protection, it would be a good idea to wear your mask or respirator while working in a ventilation cabinet, filter booth, or when using a ventilating hood, and should be mandatory if you have no means of ventilation or just have windows in your work area.

HAND PROTECTION

Because some toxins enter your body through merely touching them, cotton knit lined Neoprene coated gloves should be worn when handling any harsh cleaners, paint removers, thinners or other chemicals. The use of latex, rubber or vinyl gloves is important to minimize skin contact with the unknown composition of sanding dust, commonly encountered when sanding the composition doll parts.

Gloves should be worn when handling and cleaning dolls, especially if mold/mildew or evidence of animals or bugs is present.

CLEANUP

This is very important. Do not leave piles of sanded dust all over your work area. Clean up immediately after your sanding or painting project is completed. Dispose of paint rags and rags used to clean brushes. Empty all wastebaskets or containers. Frequent cleaning maintains a low-dust condition. Dust in and around your work area frequently. Use a damp rag to do this as dusters and brooms only scatter the dust. Vacuum the floor. Be sure to replace filters after each use in ventilating cabinets with disposable filters.

OTHER COMMON SENSE SUGGESTIONS

If you are demonstrating your work and other people enter your work area, be sure that everyone is provided with protective accessories as needed.

It is best not to smoke, or have an open flame in your area, because of the flammable or explosive properties found in many of the repair supplies.

Food or beverages should not be brought in or consumed in your work area as small dust particles or other contaminants may settle and then become ingested when you eat or drink.

Wear face mask, safety glasses and ventilate when using a soldering iron.

TIPS FOR THOSE WHO TEACH CERAMICS

I have fond memories of taking a ceramic class several years ago, in a private home. The ladies sat all around a long table in the dining room, sanding the seams off the greenware or painting delicate decorations on their creations. Beverages sat on the table, and many ladies enjoyed smoking and talking about their daily lives. By the end of the evening the sanded dust had settled everywhere and we went home. Even today I can walk into some ceramic shops and I would be able to write my name in the dust. I hope that ceramic teachers will be inspired to follow my previously discussed suggestions. Since you are setting an example and teaching others the proper ways of doing things, start yourself and others on the right track for safety. Additionally, I suggest each student could be provided with, or could bring his/her own dust mask and gloves. Be sure to provide a well-ventilated area where work is to be done. Have each student be responsible for cleaning up their work area before leaving.

PREVENTATIVE HEALTH MEASURES

Make sure your physician is informed of your involvement in ceramics, making dolls or being a doll doctor, if this means you maintain a close involvement with potentially hazardous chemicals or supplies. Tell the doctor the ingredients of your supplies. He may wish to write this in your health chart, in case future reference is necessary.

Keep your tetanus shot up-to-date in case you come in contact with rusty wire or pins which may puncture your skin.

SOURCES FOR EQUIPMENT, PROTECTIVE ACCESSORIES AND INFORMATION

Ventilation Hoods: Electrical supply stores or other companies which sell ventilating equipment. Many are listed in the yellow pages of the telephone book.
Ventilating Units/Wall Ducts, Cabinets or Booths: Look under ventilation contractors or ventilation equipment in the yellow pages of the telephone book. Also, some airbrush companies, industrial and laboratory supply houses sell this equipment.
Garments, Gloves, Masks, Safety Glasses: Hardware and drug stores, safety equipment and clothing companies listed in the yellow pages and many airbrush supply companies.

Some manufacturers of ceramic supplies are now making information available about their products, as most containers do not bear a list of ingredients. You may wish to contact them directly for this information.

Go to your public library and consult the many books available, specifically about hazardous materials or any other related books published by the National Safety Council.

Now it is up to you. As the saying goes, "The life you save may be your own!" □

ACKNOWLEDGMENTS

Dr. Robert H. Wilson, Chief, Environmental Health and Safety Department at the University of Rochester, Rochester, New York.

Better Homes and Gardens Family Medical Guide.

Hobby House Press, Inc., Reprint of *Doll-Making and Repairing/ Formulas For Making Composition.*

Paasche Airbrush Company, 1909-1929 Diversey Parkway, Chicago, Illinois 60614.

Illustration 6. Sanding a doll leg with a miniature power tool with a flexible shaft. Note the safety glasses, face mask, gloves and bib-apron.

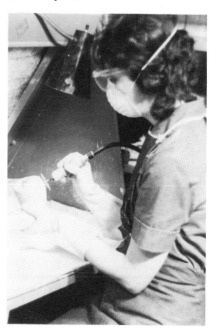

Notes on Preventing Avoidable Damage to Fine Antique Dolls

by **Robert & Karin MacDowell**

Photographs by the **Authors**

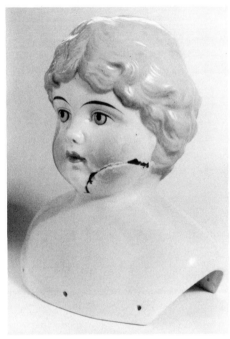

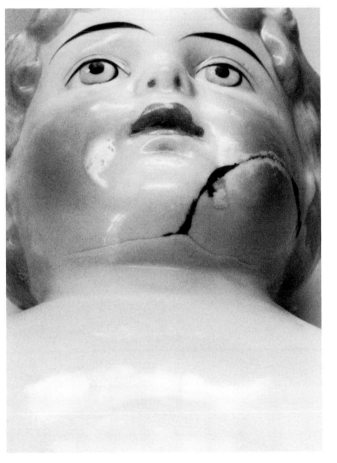

ABOVE: Illustration 1A. China head doll bonded together inaccurately, pieces out of alignment.

Illustration 1B. Detail showing mis-alignment. Since pieces did not fit correctly, grinding of edges was done, causing irreversible loss of porcelain surfaces and cheek painting detail. Chips along cracks were filled with two different materials — one, very dark and difficult to cover with light airbrushing, the other material did not bond well and is flaking off.

Following are examples of the types of problems which we encounter on a daily basis, all of which could have been avoided. Such practices do irreversible damage, which permanently devalues the objects.

Previously-done restoration work must almost always be dismantled. Such work is time-consuming and can sometimes result in doubling project cost.

Some types of damage render a project completely beyond consideration; for example, serious loss of eyebrow details caused by sandpaper or other abrasives or grinding. Some adhesives and coatings are not fully removable and, at best, leave permanent stains and discolorations. To remove all traces of adhesive from a badly assembled project is extremely difficult; if not done perfectly, pieces can never be properly aligned in the following assembly.

Persons who have not thoroughly familiarized themselves with the ethical considerations, compatible repair materials and appropriate procedures should never attempt even basic restoration work. Damage is bound to result; the finished product is unlikely to appear truly satisfactory and will have to be done over, professionally, at much higher cost than would have resulted if the initial "restoration had not been attempted.

Destruction of original material or finish is never justified. A good example would be the removal of cracking or cupping paint from a composition doll and/or completely repainting. If this is done, all originality is lost, irretrievably, forever. Methods are now known for re-attaching flaking or cupping paint. The process is time-consuming, but does preserve the original in a professionally acceptable manner. □

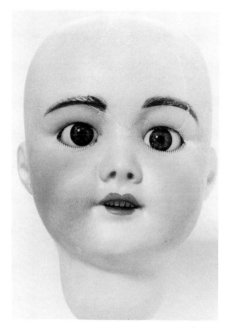

Illustration 2A. S.F.B.J. 301; pieces badly aligned, eyes could have been set much more attractively, chip in lower right eyelid, white material hand-brushed liberally around cracks, head was left uncleaned and work done over soiled surfaces.

Illustration 3A. A.M. 351 Character Baby. Repairer was unable to finish assembly because first piece was not accurately bonded. Nasty chip missing from left side of left eye. Head not cleaned, extremely heavy accretion of adhesive on outside surfaces.

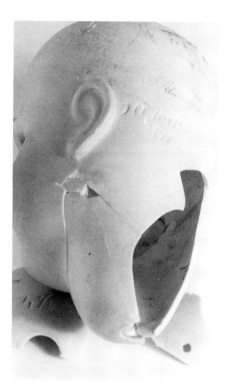

Illustration 4A. Heinrich Handwerck — Simon & Halbig. Head not cleaned, old wig adhesive should be removed. Pieces so badly aligned that completion of assembly impossible. Numerous small pieces missing.

Illustration 2B. Eyes have been removed from sleep-eye rocker assembly and set stationary. Eyes set with two kinds of wax (neither appropriate) and hard plaster-like material. One wonders, now, if the eyes are original and, if so, could they have been re-installed in the sleeping configuration. Cork piece inside neck and remains of plaster pieces are conclusive evidence that doll once had sleep eyes. If necessary to remove eyes from rocker and set them stationary, soft, un-colored wax and a small amount of soft plaster-of-paris would have yielded better results. Inside of head could have been cleaned. The head is worthy of considerably more caring, well-directed effort.

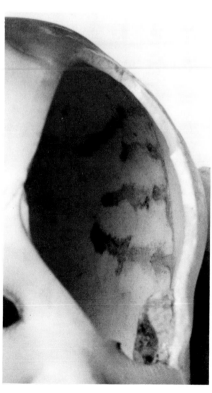

Illustration 3B. Inside of head not cleaned, heavy lines caused by excess adhesive which ran from bonded joint, entrapping underlying soil. Excess adhesive should always be removed to prevent stains.

Illustration 4B. Showing results when excess adhesive squeezes from joints and is not immediately removed — a thick, yellowed un-tidy area which may prove difficult to remove and which may leave permanent staining along bond lines. Excess adhesive does nothing significant to improve strength of bonding; it is the adhesive inside the bondline which provides most of the required stability.